Fodor's InFocus

CAYMAN ISLANDS

2nd Edition

Fodor's Travel Publications . New York, Toronto, London, Sydney, Auckland

www.fodors.com

Be a Fodor's Correspondent

Your opinion matters. It matters to us. It matters to your fellow Fodor's travelers, too. And we'd like to hear it. In fact, we *need* to hear it. When you share your experiences and opinions, you become an active member of the Fodor's community. Here's how you can help improve Fodor's for all of us.

Tell us when we're right. We rely on local writers to give you an insider's perspective. But our writers and staff editors also depend on you. Your positive feedback is a vote to renew our recommendations for the next edition.

Tell us when we're wrong. We update most of our guides every year. But things change. If any of our descriptions are inaccurate or inadequate, we'll incorporate your changes in the next edition and will correct factual errors at fodors.com *immediately*.

Tell us what to include. You probably have had fantastic travel experiences that aren't yet in Fodor's. Why not share them with a community of like-minded travelers? Share your discoveries and experiences with everyone directly at fodors.com. Your input may lead us to add a new listing or a higher recommendation.

Give us your opinion instantly at our feedback center at www.fodors.com/feedback. You may also e-mail editors@fodors.com with the subject line "Cayman Islands Editor." Or send your nominations, comments, and complaints by mail to Cayman Islands Editor, Fodor's, 1745 Broadway, New York, NY 10019.

Happy Traveling!

Tim Jarrell, Publisher

FODOR'S IN FOCUS CAYMAN ISLANDS

Series Editor: Douglas Stallings

Editor: Douglas Stallings
Writer: Jordan Simon

Production Editors: Evangelos Vasilakis, Carolyn Roth
Maps & Illustrations: David Lindroth, *cartographer*; Bob Blake and Rebecca Baer, *map editors;* William Wu, *information graphics*
Design: Fabrizio La Rocca, *creative director*; Guido Caroti, *art director*; Chie Ushio, *designer*; Melanie Marin, *senior picture editor*
Cover Photo: Stephen Frink/The Image Bank/Getty Images
Production Manager: Amanda Bullock

2nd Edition

ISBN 978-1-4000-0478-2
ISSN 1941-0220

SPECIAL SALES

This book is available for special discounts for bulk purchases for sales promotions or premiums. Special editions, including personalized covers, excerpts of existing books, and corporate imprints, can be created in large quantities for special needs. For more information, write to Special Markets/Premium Sales, 1745 Broadway, MD 6-2, New York, NY 10019, or e-mail specialmarkets@randomhouse.com.

AN IMPORTANT TIP & AN INVITATION

Although all prices, opening times, and other details in this book are based on information supplied to us at press time, changes occur all the time in the travel world, and Fodor's cannot accept responsibility for facts that become outdated or for inadvertent errors or omissions. **So always confirm information when it matters,** especially if you're making a detour to visit a specific place. Your experiences—positive and negative—matter to us. If we have missed or misstated something, **please write to us.** We follow up on all suggestions. Contact the Cayman Islands editor at editors@fodors.com or c/o Fodor's at 1745 Broadway, New York, NY 10019.

PRINTED IN CHINA
10 9 8 7 6 5 4 3 2

CONTENTS

DID YOU KNOW?

The endangered Lesser Caymans iguana that is endemic to Little Cayman and Cayman Brac was recently introduced in Grand Cayman.

ABOUT THIS BOOK

Our Ratings

We wouldn't recommend a place that wasn't worth your time, but sometimes a place is so experiential that superlatives don't do it justice: You just have to be there to know. These sights, properties, and experiences get our highest rating, **Fodor's Choice**, indicated by orange stars throughout this book. Black stars highlight sights and properties we deem **Highly Recommended**, places that our writers, editors, and readers praise again and again for consistency and excellence.

Credit Cards

Want to pay with plastic? **AE, D, DC, MC, V** after restaurant and hotel listings indicate whether American Express, Discover, Diners Club, MasterCard, and Visa are accepted.

Restaurants

Unless we state otherwise, restaurants are open for lunch and dinner daily. We mention dress only when there's a specific requirement and reservations only when they're essential or not accepted— it's always best to book ahead.

Hotels

Unless we tell you otherwise, you can assume that the hotels have private bath, phone, TV, and air-conditioning. We always list facilities but not whether you'll be charged an extra fee to use them, so when pricing accommodations, find out what's included.

Many Listings

★	Fodor's Choice
★	Highly recommended
✉	Physical address
✦	Directions
✈	Mailing address
☎	Telephone
🖷	Fax
⊕	On the Web
✉	E-mail
✎	Admission fee
☉	Open/closed times
Ⓜ	Metro stations
▭	Credit cards

Hotels & Restaurants

🏨	Hotel
⇱	Number of rooms
⚲	Facilities
⊺◯⊺	Meal plans
✕	Restaurant
⚑	Reservations
⟍	Smoking
⛿	BYOB
✕🏨	Hotel with restaurant that warrants a visit

Outdoors

🏌	Golf
⛺	Camping

Other

⏲	Family-friendly
⇨	See also
✉	Branch address
☞	Take note

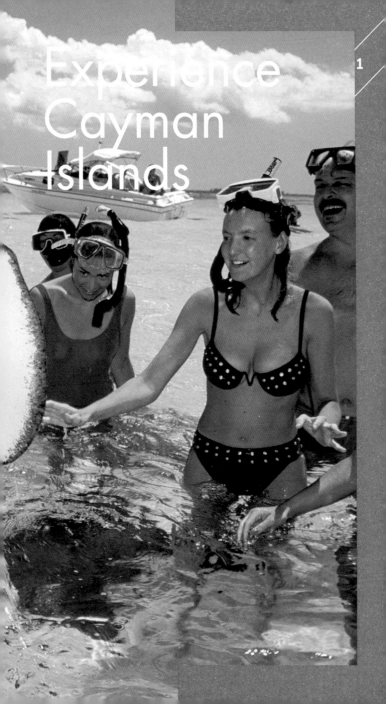

Experience
Cayman
Islands

WHAT'S WHERE

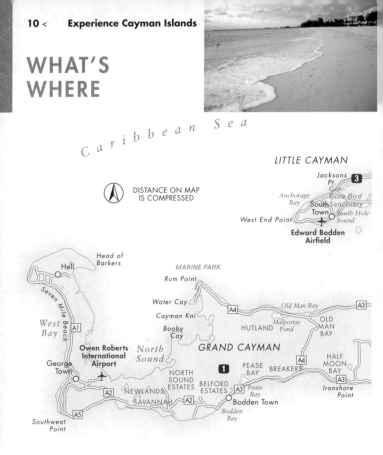

Caribbean Sea

DISTANCE ON MAP
IS COMPRESSED

LITTLE CAYMAN

Jacksons Pt. **3**

Anchorage Bay
South Town
Gore Bird Sanctuary

West End Point
South Hole Sound

Edward Bodden Airfield

Head of Barkers

Hell

MARINE PARK
Rum Point

Water Cay

Cayman Kai

Booby Cay

West Bay

Seven Mile Beach

A1

Owen Roberts International Airport

George Town

North Sound

Old Man Bay

A4 A3

Malportas Pond

HUTLAND

OLD MAN BAY

GRAND CAYMAN

PEASE BAY A4

BREAKERS

HALF MOON BAY

A3

NORTH SOUND ESTATES

BELFORD ESTATES A3

Pease Bay

Ironshore Point

NEWLANDS

SAVANNAH

A2

Bodden Town

Southweat Point

A5

Bodden Bay

1 **Grand Cayman.** The Cayman Islands' main island offers the longest, liveliest sandy strand (Seven Mile Beach), great diving, fine dining, upscale resorts, surprisingly varied nightlife, and an attractive waterfront capital with duty-free shopping in George Town. Despite the development and congestion around Seven Mile Beach and George Town, the neighborhoods of West Bay and East End are mellow and filled with natural wonders.

2 **Cayman Brac.** The archipelago's most rugged, dramatically scenic island is known for its bullying bluff, which vaults 140 feet. The bird-watching, caving, hiking, and rock climbing (experienced only with your own gear) are phenomenal, and the island is just as spectacular underwater for divers and snorkelers. The Brac is laid-back, friendly, and cheap, with good villa values and small inns and resorts.

Booby Pt. North East Pt.
North East Bay
Tibbetts Turn
Spot Bay
Stake Bay Pt.
Deadman's Pt.
Pollard Bay
Frenchman's Fort
Cat Head Bay
Tom Jennett's Bay
West End
Sea Feather Bay
West End Pt.
Cedar Pt.
CAYMAN BRAC
Gerrard-Smith Airport

Lower Spot Bay
Crawl Bay
East Point
Charles Bight

The Bahamas
ATLANTIC OCEAN
Cuba
Haiti
Dominican Republic
Caribbean Sea
COLOMBIA
VENEZUELA
Caribbean

Spotter Bay
COLLIERS
Colliers Bay
EAST END
Lower Bay

3 Little Cayman. The smallest of the Cayman Islands is the least developed, most unspoiled in the chain. Ecotourists can get back to nature (but not the basics) at splendid little resorts catering to divers and birders. You'll find world-famous dive sites like Bloody Bay Marine Park, equally fantastic fishing (especially light-tackle), secluded beaches, and fabulous bird-watching along the shore and wetlands covering nearly half the island.

CAYMAN ISLANDS PLANNER

Island Activities	Logistics
Diving is a major draw; the Bloody Bay Wall, off the coast of Little Cayman, is one of the Caribbean's top dive destinations, but there are many sites convenient to Grand Cayman where shore diving is also good.	**Getting to the Islands:** There are plenty of nonstop flights to Grand Cayman (GCM) from the United States; then you can hop over to the Brac (CYB) and Little Cayman (LYB) on a small plane.

Diving is a major draw; the Bloody Bay Wall, off the coast of Little Cayman, is one of the Caribbean's top dive destinations, but there are many sites convenient to Grand Cayman where shore diving is also good.

On Grand Cayman, a dive or snorkeling trip to **Stingray City** is very popular. There's good off-the-beach snorkeling in West Bay Cemetery, at Rum Point, and at Smith's Cove in Grand Cayman.

On land, Grand Cayman has the most to offer, with plenty of tours and activities, including **semisubmersible tours** of the bay.

Grand Cayman's **Seven Mile Beach** is one of the Caribbean's finest long stretches of sand. Little Cayman has the best beaches of the Sister Islands, especially Owen Island and Point o'Sand.

Rock climbers have now discovered the Brac's limestone bluff.

Getting to the Islands: There are plenty of nonstop flights to Grand Cayman (GCM) from the United States; then you can hop over to the Brac (CYB) and Little Cayman (LYB) on a small plane.

Hassle Factor: Low for Grand Cayman; medium to high for Little Cayman and Cayman Brac.

Nonstops: You can fly nonstop to Grand Cayman from Atlanta (Delta), Boston (US Airways once weekly), Charlotte (US Airways), Detroit (Northwest once weekly), Fort Lauderdale (Cayman Airways), Houston (Continental once weekly), Miami (American, Cayman Airways), Minneapolis (Northwest once weekly), New York–JFK (Cayman Airways), New York–Newark (Continental once weekly), Philadelphia (US Airways once weekly), and Tampa (Cayman Airways).

On the Ground: In Grand Cayman you must take a taxi or rent a car at the airport, since most hotels are not permitted to offer airport shuttles. Hotel pickup is more readily available on Cayman Brac and Little Cayman.

Renting a Car: It's possible to get by without a car on Grand Cayman if you are staying in the Seven Mile Beach area. If you want to explore the rest of the island—or if you are staying elsewhere—you'll need a car. Though less necessary on Cayman Brac or Little Cayman, cars are available on both islands. Driving is on the left, and you need a local driving permit, available at the car-rental office for US$7.50.

Where to Stay

Grand Cayman is expensive during the high season but offers the widest range of resorts, restaurants, and activities. Both Little Cayman and Cayman Brac are more geared toward serving the needs of divers, who compose the majority of visitors. The smaller islands are cheaper than Grand Cayman, but with the extra cost of transportation, the overall savings are minimized.

Grand Cayman: Grand Cayman has plenty of medium-size resorts as well as the Ritz-Carlton, a large seven-story resort on Seven Mile Beach. The island also has a wide range of condos and villas, many in resort-like compounds on or near Seven Mile Beach and the Cayman Kai area. There are even a few small guesthouses for budget-minded visitors.

The Sister Islands: Cayman Brac has mostly intimate resorts and family-run inns. Little Cayman has a mix of small resorts and condos, most appealing to divers.

Hotel and Restaurant Costs

Restaurant prices are for a main course at dinner and include any taxes or service charges. Hotel prices are per night for a double room in high season, excluding taxes, service charges, and meal plans.

Tips for Travelers

All visitors must have a valid passport and a return or ongoing ticket to enter the Cayman Islands.

The minimum legal drinking age in the Cayman Islands is 18.

Electricity is reliable and is the same as in the United States (110 volts/60 cycles). U.S. electrical appliances will work just like at home.

You should not need to change money in Grand Cayman, since U.S. dollars are readily accepted. ATMs generally offer the option of U.S. or Cayman dollars. The Cayman dollar is pegged to the U.S. dollar at the rate of approximately CI$1.25 to $1. Be sure you know which currency is being quoted when making a purchase.

What It Costs in U.S. Dollars

	¢	$	$$	$$$	$$$$
Restaurants	under $8	$8–$12	$12–$20	$20–$30	over $30
Hotels*	under $80	$80–$150	$150–$250	$250–$350	over $350

*Indicates hotels on the European Plan (EP—no meals), Continental Plan (CP—with continental breakfast), or Breakfast Plan (BP—with full breakfast). **Indicates hotels on the Modified American Plan (MAP—with breakfast and dinner), Full American Plan (FAP—including all meals but no drinks), or All-Inclusive (AI—with all meals, drinks, and most activities).

TOP EXPERIENCES

Dive Bloody Bay Wall

(A) Little Cayman features an amazing array of different sites for divers and snorkelers alike, but both Jacques and Philippe Cousteau considered the **Bloody Bay Wall** (part of a remarkable marine park) one of the top three dive sites anywhere, plunging from 18 feet more than a mile down into the Cayman Trench.

Swim with stingrays

(B) Swimming at Grand Cayman's Stingray City, even wading at the adjacent sandbar, you can interact with gracefully balletic, silken stingrays, so "tame" you can feed them as they nuzzle you, practically begging pet-like for handouts. Numerous boats take you out for the unforgettable experience in North Sound.

Take in a sculpture exhibit—underwater

(C) Cayman Brac features majestic drop-offs and swim-throughs (as well as the deliberately sunk 330-foot Russian frigate MV *Capt. Keith Tibbetts*) patrolled by riotously colored marine life, but nature's artistry is matched by the world's largest (and still growing) underwater installation, the sculptor Foots's gorgeously imagined, impressively engineered Lost City of Atlantis.

Explore the fourth Cayman island

(D) Easily accessible by kayak from the Little Cayman's "mainland," **Owen Island** appeals to snorkelers and romantics, who have their choice of captivating coves (hint: those facing away from Little Cayman are rougher but invisible to prying eyes).

Try some home cooking

(**E**) Sample island fare at fair prices, such as mouth- and eye-watering jerk chicken from a roadside stall or George Town shack. And aside from jerk and fish-fry stands, a few chefs serve meals in their homes—a perfect intro to Cayman culture and cuisine.

Splurge on a fabulous meal with great wines

(**F**) The wine-pairing menu at Blue by Eric Ripert (the celebrity toque and occasional Top Chef judge, whose NYC eatery, Le Bernardin, annually ranks in world's-best lists) is the kind of epicurean experience that comes along once in a blue moon.

Have a bubbly brunch

(**G**) The Westin Casuarina's Casa Havana hosts a spectacular smorgasbord on the sand at its Sunday Champagne Brunch, which lures locals and even guests from neighboring competitors. You'll be sitting heavily in the lap of luxury after trips to the raw sushi-ceviche bar, cheese tray, and charcuterie, pasta, carving, and dim sum stations.

Eat smaller and cheaper

Several creative kitchens like Mezze, ICOA Cafe, and the Brasserie offer delectable dishes from the dinner menu at discounted lunch prices; an array of fabulous bar snacks is also on tap.

TOP EXPERIENCES

Hang out with blue iguanas

(H) These fierce-looking yet beautiful, critically endangered reptiles found a home at the Queen Elizabeth II Botanic Park. You can take a special "safari" to visit their captive breeding enclave; learning about their life cycles, mating habits, and more; then stroll the peaceful, gorgeously laid-out gardens.

Stroll and swim at Seven Mile Beach

(I) Okay, it's really closer to 5½ miles, but those who love long, broad, uninterrupted sweeps of champagne-hued sand lined with restaurants, bars, and watersports operators yet free of litter and pesky peddlers should roll the dice on Seven Mile Beach. Snorkeling rocks (almost literally on the ironshore) at either end.

Dine with Gladys at Pirates Point

(J) Little Cayman has its own Cordon Bleu–trained chef in the sweet and salty Gladys Howard, owner of **Pirates Point.** She still supervises dinners at her intimate retreat; they aren't quite as elegant or complex as what you might find at one of Grand Cayman's top spots, but they take the (mocha-chocolate) cake for inventiveness on this tiny remote island, and the bon mots and bonhomie are unmatched.

Get crafty on the Brac

Many old-time craft traditions remain alive on Cayman Brac, and while there are many noteworthy attempts to preserve that heritage on Grand Cayman such as Cayman Traditional Arts, there's nothing like sitting in a

1

shop (often the home) of a true practitioner like Annalee Ebanks (thatch-weaving) and Tenson Scott (carving caymanite).

Listen to Barefoot Man at the Reef Resort

(K) Can you imagine Jimmy Buffett going even more native? No? Then head to Pelican's Reef at this East End enclave to hear the blond Calypsonian, Barefoot Man (née George Nowak), a beloved island institution for his witty ditties and fascinating anecdotes of Caribbean life.

Bird-watch on the Sister Islands

(L) You don't have to be a dedicated bird-watcher to appreciate the profusion of avian life throughout the Cayman Islands, including several endangered species whom the ecocentric locals protect as ferociously as nesting mothers. The Booby Pond on Little Cayman and the Brac's Parrot Preserve (including scenic Lighthouse Walk on the bluff's wild, windswept edge) are just two of the gorgeous areas set aside to commune with nature.

WHEN TO GO

The high season in the Cayman Islands is traditionally winter—from December 15 to April 15—when northern weather is at its worst. During this season you're guaranteed the most entertainment at resorts and the most people with whom to enjoy it. It's also the most fashionable, the most expensive, and the most popular time to visit—and most resorts are heavily booked. You must make reservations at least two or three months in advance for the very best places (sometimes a year in advance for the most exclusive spots). Hotel prices drop 20%–50% after April 15; airfares and cruise prices also fall. Saving money isn't the only reason to visit the Cayman Islands during the off-season. Summer is usually one of the prettiest times of the year; the sea is even calmer (ideal for diving—except when tropical storms roil the waters), and things move at a slower pace. The water is clearer for snorkeling and smoother for sailing in the Cayman Islands in May, June, and July, when the big-game fish, though abundant year-round, really run riot.

Climate

Weather in the Cayman Islands is a year-round wonder. The average daily temperature is about 80°F, and there isn't much variation from the coolest to the warmest months, including the water temperature.

Rainfall averages 50 to 60 inches per year (less in the more arid Sister Islands and Grand Cayman's East End). But in the tropics rainstorms tend to be sudden and brief, often erupting early in the morning and at dusk. Toward the end of summer, of course, hurricane season begins in earnest, the first tropical wave passing by in June. Islanders pay close attention to the tropical waves as they form and travel across the Atlantic from Africa. In an odd paradox, tropical storms passing by leave behind the sunniest and clearest days you'll ever see. (And that's saying something in the land of zero air pollution.)

GREAT ITINERARIES

It's a shame that so few visitors (other than divers) spend time on more than one island in a single trip. If you have more than a week, you can certainly spend some quality time on both Grand Cayman and one of its sister islands.

If You Have 3 Days

Ensconce yourself at a resort along Grand Cayman's **Seven Mile Beach,** spending your first day luxuriating on the sand. On Day 2, get your feet wet, if you snorkel or dive, at **Stingray City & Sandbar** in West Bay, where you can feed the alien-looking gliders by hand. Splurge for a great dinner on your second night, perhaps at **Blue by Eric Ripert.** On your last day, head into **George Town** for some shopping. Have lunch with scintillating harbor views at **Breezes by the Bay** or **Casanova** before soaking up some last rays of sun.

If You Have 7 Days

Since divers need to decompress before their return flight, the last day should be spent sightseeing on Grand Cayman. **Boatswain's Beach,** the expensive but exceptional marine theme park, is a fine destination. On the East End you could hike the pristine **Mastic Trail,** then stroll through the gorgeous grounds at **Queen Elizabeth II Botanic Park.** Spend your final morning in George Town (perhaps snorkeling **Eden Rock**). Non-div-

ers, too, should explore a bit farther afield instead of spending all their time at Seven Mile Beach. A full day around West Bay, perhaps beachcombing at savagely beautiful **Barkers,** is a good choice. If you have a car, explore the East End natural attractions, lunching at the **Lighthouse.** Head east another day to visit historic **Pedro St. James Castle;** drive through the original capital, **Bodden Town;** then spend the afternoon (lunch, swimming, and water sports) at **Cayman Kai/ Rum Point.**

If You Have 10 Days

With 10 days, you can spend time on two or even all three islands. Begin on Cayman Brac; after diving the **North Coast** walls, **MV Capt. Keith Tibbetts,** and the **Lost City of Atlantis** (or just lying on the beach), save a morning to hike through the **Parrot Reserve,** perhaps out to the **East End Lighthouse** for its sensational views (or climb the Lighthouse Steps, peeking into **Peter's Cave**). On Little Cayman, chill out picnicking on **Owen Island,** and don't miss the **Booby Pond Nature Reserve.** Spend at least two nights on Grand Cayman.

WEDDINGS AND HONEYMOONS

There's no question that the Cayman Islands, especially Grand Cayman, are one of the Caribbean's foremost honeymoon destinations. Romance is in the air here, and the fittingly champagne-hued beaches, turquoise water, palm trees swaying in balmy tropical breezes, and perpetual summer sunshine put people in the mood for love. Destination weddings—no longer exclusive to celebrities and the super rich—are particularly popular on Grand Cayman, where the larger resorts have wedding planners to help you with the paperwork and details.

The Big Day

Choosing the Perfect Place. When choosing a location, remember that you really have two choices to make: the ceremony location and the reception location, if you're having one. Most couples choose to say their vows on lovely Seven Mile Beach, with the sun setting into the azure sea as their picture-perfect backdrop. Underwater weddings in full scuba gear with schools of fish as impromptu witnesses are also possible (kissing with mask on optional). Cathy Church can photograph your underwater wedding *(see ⇨ Shopping in Chapter 2)*. You can literally leave things up in the air, getting hitched while hovering in a helicopter ("I do; Roger and out," responded one blushing bride over the propeller noise). As for the reception, you can opt for most of the same choices, as well as restaurants. If you decide to go outdoors, remember the seasons—yes, the Caribbean has seasons. If you're planning a wedding outdoors, be sure you have a backup plan in case it rains. Also, if you're planning an outdoor wedding at sunset—which is very popular—be sure you match the time of your ceremony to the time the sun sets at that time of year.

Finding a Wedding Planner. If you're planning to invite more than a minister and your loved one to your wedding ceremony, seriously consider an on-island wedding planner, who can help select a location, help design the floral scheme and recommend a florist as well as a photographer, help plan the menu, and suggest any local traditions to incorporate into your ceremony.

Of course, all the larger resorts have their own wedding planners on-site. If you're planning a resort wedding, work with the on-site wedding coordinator to prepare a detailed list of the exact services he or she will provide. If your idea of your wedding doesn't match the resort's services, try a different resort. Or look for independent wedding planners, who do not work directly for resorts.

Legal Requirements. Documentation can be prepared ahead of time or in one day while on the island. A minimal residency waiting period, blood test, and shots aren't required.

You need to supply a Cayman Islands international embarkation/disembarkation card, as well as proof of identity (a passport or certified copy of your birth certificate signed by a notary public), and age (those under 18 must provide parental consent). If you've been married before, you must provide proof of divorce with the original or certified copy of the divorce decree if applicable or a copy of the death certificate if your previous spouse died. You must list a marriage officer on the application, and you need at least two witnesses; if you haven't come with friends or family, the marriage officer can help you with that, too. A marriage license costs CI$160 (US$200).

Wedding Attire. In the Caribbean, basically anything goes, from long, formal dresses with trains to white bikinis. Floral sundresses are fine, too. Men can wear tuxedos or a simple pair of solid-color slacks with a nice white linen shirt. If you want formal dress and tuxedo, it's usually better to bring your formal attire with you.

Photographs. Deciding whether to use the photographer supplied by your resort or an independent photographer is an important choice. Resorts that host a lot of weddings usually have their own photographers, but you can also find independent, professional island-based photographers, and an independent wedding planner will know the best in the area. Look at the portfolio (many photographers now have web sites), and decide if this person can give you the kind of memories you are looking for. If you're satisfied with the photographer that your resort uses, make sure you see proofs and order prints before you leave the island.

The Honeymoon

Do you want champagne and strawberries delivered to your room each morning? A maze of a swimming pool in which to float? A five-star restaurant in which to dine? Then a resort is the way to go, and Grand Cayman offers options in different price ranges. Whether you want a luxurious experience or a more modest one, you'll certainly find someplace romantic to which you can escape. You can usually stay on at the resort where your wedding was held. On the other hand, maybe you want your own private home in which to romp naked—or maybe your own kitchen in which to whip up a gourmet meal for your loved one. In that case, a private vacation-rental home or condo is the answer.

SNAPSHOT OF THE CAYMAN ISLANDS

Once upon a time the Cayman Islands lazed virtually lost, an afterthought south of Cuba and northwest of Jamaica. Virtually all the islands remained blissfully undeveloped, tranquil on verge of tranquilizing. Only the occasional DuPont and Rockefeller or true dive and sportfishing aficionado came to Zen and zone out. No longer.

This British overseas territory, which consists of Grand Cayman, smaller Cayman Brac, and Little Cayman, is one of the Caribbean's most popular destinations. Today's Cayman Islands are seasoned with suburban prosperity (particularly Grand Cayman, where residents joke that the national flower is the satellite dish and the national bird is the building crane) and stuffed with crowds (the hotels that line the famed Seven Mile Beach are often full, even in the slow summer season). Most of the 53,000-odd Cayman Islanders live on Grand Cayman, where the cost of living is at least 20% higher than in the United States, but you won't be hassled by panhandlers or feel afraid to walk around on a dark evening (the crime rate is very low). Add political and economic stability to the mix, and you have a fine island recipe indeed.

Grand Cayman has long been known for two offshore activities: banking (or as locals call it with a wink toward their own marauding history, "the new piracy," as corsairs gave way to corporate raiders) and scuba diving. With 296 banks and another 350-odd offshore financial institutions, not to mention insurance companies, the neat, prosperous capital, George Town, usually bustles with activity, but never more so than when two to seven cruise ships are docked in the harbor, an increasingly common occurrence.

It's an unprepossessingly flat, scrub-blanketed landfall. But, like the rest of the chain, Grand Cayman had water of such pristine purity that its rippling colors would defy gemologists' descriptions: Artists rave about it much as they do about the quality of the New Mexican sky. And it has a 6-mile-long beach. The hue of antique lace, powdery sand as refined as flour, with waving sea oats beckoning like come-hither courtesans and dunes as curvaceous as Goya's *Naked Maja*, it's one of those beaches that exude a scent and sensuality as potent as pheromones.

Even in the late 1970s, the beach was virtually unscathed. But the wildly famous, violently beautiful, and merely affluent are restless, forever seeking a new hot/cool sun spot as assiduously as pigs rooting for truffles. Grand Cayman couldn't remain undeveloped for long. Not when you throw in the islands' British tax-free status, government incentives to build, and the invitingly temperate subtropical climate. Today nonstop development creeps along Seven Mile Beach. Condo resorts and private homes rival those in the Hamptons and are as immaculately manicured as the clientele. How developed has Seven Mile Beach become? It's axiomatic that every Caribbean island produces a tourist magazine including a few pages on investment. The tiny Cayman Islands produce five or six glossies, which essentially devote half their editorial to banking, insurance, and real estate, relegating dining and sightseeing to secondary status.

While many seasoned, sophisticated travelers adore Grand Cayman, one fellow writer merely quotes Gertrude Stein: "There's no there there." Grand Cayman is definitely more developed, Americanized, and homogenized than some islands, particularly along Seven Mile Beach. What French politician Jack Lang long ago decried as Coca-colonization, the proliferation of KFC, Subway, Burger King, TCBY, and other chains littering the island-scape provides fast-food-for-thought; there's even a new multiplex cinema. So, yes, this is no longer an isolated paradise. But the Cayman government is determined to balance growth with environmental stewardship. Grand Cayman's allure is precisely that precarious balance and subliminal tension between its pockets of unspoiled natural beauty and something-for-everyone, sun-sand-surf mega-development along the calmer northwest coast.

Grand Cayman offers all the conveniences and convenience stores of home, a comforting sight for many repeat guests that also makes Grand Cayman the perfect entry-level Caribbean destination. Its phenomenal popularity lies in its dependability, ease, efficiency, safety, familiarity, and user-friendliness. There are nonstop flights from New York, Miami, and other major airports. Dollars are accepted everywhere (watch the exchange rate, as CI dollars are worth 20% more than their U.S. counterpart). Everyone speaks English, with a graceful tropical lilt. The locals are unusually friendly. The restaurants are uniformly above average, often innovative. Accommodations are reassuringly American-style: smaller glorified motels, all-suites and all-inclusive hotels, time-share condos, or self-contained glam resorts. The west coast, Seven Mile Beach, is one long, glorious, resort-lined swath of sand where you can indulge in almost every conceivable water sport, or bask undisturbed by obnoxious vendors.

The so-called Sister Islands of Cayman Brac and Little Cayman appeal mostly to divers, but anyone seeking total tranquility and a green-conscious vacation for less green will delight in their old-time Caribbean ambience and pristine beaches. Even on Grand Cayman there are peaceful, untrammeled areas. Past Bodden Town going east you still find the "real" old-time Cayman. The joke on the East End is that you needn't worry if you're not from the British Commonwealth: "Drive right, you can drive on the left, you can drive in the middle." You'll find old ladies weaving thatch on the beach and the scent of jerk chicken commingling with the salt air while colorful laundry flutters on the line like so many pennants and flags.

In September 2004 Grand Cayman was hit hard by Hurricane Ivan, but the landscape has now largely regained its lush greenery, although the effects on the mangroves and large trees are still visible. There is a lot of new construction (including the mammoth, environmentally sensitive, and brilliantly engineered Camana Bay residential/commercial "city") and plenty of traffic, so check with a local to plan driving time. It can take 45 minutes during rush hours to go 8 mi (13 km) in the Seven Mile Beach/George Town area.

The Making of the Cayman Islands

Who else but Christopher Columbus would be credited with the first European sighting of the Cayman Islands? Given that no aboriginal remains have been discovered, there's even a slight chance that his crew's were the first human eyes to look upon the islands, though specks appear in the right place on the Cantino Planisphere map published in 1502. On his fourth and final voyage in 1503, Columbus, en route from Panama to Hispaniola, was blown off course by blustery winds and blundered onto Cayman Brac and Little Cayman. The former's distinctive bluff has long since been a navigational landmark for mariners. On May 10, 1503, his son Ferdinand wrote in his log: "We were in sight of two small low islands filled with tortoises, as was the sea all about, in so much as they resemble little rocks." Though the ships didn't stop, Columbus claimed them for Spain, dubbing them "Las Tortugas" (the turtles).

The islands slept for nearly a century, until Sir Francis Drake sailed by in 1585–86 and renamed them Caymanas, after the Carib word for the then-abundant 10-foot crocodiles, "many . . . large lizards which are edible." Fast-forward to the Treaty of Madrid in 1670, after England seized them and Jamaica from Spain as spoils in the endless colonial tug-of-war that embroiled the Caribbean.

The islands remained largely unsettled, used as a pit stop (especially for wood, fresh water, and turtles) by pirates and mercantile vessels alike. Slowly, immigrants arrived from all over Western Europe, including refugees from the Spanish Inquisition and deserters from the British army in Jamaica, although the population remained under 1,000 in 1800, half of it slaves. It was an inhospitable place, ill suited to agriculture, covered in jagged ironshore, and filled with pestilential swamps.

Legend has it that pirates buried loot here, though concrete evidence is lacking. The few settlers harvested cotton and turtles for export, leading hardscrabble lives, eking out an existence on what root crops and fruits they could grow for sustenance. Ships often ran aground on the treacherous reefs and were then salvaged by the locals (who weren't above disorienting vessels with beacon fires). Wrecking proved the most profitable sideline. The most famous such disaster, the wreck of the *Ten Sails*, occurred when a ship struck an East End reef in 1794, and nine others fell like dominoes. According to local lore, the Caymanians proved so resourceful—even heroic—that an appreciative King George III granted the islands tax-free status.

The first democratic elections were held in 1831. Slavery was abolished in 1835, and most freemen remained. By 1900 the population had quintupled, though islanders still led hard lives, largely isolated from the outside world. Cotton, mahogany, sarsaparilla, thatch rope (mostly exported to Jamaica), fishing, turtling, and shipbuilding were the primary sources of income until the mid-20th century.

The population was approximately 3,000 in the 1950s; many islanders had left in search of a better life on Jamaica or elsewhere. Then Cayman struck the two sources of offshore gold that would revitalize the country. Divers discovered the precipitous walls and pristine reefs. The late Bob Soto established the Caribbean's first true dive operation on Grand Cayman in 1957, arguably establishing the regional birthplace of recreational scuba diving. Today there are more than 40 dive shops offering excursions to more than 200 dive sites for every level of enthusiast. The destination received a boost when Jacques Cousteau and his son Philippe raved about the underwater wonderland, naming Bloody Bay off Little Cayman one of the world's top three dive sites.

Sport fishermen also found the waters just fine; when the Southern Cross Club was built on Little Cayman in 1958 by the CEO of Sears-Roebuck and CFO of General Motors as a private club for their wealthy pals, the island's resident population was a grand total of three. With as many as 40,000 marlin and swordfish routinely hooked each year, the government established stringent rules; catch-and-release was vigorously promoted. The islands also helped pioneer ecotourism, creating several marine parks, bird sanctuaries, and other nature reserves.

The Owen Roberts Airport was constructed in the late 1950s, which in turn expedited the shipping of large machinery and materials. The first building boom resulted. Meanwhile, when Jamaica gained independence in 1962, the Cayman Islands opted to remain a British overseas territory; Cayman operates semi-autonomously, with parliamentary elections and a crown-appointed governor.

At the same time, the tax structure was fashioned as one giant incentive, luring hundreds of international financial institutions to the islands. Banking assets exceed (conservatively) US$500 billion. There are now 40,000 registered companies, including more than 600 banks and trusts—the world's fifth-largest financial center. In a mere three decades, a sleepy, mosquito-ridden backwater was transformed into a first-rate First World financial and tourism center, its infrastructure and standard of living the envy of the Caribbean. And now that the authorities have cleaned up after money-laundering scandals in the 1990s and the devastation of Hurricane Ivan in 2004, the Cayman Islands can no longer promote their former catchy marketing campaign, "The Islands that Time Forgot." Well, at least not Grand Cayman.

The People of the Cayman Islands

The Cayman Islands are unique in that, unlike the rest of the Caribbean basin, no traces of habitation by indigenous people have been found by archaeologists or anthropologists. No haunting ruins attest to early settlement, though the wrecks just offshore attest to the cruel beauty of the reefs that ironically drive tourism. It may be that rare case where the politically incorrect term "discovered by Columbus" applies, though some scholars suggest that Arawaks and, especially, Caribs (skilled shipbuilders known for their 80-foot seaworthy canoes) would have stopped for provisioning between Jamaica and Cuba much as later mariners did.

Cayman was eventually settled by the British, who brought the slave trade with them (though the poor, porous soil was ill suited to cultivation). But after World War II the population had dwindled to a few thousand at most on the virtual ghost islands; most of the population had left for Jamaica and other islands in search of a better life.

That all changed with the advent of its two offshore bonanzas, which mushroomed in the 1960s. Today nearly everyone takes pride in pointing out that 113 nationalities compose the current full-time populace (that figure is as low as 87 depending on the source). Residents, especially dewy-eyed expats, cite their coexistence on these tiny specks of land as proof of harmony if not Utopia. So defining what exactly constitutes a Caymanian becomes as elusive as that proverbial sand slipping through your fingers, a mostly genteel controversy.

Indeed, more than half the population of Little Cayman (not counting the birds, though many are migratory as well) is North American or British. Then there are the Cayman-born, who take their own proprietary view and sometimes feel disenfranchised, especially on prosperous Grand Cayman. Several Cayman-born artists speak of feeling pressured to deliver less edgy,

more generic work to the government-funded cultural institutions. And even the expats decry the high prices and harsh immigration, employment, and rollover laws.

Despite its geographic and cultural isolation from most of the region, Cayman (which is the preferred term for the country; *never* say "the Caymans") is close to its nearest island sisters in many respects. Culture is heavily influenced by Jamaica's proximity and sizable residential population. The area has developed close ties to the United States and Canada, as well as its mother country, Great Britain. U.S. products line grocery-store shelves, and U.S., Canadian, and British investors finance many of the large real-estate developments. Europeans have invested in some of the most exciting restaurants and small hotels.

One noteworthy aspect of Caymanian culture is its conservatism. This isn't surprising given the billions stowed in its banks. But between its British overseas territory status and proximity to the United States, Cayman can seem downright puritanical, especially for a fun-in-the-sun vacation destination. Churches are ubiquitous, and even Grand Cayman virtually shuts down on Sundays and religious holidays. The island's conservatism was partly responsible for the one major P.R. nightmare, when a gay-chartered cruise ship was denied berthing rights in 1998 (the minister of tourism allegedly voiced concern that the passengers could not "uphold the standards of appropriate behavior"). In the ensuing fracas, the British government decriminalized homosexuality, but even a decade later the debate simmers.

In most respects, however, Caymanians adopt a live-and-let-live philosophy. They're genuinely welcoming, especially on the sister islands, and expect the same courtesies to be observed. If you really want to fit in, address islanders as Mr. and Miss (even married women) followed by their first, not surname.

Spanish Galleons and Pirates

In 1586 Sir Francis Drake and his privateers, with the tacit approval of Queen Elizabeth I, were the first raiders to arrive in the Cayman Islands, finding safe harbors aplenty from which to prey on Spain's gold-laden galleons. So began a history of piracy, both encouraged and downplayed by Caymanian historians, the former because it makes for colorful copy, the latter because the locals were hardly models of moral behavior themselves, deliberately wrecking then plundering ships on the hazardous reefs.

Like any other mariners during the 17th and 18th centuries, buccaneers prowled these waters, especially in search of provisions, crew replacements, and a remote spot to effect repairs. The islands lay squarely on the trade route from Central America to Cuba and back to Spain. Local lore swears that bountiful treasure remains buried, especially in Bodden Town and the Brac's many caves and coves, to this day.

Reputedly the era's most infamous rapscallions sought hideouts both for themselves and their booty: Henry Morgan, Edward "Blackbeard" Teach, Anne Bonney, Edward Low, George Lowther, and Neal Walker, to name-drop a few. Though undoubtedly buccaneers knew these waters, most historians suggest they played a relatively small role in Caymanian history. Whatever the truth, divers and snorkelers believe they've discovered buried treasure in the glittering underwater tiara of bejeweled coral reefs.

Geography, Flora, and Fauna of the Cayman Islands

These isolated slivers of sun-seared limestone offer an astonishing variety of terrains (above and below water), with richly diverse flora and fauna to match. That very geographic separation enabled species to evolve slightly differently from their mainland—even Jamaican and Cuban—counterparts, developing unique mutations and other characteristics.

A felicitous combination of factors—climate, underwater currents, water temperature, and geology—painted Cayman's multifaceted aquatic canvas. Other than the Brac's dramatic vaulting bluff, the Cayman Islands are pancake-flat. Few realize that they perch upon the peaks of a sheer submerged mountain range that defines the Cayman Trench, whose northern ridge plummets more than 25,000 feet, the deepest point in the Caribbean Sea. These topographical features form the stunning drop-offs and vertical walls within a few hundred yards of shore that seduce scuba divers from the world over. It seems a perfect setting for a Jules Verne adventure.

The healthy coral reef systems provide homes for hundreds of species of marine life, from Lilliputian grunts to leviathan groupers, not to mention mollusks, crustaceans, sponges, and sea fans, all in showy colors. Cayman is world-renowned for its marine life, but terra firma is almost as varied. Mangrove swamp composes almost half the total landmass, providing an important breeding ground for fish and birds; their protection is a major mandate

of the National Trust for the Cayman Islands.

Almost half the 250 avian species identified in Cayman are seacoast or open-sea birds, including the migrants traversing the North and South American continents. Species include several types of boobies, West Indian whistling ducks, frigate birds, ospreys, purple gallinules, and coots. The colorful Cayman Brac parrot has earned its own protected reserve, as has the red-footed booby, making the Brac and Little Cayman particular favorites with birders. More than 650 different plant species have been documented, and the forests are far more diverse than those at northern latitudes; in parts of the Brac, cacti incongruously grow next to orchids and mahogany trees. Grand Cayman is home to one of the planet's most endangered species, the blue iguana, and an ongoing project is attempting with some success to breed and reintroduce the animal to the wild.

DID YOU KNOW?

More than 40 dive shops take divers to more than 200 individual sites; the Cayman Islands' first dive operation opened in 1957.

2

Exploring Grand Cayman

WITH SHOPPING

WORD OF MOUTH

"We . . . stopped at the [Queen Elizabeth II] Botanic [Park] on the way [back to our resort] which was wonderful. Blue iguanas and lots of lush foliage made it a stop worth doing."

—starfish 1

By Jordan Simon

THOUGH GRAND CAYMAN IS MOST CELEBRATED for its aquatic activities, there's no shortage of diversions to please landlubbers, history buffs, the ecocentric, and families, from turtle and butterfly farms to ruined fortifications. It's just as alluring on land as under water, gleaming with a ravishing dryness. Though not lush, the surrounding scenery can spiral from arid semi-desert to tropical hardwood forests that pierce the sky like cathedral spires. Many attractions admirably attempt to foster greater understanding of the environment and the importance of responsible stewardship of our resources.

Window-shopping in the captivating capital, George Town, ranks as many visitors' favorite form of recreation and sightseeing. Not only will you find no additional sales tax, but there's duty-free merchandise aplenty. And though most people's image of Grand Cayman is bustling Seven Mile Beach, there are downright rural, pastoral pockets where if time doesn't stand still, it slows to a turtle's steady crawl. This is where travelers can experience the "real" Cayman, including craft traditions such as thatch weaving that have nearly vanished.

EXPLORING GRAND CAYMAN

The historic capital of George Town, on the southeast corner of Grand Cayman, is easy to explore on foot. If you're a shopper, you can spend days here; otherwise, an hour will suffice for a tour of the downtown area. To see the rest of the island, rent a car or scooter or take a guided tour. The portion of the island called West Bay is noted for its jumble of neighborhoods, many featuring ornate Edwardian homes built by seafarers, nautical tour companies (and real fishing fleet) at Morgan's Harbour, and a few attractions. When traffic is heavy, it's about a half-hour to West Bay from George Town, even with the newer bypass road that runs parallel to West Bay Road. The less-developed North Side and East End have natural attractions from blowholes to botanical gardens, as well as the remains of the island's original settlements. Plan on at least 45 minutes for the drive out from George Town (more than an hour during rush hours). You need a day to explore the entire island—including a stop at a beach for a picnic or swim.

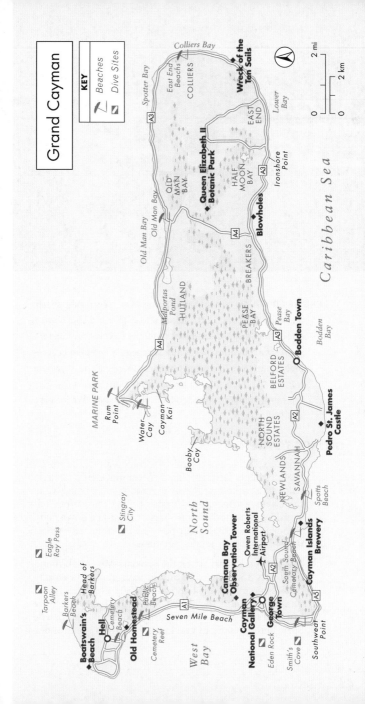

Grand Cayman

KEY

⊼ Beaches
◪ Dive Sites

0   2 mi
0   2 km

Colliers Bay

Spotter Bay

East End Beaches

COLLIERS

◆ **Wreck of the Ten Sails**

◆ **Queen Elizabeth II Botanic Park**

Old Man Bay

Old Man Bay

OLD MAN BAY

HALF MOON BAY

EAST END

Lower Bay

Ironshore Point

HUTLAND

Malportas Pond

A4

BREAKERS

◆ **Blowholes**

PEASE BAY

Pease Bay

A3

◆ **Bodden Town**

Bodden Bay

Caribbean Sea

MARINE PARK

Rum Point

Cayman Kai

Water Cay

Booby Cay

BELFORD ESTATES

NORTH SOUND ESTATES

NEWLANDS

SAVANNAH

A2

◆ **Pedro St. James Castle**

Spotts Beach

North Sound

Stingray City ◪

Eagle Ray Pass ◪

Tarpoon Alley ◪

Barkers Beach

Head of Barkers

◆ **Boatswain's Beach**

○ **Hell**

Cemetery Beach

Public Beach

◆ **Old Homestead**

Cemetery Reef

West Bay

Seven Mile Beach

A1

◆ **Camana Bay Observation Tower**

Owen Roberts International Airport

◆ **Cayman National Gallery**

Eden Rock

○ **George Town**

Smith's Cove

Southwest Point

South Sound

Cemetery Beach

A2

A5

◆ **Cayman Islands Brewery**

Caribbean Sea

An aerial view of West Bay

CRUISE CRUSH. On certain days George Town, Seven Mile Beach, and even West Bay's attractions crawl with cruise-ship hordes. Check the Cayman Island Port Authority (⊕ *www.caymanport. com/schedule.htm*) for the latest schedule and plan accordingly, unless you like being trampled. There may be anywhere from one to three ships at anchor off George Town any day of the week, but more ships tend to call on Tuesday, Wednesday, and Thursday.

GEORGE TOWN

Begin exploring the capital by strolling along the waterfront, Harbour Drive, to **Elmslie Memorial United Church,** named after the first Presbyterian missionary to serve in the Caymans. Its vaulted timber ceiling (built from salvaged wreck material in the shape of an upside-down hull), wooden arches, mahogany pews, and tranquil nave reflect the island's deeply religious nature.

Just north near Fort Street, the **Seamen's Memorial Monument** lists 153 names on an old navigational beacon; a bronze piece by Canadian sculptor Simon Morris, titled *Tradition*, honors the almost 500 Caymanians who have lost their lives at sea. Dive-industry pioneer Bob Soto, wife Suzy, and daughter-in-law Leslie Bergstrom spearheaded

BEST BETS

■ **Feeling Blue.** Visiting the endangered blue iguana compound at the glorious Queen Elizabeth II Botanic Park.

■ **Petting a Turtle.** Though it's hideously expensive, Boatswain's Beach encapsulates everything that makes Cayman special. And admission to its world-class turtle research center/farm, true edu-tainment, is cheaper.

■ **Getting Touched by History.** Pedro St. James Castle bears eloquent testimony to Caymanian struggles for democracy, freedom, and survival against the elements.

■ **National Trust–worthy.** The National Trust is an admirable institution dedicated to preserving the Caymanian environment and culture. If you're on island when they're running a tour (perhaps to the bat caves or historic homes) or a demonstration (cooking, thatch weaving), go!

■ **Whatta Guy.** When he's not off adventuring, acclaimed marine biologist-artist Guy Harvey is usually in his amazing gallery-shop; buy a print, ask him to sign it, and converse on conservation.

the project, which Prince Edward unveiled during the 2003 quincentennial celebrations.

A few steps away lie the scant remains of **Fort George,** constructed in 1790 to repel plundering pirates; it also functioned as a watch post during World War II to scan for German subs.

In front of the court building, in the center of town, names of influential Caymanians are inscribed on the **Wall of History,** which also commemorates the islands' quincentennial. Across the street is the Cayman Islands **Legislative Assembly Building,** next door to the **1919 Peace Memorial Building.** A block south is the horseshoe-shaped **General Post Office,** built in 1939 at the tail end of the Art Deco period. Let the kids pet the big blue iguana statues.

★ Fodor'sChoice **Cayman Islands National Museum.** Built in 1833, the historically significant clapboard home of the national museum has had several different incarnations over the years, serving as courthouse, jail, post office, and dance hall. It features an ongoing archaeological excavation of the Old Gaol and excellent 3-D bathymetric displays, murals, dioramas, and videos that illustrate local geology, flora and fauna, and island history. The first floor focuses on natural

Cayman Islands
National Museum, 1

National Gallery, 2

National Trust, 3

history, including a microcosm of Cayman ecosystems, from beaches to dry woodlands and swamps, and offers such interactive elements as a simulated sub. Upstairs, the cultural exhibit features renovated murals, video history reenactments, and 3-D back panels in display cases holding thousands of artifacts ranging from a 14-foot catboat with animatronic captain to old coins and rare documents painting a portrait of daily life and past industries such as shipbuilding and turtling, stressing Caymanians' resilience when they had little contact with the outside world. There are also temporary exhibits focusing on aspects of Caymanian culture, a local art collection, and interactive displays for kids. ✉ *Harbour Dr., George Town* ☎ *345/949–8368* ⊕ *www.museum.ky* 🎟 *$5* ☺ *Weekdays 9–5, Sat. 10–2.*

★ **National Gallery.** A worthy nonprofit organization, the museum was established in 1996 to display and promote the range of Caymanian artists and craftspeople, both established and grassroots. The gallery coordinates a wealth of first-rate outreach programs for everyone from infants to inmates. It usually mounts six major exhibitions a year, including three large-scale retrospectives or thematic shows and multimedia installations. Director Natalie Coleman

Maritime Heritage Trail

The National Trust for the Cayman Islands, National Museum, National Archive, Sister Islands Nature Tourism Project, and Department of the Environment have collaborated on a series of land-based sightseeing trails on Grand Cayman and the sister islands that commemorate the country's maritime heritage. Shore-side signs around the islands denote points of access and explain their historic or natural significance, from shipwreck sites to shorebird-sighting spots, chandlers' warehouses to lighthouses.

Brochures and posters are available at the National Trust and Tourism offices on each island, as well as at many hotels. They provide additional information on turtling, shipbuilding, salvaging, fishing, and other sea-based economies. The project provides visitors with interactive edutainment as they explore the islands.

also brings in international shows that somehow relate to the island, often inviting local artists for stimulating dialogue. The gallery hosts public slide shows, a lunchtime lecture series running in conjunction with current exhibits, Art Flix (video presentations on art history, introduced with a short lecture and followed by a discussion led by curators or artists), and a CineClub (movie night). The gallery has also developed an Artist Trail Map with the Department of Tourism and can facilitate studio tours. The gallery hopes its large new quarters near Seven Mile Beach on Harquail Bypass will open by fall 2010; until then it remains in its original George Town building. ⊠ *Ground floor, Harbour Place, S. Church St., George Town* ☎ *345/945–8111* ⊕ *www.nationalgallery.org.ky* ⌒ *Free* ⊙ *Weekdays 9–5, Sat. 11–4.*

NEED A BREAK? **Full of Beans Cafe** (⊠ *Pasadora Place, Smith Rd., George Town* ☎ *345/943–2326*) offers a surprisingly large, eclectic, Asian-tinged menu utilizing ultra-fresh ingredients. Standouts include homemade carrot cake, mango smoothies, cranberry-Brie-pecan salad, portobello panini, and lobster medallions with beet and cucumber salads drizzled in ginger-lime oil. Owner Cindy Butler fashions a feast for weary eyes as well, with rotating artworks and stylish mosaic mirrors contrasting with faux-brick walls and vintage hardwood tables. There is another location in the heart of downtown.

National Trust. For a wonderful map of the historic and natural attractions, go to the office of the National Trust. The Trust sells books and guides to Cayman. The fabulous Web site has more than 50 information sheets on cultural and natural topics from iguanas to schoolhouses. Take advantage of the regularly scheduled sociable yet educational activities, from boat tours through the forests of the Central Mangrove Wetlands to cooking classes where a local celebrity chef demonstrates the art of preparing traditional local dishes. Stop there first before you tour the island. Be forewarned: Though the office is walkable from George Town, it's an often hot 20-minute walk from downtown. ⊠ *Dart Park, 558 S. Church St., George Town* ☎ *345/749–1121* ⊕ *nationaltrust.org.ky* ⊗ *Mon.–Fri., 9–1 and 2–5:30.*

ELSEWHERE ON THE ISLAND

SEVEN MILE BEACH

☾ **Camana Bay Observation Tower.** This 75-foot structure pro-
★ vides striking 360-degree panoramas of otherwise flat Grand Cayman, sweeping from George Town and Seven Mile Beach to the North Sound. The double-helix staircase is impressive in its own right. Running alongside the steps (though an elevator is also available), a floor-to-ceiling mosaic replicates the look and feel of a dive from sea bed to surface. Constructed of countless tiles in 114 different colors, it's one of the world's largest marine-theme mosaic installations. Benches and lookout points encourage you to take your time and admire the views as you ascend. Afterward you can enjoy 500-acre Camana Bay's gardens, waterfront boardwalk, and pedestrian paths lined with shops and restaurants, or frequent live entertainment. ⊠ *Extending between Seven Mile Beach and North Sound, 2 mi (3 km) north of George Town, Camana Bay* ☎ *345/640–3500* ⊕ *www.camanabay.com* ⊡ *Free* ⊗ *Sunrise–10* PM.

WEST BAY

★ **Fodor's Choice Boatswain's Beach.** Cayman's premier attraction,
☾ the Turtle Farm, has been rebranded and transformed into a marine theme park. The expanded complex now has several souvenir shops and restaurants. Still, the turtles remain a central attraction, and you can tour ponds in the original research-breeding facility with thousands in various stages of growth, some up to 600 pounds and more than 70 years old. Turtles can be picked up from the tanks, a real treat for children and adults as the little creatures flap their fins

A traditional Cayman cottage at Boatswain's Beach

and splash the water. Four areas—three aquatic and one dry—cover 23 acres; different-colored bracelets determine access (the steep full-pass admission includes snorkeling gear). The park helps promote conservation, encouraging interaction (a Tidal Pool houses invertebrates like starfish and crabs) and observation. Animal Program Events include Keeper Talks, where you might feed birds or iguanas, and biologists speaking about conservation and its importance to the ecosystem. The freshwater **Breaker's Lagoon,** replete with cascades plunging over moss-carpeted rocks evoking Cayman Brac, is the islands' largest pool. The saltwater **Boatswain's Lagoon,** replicating all the Cayman Islands and the Trench, teems with 14,000 denizens of the deep milling about a cannily designed synthetic reef. You can snorkel here (lessons and guided tours are available). Both lagoons have underwater four-inch-thick acrylic panels that look directly into **Predator Reef,** home to six brown sharks, four nurse sharks, and other predatory fish such as tarpons, eels, and jacks. These predators can also be viewed from terra (or terror, as one guide jokes) firma. Make sure you check out feeding times! The free-flight **Aviary,** designed by consultants from Disney's Animal Kingdom, is a riot of color and noise as feathered friends represent the entire Caribbean basin, doubling as a rehabilitation center for Cayman Wildlife and Rescue. A winding interpretive **nature trail** culminates in the Blue Hole, a collapsed cave once filled with water. Audio tours are available with different

Camana Bay

Dubbed a "new town" (in all senses of the term), ambitious in scope and philosophy, the mixed-use, master-planned Camana Bay stretches along 500 acres from Seven Mile Beach to the North Sound. It's a sustainable, traditionally, and colorfully Caribbean—yet technologically cutting-edge—design, and ecologically sensitive to boot. Specifically designed by more than 100 consultants from several leading local and global firms as a gathering center to live, work, and play, Camana Bay has been carefully developed in three phases (the final phase is expected to be completed by 2012 and will include hotels and a marina, alongside residential and office development).

The four residential-office-retail courtyards feature unique feels and color schemes unifying native flora with surrounding walls, walks, and mosaics.

Streets were aligned to mitigate heat and to capture breezes. Plants were carefully chosen to attract birds and butterflies, and the development has green space galore, including artificial islands and harbors, as well as water features like canals and fountains.

The pedestrianized main street, called the Paseo, is lined with mostly high-end shops that are open late, restaurants, and entertainment (including a weekly farmer's market and a movie theater complex). The Paseo culminates in the Crescent, a waterfront plaza with restaurants, more gardens, interactive fountains, an esplanade, amphitheater, and public venues for fireworks to festivals. There are also jogging/biking trails, pocket parks, open spaces, and a beach. Residents and visitors are encouraged to park their cars and stroll (enhancing the green lifestyle) or just hang out.

focuses, from butterflies to bush medicine. The last stop is the living museum, **Cayman Street**, complete with facades duplicating different types of vernacular architecture; an herb and fruit garden; porch-side artisans, musicians and storytellers; model catboats; live cooking on an old-fashioned "caboose" oven; and interactive craft demonstrations from painting mahogany to thatch weaving. ⊠ *825 Northwest Point Rd., Box 812, West Bay* ☎ *345/949–3894* ⊕ *www.boatswainsbeach.ky* ☜ *Comprehensive ticket $45, Turtle Farm alone $30* ☉ *Daily 8:30–4:30.*

Hell. Quite literally the tourist trap from Hell, especially when overrun by cruise ship passengers, this attraction does offer free admission, fun photo ops, and sublime surrealism.

Its name refers to the quarter-acre of menacing shards of charred brimstone thrusting up like vengeful spirits (actually blackened and "sculpted" by acid-secreting algae and fungi over millennia). The eerie lunarscape is now cordoned off, but you can prove you had a helluva time by taking a photo from the observation deck. The attractions are the small post office and a gift shop where you can get cards and letters postmarked from Hell, not to mention wonderfully silly postcards titled When Hell Freezes Over (depicting bathing beauties on the beach), The Devil Made Me Do It bumper stickers, Scotch bonnet–based Hell sauce, and The Coolest Shop in Hell T-shirts. Ivan Farrington, the owner of the Devil's Hang-Out store, cavorts in a devil's costume (horn, cape, and tails), regaling you with demonically bad jokes. ⊠ *Hell Rd., West Bay* ☎ *345/949–3358* ⊛ *www.hell. ky* ⊜ *Free* ⊙ *Daily 9–6.*

EAST END AND NORTH SIDE

The Tourism Attraction Board and 14 leading eastern-district businesses (from Ocean Frontiers dive shop to Kaibo Beach Bar) and attractions developed the **"Discover the East" Adventure Card** to encourage visitors (and locals) to experience the beauty, culture, and heritage of Grand Cayman's eastern districts. The $16 card provides free admission to the Queen Elizabeth II Botanic Park and to Pedro St. James (normally $10 each), as well as gifts and discounts throughout Bodden Town, Cayman Kai, North Side, and the East End, from free desserts with dinner to $20 off diving.

☼ **Blowholes.** When the easterly trade winds blow hard, crashing waves force water into caverns and send impressive geysers shooting up as much as 20 feet through the ironshore. The blowholes were partially filled during Hurricane Ivan in 2004, so the water must be rough to recapture their former elemental drama. ⊠ *Frank Sound Rd., roughly 10 mi (16 km) east of Bodden Town, near East End.*

Bodden Town. In the island's original south-shore capital you can find an old cemetery on the shore side of the road. Graves with A-frame structures are said to contain the remains of pirates. There are also the ruins of a fort and a wall erected by slaves in the 19th century. The National Trust runs tours of the restored 1840s Mission House. A curio shop serves as the entrance to what's called the Pirate's Caves ($8), partially underground natural formations that are more hokey (decked out with fake treasure chests and

DID YOU KNOW?

The blowholes on Grand Cayman's southern shore were formed when waves pushed sea water through the ceilings of caves under the ironshore, sending the spray up into the air.

Cayman House and Garden

The few original Caymanian cottages that exist represent a unique architectural vernacular cannily adapted to the climate and available resources. Foundation posts and floors were constructed from durable, termite-resistant ironwood. Wattle-and-daub walls were fashioned from basket-woven sticks plastered on both sides with lime daub (extracted coral burned with various woods). The earliest roofs were thatched with woven palm fronds (later shingled or topped with corrugated zinc); their peak helped cool houses, as hot air rises. The kitchen was separate, usu-ally just a "caboose" stove for cooking.

The other unusual custom, "backing sand," originated as a Christmas tradition, then be-came a year-round decorative statement. Women and children would tote woven-thatch bas-kets by moonlight to the beach, bringing "back" glittering white sand to cover their front yards. They'd rake intricate patterns and adorn the sand with sinu-ous conch-shell paths. The yard was also swept Saturdays so it would look well tended after Sunday services. A side benefit was that it helped reduce in-sect infestation.

mannequins in pirate garb, with an outdoor petting zoo) than spooky.

☙ The **Mission House** is a classic gabled two-story Cay-manian home on wooden posts, with wattle-and-daub accents, dating to the 1840s and restored by the National Trust. The building earned its sobriquet thanks to early missionaries, teachers, and families who lived here while helping establish the Presbyterian ministry and school in Bodden Town. Shards of 19th-century glass and ceram-ics found on-site and period furnishings are on display. The posted opening hours are irregular, especially dur-ing the off-season. ✉ *63 Gun Square Rd., Bodden Town* ☎ *345/947–5805 or 345/925–6036* ⊕ *www.nationaltrust. org.ky* 🕾 *CI$5* ☉ *Tues.–Sat. 9–5:30.*

You enter the **Pirate's Caves** through a surprisingly good curio shop (the owner is noted for jewelry fashioned from doubloons). Outside, ceramic "skulls" embedded into banyan trees and mini gravestones enhance the supposed spookiness. Younger kids should adore the playground and mini zoo with freshwater Brazilian stingrays, turtles, par-rots, macaws, iguanas, agoutis (a large rodent), mountain goats, and farm animals like chickens, the pig Percy, and the horse Spirit. The caves themselves are pure yo-ho-hokum, tricked up with more faux "skeletons," swords jutting from limestone formations, and other rusted artifacts of dubious authenticity (such as fake treasure chests), lanterns, and conch shells, as well as an authentic fossilized bone or two. Beware the steep descent (with only rope handrails). Very informative sheets on history and the native plants are provided, as well as good interpretive signage within the grounds. ⊠ *South Shore Rd., Bodden Town* ☎ *345/947–3122* ⊠ *$8* ⊙ *Daily 9–6.*

Cayman Islands Brewery. This brewery occupies the former Stingray facility; free tours are available, but you must call ahead to ensure someone is available to squire you around. Caybrew is a full-bodied yet light lager with a crisp hop finish. The guide will explain the iconic imagery of the bottle and label, and the nearly three-week process: seven days' fermentation, ten days' lagering (storage), and one day in the bottling tank. The brewery's ecofriendly features are also championed: Local farmers receive the spent grains used to produce the beer to serve as cattle feed at no charge, while waste liquid is channeled into one of the Caribbean's most advanced water treatment systems. Then enjoy your complimentary tasting with the knowledge that you're helping the local environment and economy. ⊠ *366 Shamrock Rd., Red Bay* ☎ *345/947–6699* ⊕ *www.cib.ky* ⊠ *Free* ⊙ *Weekdays 9–5, Sat. 10–5.*

★ FodorśChoice **Pedro St. James Castle.** Built in 1780, the great-
ℭ house is Cayman's oldest stone structure and the only remaining late-18th-century residence on the island. In its capacity as courthouse and jail, it was the birthplace of Caymanian democracy, where in December 1831 the first elected parliament was organized and in 1835 the Slavery Abolition Act signed. The structure still has original or historically accurate replicas of sweeping verandahs, mahogany floors, rough-hewn wide-beam ceilings, outside louvers, stone and oxblood- or mustard-color lime-wash-painted walls, brass fixtures, and Georgian furnishings (from tea caddies to canopy beds to commodes). Paying obsessive attention to detail, the curators even fill glasses with faux wine. The mini-museum also includes a hodge-podge of displays from slave emancipation to old stamps. The buildings are surrounded by 8 acres of natural parks and woodlands. You can stroll through landscaping of native Caymanian flora and experience one of the most

Pedro St. James Castle

spectacular views on the island from atop the dramatic Great Pedro Bluff. First watch the impressive multimedia theater show, complete with smoking pots, misting rains, and two film screens where the story of Pedro's Castle is presented on the hour. The poignant Hurricane Ivan Memorial outside uses text, images, and symbols to represent important aspects of that horrific 2004 natural disaster. ⊠ *Pedro Castle Rd., Box 305, Savannah* ☎ *345/947–3329* ⊕ *www.pedrostjames.ky* ⊠ *$10* ⊙ *Daily 9–5.*

★ **Fodor's Choice Queen Elizabeth II Botanic Park.** This 65-acre wilderness preserve showcases a wide range of indigenous and nonindigenous tropical vegetation, approximately 2,000 species in total. Splendid sections include numerous water features from limpid lily ponds to cascades; a Heritage Garden with a traditional cottage and caboose kitchen includes crops that might have been planted on Cayman a century ago; a Floral Colour Garden, arranged by color, the walkway wandering through sections of pink, red, orange, yellow, white, blue, mauve, lavender, and purple. A 2-acre lake and adjacent wetlands include three islets that provide a habitat and breeding ground for native birds just as showy as the floral displays: green herons, black-necked stilts, American coots, blue-winged teal, cattle egrets, and rare West Indian whistling ducks. The nearly mile-long Woodland Trail encompasses every Cayman ecosystem from wetland to cactus thicket, buttonwood swamp to lofty

Queen Elizabeth II Botanic Park

woodland with imposing mahogany trees. You'll encounter birds, lizards, turtles, agoutis, and more, but the park's star residents are the protected endemic blue iguanas, found only in Grand Cayman. The world's most endangered iguana, they're the focus of the National Trust's Blue Iguana Recovery Program, a captive breeding and reintroduction initiative. This section of the park is usually closed to the general public, though released "blue dragons" hang out in the vicinity. The Trust conducts 90-minute behind-the-scenes safaris Monday–Saturday at 11 AM for $30. ✉ *367 Botanic Rd., North Side* ✉ *Box 203, North Side, Grand Cayman* ☎ *345/947–9462* ⊕ *www.botanic-park.ky* ✆ *$10* ⊙ *Apr.–Sept., daily 9–6:30; Oct.–Mar., daily 9–5:30; last admission 1 hr prior to closing.*

Wreck of the Ten Sails Park. This lonely, lovely park on Grand Cayman's windswept eastern tip commemorates the island's most (in)famous shipwreck. On February 8, 1794, the *Cordelia*, heading a convoy of 58 square-rigged merchant vessels en route from Jamaica to England, foundered on one of the treacherous East End reefs. Its warning cannon fire was tragically misconstrued as a call to band more closely together due to imminent pirate attack, and nine more ships ran aground. The local sailors, who knew those rough seas, demonstrated great bravery in rescuing all 400-odd seamen. Popular legend claims (romantically but inaccurately) that King George III granted the islands an eternal tax exemption. Queen Elizabeth II dedicated the park's plaque in 1994. Interpretive signs document the historic details. The ironically peaceful headland provides magnificent views of the reef (including more recent shipwrecks); bird-watching is superb from here half a mile south along the coast to the Lighthouse Park, which is being developed on a craggy bluff by the National Trust. ✉ *Gun Bay, East End* ☎ *345/949–0121 (National Trust)* 🎫 *Free* ⊙ *Daily*.

SHOPPING

On Grand Cayman the good news is that there's no sales tax *and* plenty of duty-free merchandise including jewelry, china, crystal, perfumes, and cameras. Savings on luxury goods, though rarely as great as good sales in big cities or at outlet malls in the United States, range between 10% and 25%. Notable exceptions are liquor, which is available minus that tariff only at specially designated shops, and haute couture (though the ritzier resort shops stock some designer labels). "Brand Cayman" is the local nickname for the glamorous shops along Cardinal Avenue, the local answer to New York's Madison Avenue and Beverly Hills's Rodeo Drive. Esteemed names include Waterford and Wedgwood, Cartier, and Cayman's own Bernard K. Passman.

Worthy local items include woven thatch mats and baskets, jewelry made from a marble-like stone called Caymanite (from Cayman Brac's cliffs, a striated amalgam of several metals), and authentic sunken treasure often fashioned into jewelry, though the last is never cheap (request a certificate of authenticity if one isn't offered). You'll also find individual artists' ateliers and small, colorful craft shops whose owners often love discussing the old days and traditions. Bear in mind that most major attractions feature extensive and/or intriguing gift shops, whether Boatswain's Beach or the National Gallery.

Local palate pleasers include treats made by the Tortuga Rum Company (both the famed cakes and the actual distilled spirit, including a sublime 12-year-old rum), Cayman Honey, Cayman Taffy, and Cayman Sea Salt (from the ecofriendly "farm" of the same name). Also seek out such gastronomic goodies as jams, sauces, and vinegars from Hawley Haven and Whistling Duck Farms on the eastern half of the island. Cigar lovers, take note: Some shops carry

Blue Dragons

CLOSE UP

Co-sponsored by the Botanic Park and the National Trust, the **Blue Iguana Recovery Program** (⊕ *www.blueiguana.ky*) is a model captive breeding plan for the remarkable reptiles that only two decades ago faced total extinction. The Grand Cayman blue iguana lived on the island for millennia until man arrived, its only natural predator the racer snake. Until recently they were the world's most critically endangered species, functionally extinct with only 25 remaining in the wild. BIRP has released 200 into the Salina Reserve, with an ultimate repopulation goal of 1,000 if they can breed successfully in the wild.

The National Trust conducts safaris six mornings a week, giving you a chance to see hatchlings in the cages, camouflaged toddlers, and breeding-age adults like Mad Max and Blue Blue. Most of the iguanas raised here are released at two years by the Wildlife Conservation Society with a microchip implant tag for radio tracking and color-coded beading ("their navel rings," jokes a guide) for unique identification. Tones fluctuate according to lighting and season, brightening to azure during the April–May breeding period. Guides explain the gestation and incubation periods and the pairing of potential mates ("some are too dominant, and we don't want inbreeding like Appalachian hillbillies, leading to potential mutations or sterility").

If you can't make it to the park, look for the 15 larger-than-life one-of-a-kind outdoor sculptures commissioned from local artists scattered around the island. You can download maps of the Blue Dragon Trail from the BIRP, National Trust, and Botanic Park sites. Many hotels also stock leaflets with maps and fun facts (the iguanas live up to 70 years, grow to 6 feet in length, and weigh 25 pounds). You can even purchase custom blue iguana products (helping fund research), such as Joel Friesch's limited-edition hand-painted bobbleheads (blues bob their heads rapidly as a territorial warning) packaged in a bright yellow hard cardboard box. You can also volunteer for a working vacation (or longer field-work study stint) online.

famed Cuban brands, but you must enjoy them on the island; bringing them back to the United States is illegal.

AREAS AND MALLS

An almost unbroken line of strip malls runs from George Town through Seven Mile Beach, most of them presenting shopping and dining options galore. The ongoing Camana Bay mega-development already glitters with glam shops, including Island Companies' largest and grandest store offering the hautest name-brand jewelry, watches, and duty-free goods.

GEORGE TOWN

Bayshore Mall (⊠ *South Church St., George Town*), optimally located downtown and one of the newest shopaholics' targets (you can't miss the cotton-candy colors), contains a Kirk Freeport department-store branch (Tag Heuer to Herend porcelain, Mikimoto to Mont Blanc), swank Lalique and Lladró boutiques, La Parfumerie (which often offers makeovers and carries 450 beauty brands), and other usual luxury culprits.

Cayside Courtyard (⊠ *Harbour Dr., George Town*) is noted for its specialty jewelers and antiques dealers.

Duty Free Plaza (⊠ *S. Church St., George Town*) caters to more casual shoppers with the T-shirt Factory, Island Treasures, Havana Cigars, Blackbeard's Rumcake Bakery, and the Surf Shop. The mall also contains a kid-pleasing 12,000-gallon saltwater aquarium with sharks, eels, and stingrays.

Island Plaza (⊠ *Harbour Dr., George Town*) counters with 15 duty- and tax-free stores, including Swarovski Boutique, Island Jewellers, and Churchill's Cigars (with bars to de-stress in after binge shopping).

★ **Kirk Freeport Plaza** (⊠ *Cardinal Ave., George Town*), home to the Kirk Freeport flagship department store, is ground zero for couture; it's also known for its boutiques selling fine watches and jewelry, china, crystal, leather, perfumes, and cosmetics, from Baccarat to Bulgari, Raymond Weil to Waterford and Wedgwood (the last two share their own autonomous boutique). Just keep walking—there's plenty of eye-catching, mind-boggling consumerism in all directions: Boucheron, Cartier (with its own mini-boutique), Chanel, Clinique, Christian Dior, Clarins, Estée Lauder, Fendi, Guerlain, Lancôme, Yves Saint Laurent, Issey Miyake, Jean Paul Gautier, Nina Ricci, Rolex, Roberto Coin, Rosenthal and Royal Doulton china, and more.

Words and Music

Local books and CDs make wonderful gifts and souvenirs. Recapture the flavor of your stay with *Miss Cleo's Cayman Kitchen*—subtitled "Treasured Recipes from the East End"—by Cleopatra Conolly, or *Cook' in Little Cayman,* by irrepressible Gladys Howard, a longtime resort owner who studied under James Beard and Julia Child. Plunge into *Diary of a Dirtbag Divemaster* by Little Cayman's Terry Thompson; it's a fact-inspired fiction recounting the escapades of six dive instructors working on a small Caribbean island. Another Little Cayman expat, Gay Morse, relates her own amusing behind-the-scenes anecdotes about teaching scuba and helping operate a small resort, *So You Want to Live on an Island?* H. George "Barefoot Man" Nowak's *Which Way to the Islands?* is another hilarious collection of only-in-the-Caribbean stories. Noted artist Nasaria Suckoo-Chollette

pens poems and short stories based on local culture and folklore, including Story Telling Rundown. On a more serious note, celebrated photographer Courtney Platt documented the devastation wrought by Hurricane Ivan in the 330 striking images composing *Paradise Interrupted.*

Sway back home to soca, reggae, calypso, and Carib-country beats. Grand Cayman has several recording studios, including the state-of-the-art Hopscotch, whose Platinum label records both Lammie and MOJ. Garden Studios is owned by popular group Hi Tide. C and B Studio records exclusively for Sea and B—Earl la Pierre and Barefoot Man (the latter alone has 27 CDs and counting). Other worthwhile local recording artists include jazz masters Gary Ebanks and Intransit, hard rockers Ratskyn and Cloudburst, and sultry soulster Karen Edie.

Stores in the **Landmark** (⊠ *Harbour Dr., George Town*) sell perfumes, treasure coins, and upscale beachwear; Breezes by the Bay restaurant is upstairs.

SEVEN MILE BEACH

Galleria Plaza (⊠ *West Bar Rd., Seven Mile Beach*), nicknamed Blue Plaza for its azure hue, features several galleries and exotic home-accessories stores dealing in Oriental rugs or Indonesian furnishings, as well as more moderate souvenir shops hawking T-shirts and swimwear.

The Strand Shopping Centre (⊠ *West Bay Rd., Seven Mile Beach*) has branches of Tortuga Rum and Blackbeard's Liquor, and banks galore—the better to withdraw cash for shops with cachet like Polo Ralph Lauren and another Kirk Freeport (this branch particularly noteworthy for china and crystal, from Kosta Boda to Baccarat, as well as a second La Parfumerie).

West Shore Shopping Centre (✉ *West Bay Rd., Seven Mile Beach*), dubbed Pink Plaza for reasons that become obvious upon approach, offers upscale boutiques and galleries (tenants range from Sotheby's International Realty to the Body Shop).

SPECIALTY STORES

ART

The art scene has exploded in the past decade, moving away from typical Caribbean motifs and "primitive" styles. Cayman's most famous artist had been the late Gladwyn Bush, fondly known as Miss Lassie, who died in 2003. She began painting her intuitive religious subjects after a "vision" when she was 62. She also decorated the facade, interior walls, furnishings, even appliances of her home (which at this writing was being converted into a museum, at the junction of South Shore Road and Walkers Road). Bush was awarded the MBE (Most Excellent Order of the British Empire) in 1997, and her work is found in collections from Paris to Baltimore (whose American Visionary Art Museum owns several canvases). Bendel Hydes is another widely respected local (who moved to SoHo more than two decades ago yet still paints Caymanian-inspired works that capture the islands' elemental colors and dynamic movement). Leading expat artists include Joanne Sibley and Charles Long, both of whom create more figurative Cayman-theme art from luminous landscapes and shining portraits to pyrotechnically hued flora. Several artists' home-studios double as galleries, including the internationally known Al Ebanks, the controversial Luelan Bodden, and fanciful sculptor Horacio Esteban; the National Gallery has a list.

★ **Al Ebanks Studio Gallery** (✉ *186B Shedden Rd., George Town* ☎ *345/916–0063*) shows the eponymous artist's versatile, always provocative work in various media. Since you're walking into his home as well as atelier, everything is on display. Clever movable panels maximize space "like Art Murphy beds." His work, while inspired by his home, could never be labeled traditional Caribbean art, exhibiting vigorous movement through abstract swirls of color and textural

Goin Native Sons

In 1995 three artists founded a collaborative called Native Sons, adding a fourth in 1996, and currently featuring 10 members. Their primary goal is to develop and promote Caymanian artists. Though they work in different mediums and styles, the group resists facile characterization and challenges conventions as to what characterizes "Caribbean" art. One of the core members, Al Ebanks, has achieved major international success, but he admits that the islands can be provincial: "Cayman doesn't always recognize talent unless you're signed to a gallery overseas."

Though the National Gallery and the Cayman National Cultural Foundation both vigorously support the movement and are committed to sponsoring local artists, some Native Sons members feel their agendas can be too safe, betraying the bureaucratic, corporate mentality they admit is often necessary to raise funds for non-profit institutions. They also felt subtle pressure to conform commercially and an inherent bias toward expat artists, whose work often depicted the literally sunnier side of Caymanian life, and resented what they perceived to be censorship of rawer, edgier works, including depictions of nudity in arch-conservative Cayman. They sought to push the boundaries for both institutions and private galleries. "Yes, art is art and shouldn't be grounded in national stereotypes, though my country inspires my work... We just want balance," Ebanks says. "People look at more challenging work and ask 'Where's the boats?' We live that scene!"

Obviously this is a hot-button topic on a tiny island. Chris Christian, who originally achieved success through representational beach scenes but wanted to expand and experiment, uses the Cayman term "crabs in a bucket," describing how "artists in a small pool scratch and scramble over each other, succeeding by badmouthing others." Which is why the support structure and philosophy of Native Sons is so vital: They help each other negotiate "that constant balance between commercial success and artistic integrity."

Other members include cofounder Wray Banker, Randy Chollette, Nasaria Suckoo-Chollette, Gordon Solomon, Horacio Esteban, and Nickola McCoy. These native sons and daughters all passionately believe art isn't merely about pretty pictures and uncompromisingly believe in preserving Caymanian culture and freedom of expression.

contrasts. Though non-representational (save for his equally intriguing sculpture and ceramics), the focal subject from carnivals to iguanas is always subtly apparent. Ask him about the Native Sons art movement he co-founded.

Artifacts (✉ *Cayside Courtyard, Harbour Dr., George Town* ☎ *345/949–2442⊕ www.artifacts.com.ky*), on the George Town waterfront, sells Spanish pieces of eight, doubloons, and Halcyon Days enamels (hand-painted collectible pill-boxes made in England), as well as antique maps and other collectibles.

Bodden Town Art Shop (✉ *Bodden Town Rd., next to Pirate Caves, Bodden Town* ☎ *345/943–2827*) purveys a grab bag of goodies, from homemade jellies to giclee prints, woven thatch handbags to hardwood and bronze sculpture. Top local and expat artists such as Randy Chollette and Avril Ward also exhibit here.

★ **Cathy Church's Underwater Photo Centre and Gallery** (✉ *S. Church St., George Town* ☎ *345/949–7415*) has a collection of the acclaimed underwater shutterbug's spectacular color and limited-edition black-and-white underwater photos. Have Cathy autograph her latest coffee-table book and regale you with anecdotes of her globe-trotting adventures. The store also carries the latest marine camera equipment, and she'll schedule private underwater photography instruction as well on her own dive boat outfitted with special graphics-oriented computers to critique your work.

★ **Guy Harvey's Gallery and Shoppe** (✉ *49 S. Church St., George Town* ☎ *345/943–4891*) is where world-renowned marine biologist, conservationist, and artist Guy Harvey showcases his aquatic-inspired action-packed art in nearly every conceivable medium, logo tableware, and sportswear (even logo soccer balls and Zippos). The soaring two-story 4,000-square-foot space is almost more theme park than store, with monitors playing his sportfishing videos, wood floors inlaid with tile duplicating rippling water, dangling catboats "attacked" by life-like shark models, and life-size murals honoring such classics as Hemingway's *Old Man and the Sea*. Original paintings, sculpture, and drawings are expensive, but there's something (tile art, prints, lithographs, and photos) in most price ranges.

Island Glassblowing Studio (✉ *189 N. Church St., George Town* ☎ *345/946–1483 ⊕ www.islandglassblowing.com*) is run by the Zawitowski family of designers, who offer free

Not Just a Guy Thing

Guy Harvey is a man of many hats. He has a PhD in marine biology and is also a world-class angler, renowned aquatic wildlife artist, cinematographer, TV producer, presenter of a weekly TV program titled *Portraits from the Deep,* clothing designer, and dedicated environmentalist.

Anyone passing through the Fort Lauderdale airport has seen his dramatic three-story mural (a smaller mural adorns Grand Cayman's Owen Roberts Airport). His art features meticulous composition and vibrant color, capturing the adrenaline-pumping action. "I try to humanize them, give them character in my paintings," Harvey says, though hardly in dewy, Disney-esque fashion.

Growing up a 10th-generation Jamaican, he loved fishing and diving with his father from an early age. Obsessed by all things aquatic, Harvey first gained notice in art circles with a 1985 Kingston exhibit of pen-and-ink drawings based on Hemingway's *Old Man and the Sea,* a recurring theme: man and animal bonding and exhibiting grace under pressure in their struggle for survival.

He moved to Cayman during Jamaica's political upheaval in the late 1970s. He liked Cayman's similar culture and cuisine, British heritage, and proximity to both Jamaica and Florida. Harvey has used his high profile synergistically as an artist, angler, author, and documentarian to strike merchandising deals, creating apparel and houseware lines and restaurants, pouring many of the profits back into research. He still travels the world on interactive marine programs such as following tagged sharks from Belize to Brazil. These expeditions serve a dual purpose: "...saving the environment while inspiring me artistically."

Harvey has consistently supported "catch and release" ethics for game fish around the world. He works closely with many conservation organizations to help protect global fishery resources and was appointed a trustee of the International Game Fish Association in 1992; six years later he was voted the IGFA's first-ever "Lifetime Achievement Award" from the World Fishing Awards Committee. The non-profit Guy Harvey Research Institute was established with the Oceanographic Center of Nova Southeastern University in 1999 to support effective conservation and restoration of fish resources and biodiversity. At the same time, he doesn't shy away from controversy: "Dolphin safety is one of the biggest lies foisted on the public," he says.

demonstrations of their incredible skills as they almost acrobatically gather red-hot molten glass with long steel rods from a 2,000°F- furnace, then roll it in vibrantly colored powders. Figurines (dolphins to elephants) to "functional" art (vases, platters) to fetching jewelry that captures the light all glow in cobalt to coral colors that rival nature's creativity.

★ **NasArt** (⊠ *Crewe Rd., Red Bay* ☎ *345/945–8278*) is the home-studio of Luelan Bodden, virtually every surface painted with wild images and hues. One of Cayman's most exciting, controversial artists, he works in various media and is deliberately provocative with a sociopolitical slant.

★ **Pure Art** (⊠ *S. Church St., George Town* ☎ *345/949– 9133*⊕ *www.pureart.ky*), about 1½ mi (2½ km) south of George Town, purveys wit, warmth, and whimsy right from the wildly colored front steps. Its warren of rooms resembles a garage sale run amok or a quirky grandmother's attic spilling over with unexpected finds, from foodstuffs to functional art.

The **Ritz-Carlton Gallery** (⊠ *Ritz-Carlton Grand Cayman, West Bay Rd., Seven Mile Beach* ☎ *345/815–6053*) more than fulfilled one of the resort's conditions upon securing rights to build, which was to commission local arts and artisans to help decorate the public spaces. The corridor-cum-bridge spanning West Bay Road became a gallery where Trina and Chris Christian of Cayman Traditional Arts curate quarterly exhibitions of Cayman's finest (there are also themed shows devoted to photography and local kids' art). Each piece is for sale; CTA and/or the hotel will mediate in the negotiations between artist and buyer at a favorable commission.

BOOKS
Books & Books (⊠ *45 Market St., Camana Bay* ☎ *345/640– 2665*) has opened an outlet in Grand Cayman. The independent bookseller also has stores in the Miami area. Regular events include "Floetry," when poets and performers express themselves at the open mike.

CAMERAS
★ The **Camera Store** (⊠ *Waterfront Centre, N. Church St., George Town* ☎ *345/949–4551*) has friendly and knowledgeable service, lots of duty-free digital cameras, accessories, and fast photo printing from self-service kiosks.

CIGARS

Given Cayman's proximity to Cuba, the banned but tempting panatelas and robustos are readily available at reasonable prices. They are still considered contraband in the United States until the embargo is lifted.

A cigar-store Indian points the way into **Churchill's Cigars** (✉ *Island Plaza, Harbour Dr., George Town* ☎ *345/945-6141*), which sells the island's largest selection of authentic Cubanos (and other imports), including such names as Upmann, Romeo y Julieta, and Cohiba, almost fetishistically displayed in the dark, clubby surroundings. The enthusiastic staff will advise on drink pairings (bold older rum for a Montecristo No. 2, Cognac for smaller Partagas Shorts, a single-malt scotch such as Glenmorangie for the Bolivar Belicoso Fino). There's a small airport branch as well.

Havana Club Cigars (✉ *508 West Bay Rd., Seven Mile Beach* ☎ *345/946–0523* ⊕ *www.havanaclub-cigars.com*) is the brainchild of Raglan Roper, who sailed from Florida to Cayman two decades ago, stopping in Cuba en route. Immediately hooked on the cigars, cuisine, and culture, he eventually opened a Cayman shop, then expanded (he also owns a Cuban restaurant). In addition to the famed brands, the attraction is the irresistible in-house *torcedor* (cigar roller), Jesus Lara Perez, who rotates demonstrations between the stores. Jesus started working at 14 in the Cuban cigar factory La Isolina in Santa Clara, eventually becoming chief cigar roller for other leading brands.

CLOTHING

Arabus (✉ *Duty Free Bldg., 42 Edward St., George Town* ☎ *345/949–4620*) primarily carries classy, classic knockoffs—though not at rip-off prices—for both sexes, casual to dressy, in flowing silk and cushy cashmere (for back home).

Chiclit (✉ *Galleria Plaza, West Bay Rd., Seven Mile Beach* ☎ *345/943–2442*) showcases glitzy couture for model wannabes (indeed, the store mounts fashion shows for special events); designers—and styles—can range from Balenciaga to Betsey Johnson.

Natalie Bishop (✉ *Harbour Place, George Town* ☎ *345/946–7080*) designs soft flowing sundresses and swimwear in Lilly Pulitzer–style floral prints and seashell colors.

FOODSTUFFS

There are seven modern, U.S.-style supermarkets (three of them have full-service pharmacies) on Grand Cayman. Ask for the one nearest you. Together, they will spoil you for choices of fresh fruit and vegetables, a wide selection of groceries, as well as a good selection of meats, poultry, and fish. All have deli counters serving hot meals, salads, sandwiches, cold cuts, and cheeses. Kirk Supermarket carries a wide range of international foods from the Caribbean, Europe, and Asia. The biggest difference you'll find between these and supermarkets on the mainland are the prices, which are about 25%–30% more than at home.

☙ Visitors to genial **Cayman Taffy** (⊠ *West Bay Rd., Seven Mile Beach* ☏ *345/943–2333* ⊕ *www.caymantaffy.net*) can satisfy their curiosity along with their taste buds by viewing the candy-making process in restored vintage equipment dating back to the early 20th century. Then sample saltwater taffy, caramel corn, and brittle in such exotic flavors as banana, coconut, mango, and Jamaican rum. The packaging, in coconut shells or boldly painted boxes, is almost as delectable.

Foster's Food Fair-IGA (⊠ *Airport Centre, 63 Dorcy Dr., George Town* ☏ *345/949–5155* ⊠ *Strand Shopping Center, 46A Canal Point Dr., off West Bay Rd., Seven Mile Beach* ☏ *345/945–4748* ⊠ *Republix Plaza, 2373 Willie Farrington Dr., Seven Mile Beach* ☏ *345/949–3214* ⊠ *Morritt's Shopping Centre, 2206 Queens Hwy., East End* ☏ *345/947–2826* ⊠ *Countryside Shopping Center, 33 Hirst Rd., Savannah* ☏ *345/943–5155*) is the island's biggest chain, with five stores. The Airport Centre and Strand stores have full-service pharmacies. These stores are open from Monday through Saturday, 7 AM to 11 PM.

★ **Hurley's Marketplace** (⊠ *Grand Harbour Shopping Centre, Red Bay* ☏ *345/947–8488*) is open Monday through Saturday from 7 AM to 11 PM.

Kirk Supermarket and Pharmacy (⊠ *Eastern Ave. near intersection with West Bay Rd., George Town* ☏ *345/949–7022*) is open Monday through Thursday from 7 AM to 10 PM (until 11 PM Friday and Saturday) and is a particularly good source for traditional Caymanian fast food (oxtail, curried goat) and beverages at the juice bar. It also carries the largest selection of organic and special dietary products; the pharmacy stocks various homeopathic and herbal remedies.

Cayman Craft Market

This open-air marketplace run by the Tourism Attraction Board at Hog Sty Bay, smack in the middle of George Town, is artists' central, helping maintain old-time Caymanian skills. The vendors offer locally made leather, thatch, wood, and shell items. You'll also find dolls, hats, carved parrots, bead and seed jewelry, hand-painted thatch bags and bonnets, and hand-carved waurie (also spelled warri) boards—an ancient African game using seeds (or the more modern marbles).

Also available here are Sea Salt (and their luxury bath product);

Hawley Haven Farm products (Mrs. Laurie Hawley's delectable papaya, tamarind, and guava jams; spicy mango chutney; thyme vinegar; Cayman honey; and jerk sauce; as well as her painted folkloric characters on handmade sun-dried paper made with native flowers, leaves, and herbs); the Cayman Tropicals line of fragrant fruit-based hair and skin-care products; and North Side's Whistling Duck Farm specialties from soursop to seagrape jams and jellies. Every month highlights a different area of the Cayman Islands, from Cayman Brac to Bodden Town.

The **Tortuga Rum Company** (⊠ *N. Sound Rd., Industrial Park, George Town* ☎ *345/949–7701 or 345/949–7867* ⊕ *www.tortugarumcakes.com*) bakes, then vacuum-seals more than 10,000 of its world-famous rum cakes daily, adhering to the original "secret" century-old recipe. There are seven scrumptious flavors, from banana to Blue Mountain coffee. Their 12-year-old rum, blended from private stock though actually distilled in Guyana, is a connoisseur's delight for after-dinner sipping. You can buy a fresh rum cake at the airport on the way home at the same prices as at the factory store.

HANDICRAFTS AND SOUVENIRS

Bed Buddies (⊠ *Hell Rd., West Bay* ☎ *345/917–1182* ⊕ *www.bedbuddiescreation.com*) refers to husband-wife team Bonnie and Fernando Thompson, who fashion lovely jewelry, bags, and baubles from local materials, including whelk shells, coconut husks, tree resin, and distinctive seeds from cat's claw to Cayman red apple.

Pirate's Grotto (⊠ *Harbour Dr., basement level, below Landmark Shopping Center, George Town* ☎ *345/945–0244*) is a cute store with duty-free liquor and cigars (including Cubans) as well as Cayman Islands souvenirs.

JEWELRY

Although you can find black-coral products in Grand Cayman, they're controversial. Most of the coral sold here comes from Belize and Honduras; Cayman Islands marine law prohibits the removal of live coral from its own sea. Black coral grows at a glacial rate (3 inches per decade) and is an endangered species. Cayman, however, is famed for artisans working with the material; shops are recommended, but let your conscience dictate your purchases.

Balaclava Jewellers (⊠ *Governors Square, West Bay Rd., Seven Mile Beach* ☎ *345/945–5788* ⊕ *www.balaclava-jewellers.com*) is the domain of Martina and Philip Cadien, who studied at Germany's prestigious Pforzheim Goldsmithing School. The showroom sparkles appropriately, with breathtaking handcrafted pieces—usually naturally colored diamonds set in platinum or 18K white, yellow, and rose gold—framed and lovingly, almost sensuously lit. Although there are simpler strands, this is a place where flash holds sway; the prices take your breath away, but the gems are flawless.

★ The black-coral creations of **Bernard Passman** (⊠ *Cardinal Ave., George Town* ☎ *345/949–0123*) have won the approval of the British royal family, who chose him to create a wedding present for Prince Charles and Princess Diana. His fabulous flatware and fanciful candelabras would stand out in the Addams Family manse. He even creates three-dimensional bas-relief scenes with cavorting dolphins, as well as mermaids with glittering gold gilt tails and golfers (each movement of the swing depicted by a dozen clubs in 18K gold).

Locals appreciate **Grand Cayman Jewellers** (⊠ *Island Plaza, Cardinal Ave., George Town* ☎ *345/946–2333*) for its affordable line of watches, especially top-notch Swiss brands occupying their own niche, from Movado to Maurice Lacroix, and a globe-trotting inventory from Australian opals to Austrian crystal, Italian gold to Tahitian pearls.

Landmark Jewellers (⊠ *Landmark Bldg., Harbour Dr. and Cardinal Ave., George Town* ☎ *345/945–0204*) proffers sparkling savings on unique gemstone jewelry by such respected designers as Mark Henry, as well as both loose and set rubies, emeralds, sapphires, and tanzanite. The watch selection astounds, with Switzerland alone clocking in with the likes of DOXA, Ball, Frédérique Constant, Oris, and Krieger.

Magnum Jewelers (⊠ *Cardinal Plaza, George Town* ☎ *345/946–9199* ⊕ *www.magnumjewelers.com*), befitting its name, traffics in high-caliber pieces by the elite likes of Girard-Perregeaux and Harry Winston for a high-powered clientele. President Harry Chandi travels the world, his keen eye sourcing distinctive contemporary watches and bijoux (especially increasingly rare colored diamonds) for his equally glittery celebrity clientele, who also appreciate a bargain like the rest of us. Smaller spenders might appreciate the whimsical items such as pendants with hand-painted enamel sandals or crystal-encrusted purses.

★ **Mitzi's Fine Jewelry** (⊠ *5 Bay Harbour Centre, West Bay Rd., Seven Mile Beach* ☎ *345/945–5014*) is a treasure trove of salvaged 18th-century coins, silver, Caymanite pieces, and black coral; the store also carries Italian porcelain and the Carrera y Carrera line of jewelry and sculptures. Self-taught, vivacious proprietor Mitzi Callan, who specializes in handmade pieces, is usually on hand to help.

★ **24K-Mon Jewelers** (⊠ *Buckingham Sq., Seven Mile Beach* ☎ *345/949–1499* ⊕ *www.24k-monjewelers.com*) sells works of art from many jewelers, including Wyland, Merry-Lee Rae, and Stephen Douglas, as well as designs courtesy of owner-goldsmith Gale Tibbetts and her friends, incorporating everything from Swarovski crystals to Spanish doubloons. The adjacent gallery is one of the few commercial outlets for local artists such as Miguel Powery.

KIDS' STUFF

Cayman Critters (⊠ *Bayshore Mall, S. Church St., George Town* ☎ *345/945–2748*) allows you to stuff your own animal pal (the "fluff" machine resembles a whirring cotton-candy dispenser). A very cool glass floor overlooks a step-well cut directly into the limestone with an 18th-century anchorage. The wry owner cracks about "opening a sister shop called Stuff Your Husband."

Where to Eat in Grand Cayman

WORD OF MOUTH

"[W]e usually eat breakfast and lunch in our condo (ocean front) and go out for dinner. Yes, it costs more than where we live in the U.S., but LOTS less than our trip to Europe this fall. It's relative."

—luvtotravl

By Jordan
Simon

NO INDIGENOUS PEOPLES or gaggle of contentious colonial powers left much of an imprint on Grand Cayman cuisine, as was the case on many other islands. Until recently, the strongest culinary contributions to Cayman cuisine came from nearby Jamaica and, to a lesser extent, Cuba, though the worst of the British pub tradition lingered in pasties and heavy puddings. Fortunately, since the boom of the late 1970s, chefs from around the world (and the need to offer familiar ingredients and dishes to expats from as far afield as Beijing and Berlin) have seasoned a once-bland dining scene.

Today, despite its small size, comparative isolation, and British colonial trappings, Grand Cayman offers a smorgasbord of gastronomic goodies. With more than 100 eateries, something should suit and sate every palate and pocketbook (especially once you factor in fast-food franchises sweeping the islandscape like tumbleweed and stalls dispensing local specialties).

The term *"melting pot"* describes both the majority of menus and the multicultural population. It's not uncommon to find "American" dishes at an otherwise Caribbean restaurant, Indian fare at an Italian eatery (and vice versa). The sheer range of dining options from Middle Eastern to Mexican reflects the island's cosmopolitan, discriminating clientele. Imported ingredients reflect the United Nations, with chefs sourcing salmon from Norway, foie gras from Périgord, and lamb from New Zealand. Wine lists can be equally global in scope (often receiving awards from such oeno-bibles as *Wine Spectator*). Don't be surprised to find both Czech and Chilean staffers at a remote East End restaurant.

As one restaurateur quipped, "Cayman is the ultimate culture-shock absorber."

WHERE TO EAT

Grand Cayman dining is casual (even shorts are okay, at least for lunch, but *not* beachwear and tank tops). More upscale restaurants usually require slacks for dinner. Mosquitoes can be pesky when you dine outdoors, especially at sunset, so plan ahead or ask for repellent. Winter can be chilly enough to warrant a light sweater. You should make reservations at all but the most casual places, particularly during the high season.

Eat Like a Local

Caymanian cuisine evolved from whatever could be coaxed from the sea and eked out from the poor, porous soil. Farmers cultivated carb-rich crops that could remain fresh without refrigeration and furnish energy for the heavy labor typical of the islanders' hardscrabble existence. Hence pumpkins, coconuts, plantains, breadfruit, sweet potatoes, yams, and other "provisions" (root vegetables) became staple ingredients. Turtle (now farm-raised), the traditional specialty, can be served in soup or stew and as a steak. Conch, the meat of a large pink mollusk, is prepared in stews, chowders, and fritters and pan-fried (cracked). Fish—including snapper, tuna, wahoo, grouper, and marlin—is served baked, broiled, steamed, or "Cayman-style" (as an *escoveitch* with peppers, onions, and tomatoes).

"Rundown" is another classic: Fish (marinated with fresh lime juice, scallions, and fiery Scotch bonnet peppers) is steamed in coconut milk with breadfruit, pumpkin dumplings, and/or cassava. Fish tea boils and bubbles similar ingredients for hours—even days—until it thickens into gravy. The traditional dessert, heavy cake, earned its name because excluding scarce flour and eggs made it incredibly dense: Coconut, sugar, spices, and butter are boiled, mixed with seasonal binders (cassava, yam, pumpkin), and baked.

Jamaican influence is seen in oxtail, goat stew, jerk chicken and pork, salt cod, and ackee (a red tree fruit resembling scrambled eggs in flavor and texture when cooked), and manish water (a lusty goat-head stew with garlic, thyme, scallion, green banana [i.e., plantain], yam, potato, and other tubers).

Since nearly everything must be imported, prices average about 25% higher than those in a major U.S. city. Many restaurants add a 10%–15% service charge to the bill; be sure to check before leaving a tip (waiters usually receive only a small portion of any included gratuities, so leave something extra at your discretion for good service). Alcohol can send your meal tab skyrocketing. Buy liquor duty-free, either at the airport before your flight to the Cayman Islands or in one of the duty-free liquor stores that can be found in almost every strip mall on Grand Cayman, and enjoy a cocktail or nightcap from the comfort of your room or balcony. Cayman customs limits you to two bottles per person. Lunch often offers the same or similar dishes at a

BEST BETS

★ **Fodor's** Choice
Blue by Eric Ripert, Casa
Havana

BEST VIEWS
Cracked Conch, Grand Old
House, Luca, Morgan's Harbour, Osetra Bay, Over the
Edge, Reef Grill at Royal
Palms

BEST FOR ROMANCE
Bacchus, Blue by Eric Ripert,
Casa Havana, Grand Old
House, Reef Grill at Royal

Palms, Roland's Garden

BEST FOR FAMILIES
Al La Kebab, Chicken!
Chicken!, Cimboco

BEST FOR LOCAL CUISINE
Chicken! Chicken!, Cimboco,
Over the Edge

MOST POPULAR
Al La Kebab, Guy Harvey's
Island Grill, Eats Café, ICOA
Fine Foods, Morgan's Harbour,
Ragazzi, Yoshi Sushi

considerable discount. Finally, when you are figuring your
dining budget, remember that the Cayman dollar is worth
25% more than the U.S. dollar, and virtually all menus are
priced in Cayman dollars.

WHAT IT COSTS IN U.S. DOLLARS					
	¢	$	$$	$$$	$$$$
At dinner	under $8	$8–$12	$12–$20	$20–$30	over $30

Prices are per person for a main course at dinner, excluding service charges or taxes.

GEORGE TOWN AND ENVIRONS

$$$–
$$$$

✕ **Bacchus Restaurant and Wine Bar.** *Seafood.* This cozy oeno-
phile's den may offer a lineup of 350-plus wines spanning
Australia to Austria, but it's utterly unstuffy (conveyed by
murals of reveling diners and quotes stenciled everywhere,
such as "What I like to drink most is wine that belongs
to others"–Diogenes). Chef-owner Keith Griffin promises
"no sunsets, no fish feeding—it's all about the food." In
other words, no gimmickry, though his constantly changing
menu is a mischievous melange of influences and ingre-
dients. Accents alone, from compotes to coulis, include
chili-caramel dip (for crispy sesame-coconut shrimp), mus-
tard-olive crust (for rack of lamb with Cabernet-cranberry
sauce and bacon-jalapeño mashed potatoes), and coconut-
lime dressing (for tea-cured yellowfin tuna seviche with

Conch fritters at Bacchus Restaurant and Wine Bar

toasted sesame-wakame salad). He'll fearlessly blacken, spice-rub, grill, deglaze, braise, stir-fry, barbecue, smoke, and poach, often delighting in unorthodox pairings that titillate every set of taste buds. Best of all, Griffin believes in sharing, with lavish happy-hour specials and all-you-can-eat-and-drink champagne-and-lobster Tuesday and Thursday for CI$49.95 per person; three-course dinners (including two wine pairings) Monday, Wednesday, and Saturday for CI$39.95; not to mention fondue nights. ⊠ *19 Fort St., George Town* ☎ *345/949–5747* ⊕ *www.bacchus.ky* ⌲ *Reservations essential* ▭ *AE, D, MC, V* ⊘ *Closed Sun.*

$$$–
$$$$ ✕ **The Brasserie.** *Eclectic.* Actuaries, bankers, and CEOs frequent this contemporary throwback to a colonial country club for lunch and "attitude adjustment" happy hours for cocktails and complimentary canapés. Inviting fusion cuisine includes terrific bar tapas like the Foie Whopper kobe burger with cave-aged Gouda and red curry aioli, and melted Brie with white truffle and mango marmalade. On Wednesday, you can get an eight-course "blind tasting" driven by marketplace cuisine for CI$75 (CI$105 with wine). You'll find that any dish deftly balances flavors and textures without sensory overload: This is serious food with a sense of playfulness. Save room for desserts, from an artisanal cheese plate to an ice-cream-and-sorbet tasting menu to elaborate architectural confections. Lunch is more reasonably priced but equally creative; the adjacent new Market excels at take-out, and the wine list is well-

Where to Eat in
George Town

| Bacchus Restaurant & Wine Bar, **4** |
| The Brasserie, **8** |
| Breezes by the Bay, **2** |
| Casanova Restaurant by the Sea, **5** |
| Champion House II, **7** |
| Grand Old House, **9** |
| Guy Harvey's Island Grill, **1** |
| Lobster Pot, **6** |
| MacDonald's, **3** |

considered. ⊠ *171 Elgin Ave., Cricket Sq., George Town* ☎ *345/945–1815* ⊕ *www.brasseriecayman.com* ⌕ *Reservations essential* ⊟ *AE, MC, V* ⊘ *Closed weekends.*

\$\$–\$\$\$ ✕ **Breezes by the Bay.** *Caribbean.* There isn't a bad seat in the house at this nonstop feel-good fiesta festooned with tiny paper lanterns, Christmas lights, ship murals, and Mardi Gras beads (you're "lei'd" upon entering). Wraparound balconies take in a dazzling panorama from South Sound to Seven Mile Beach. It's a joyous nonstop happy hour all day every day, especially at Countdown to Sunset. Signs promise "the good kind of hurricanes," referring to their 23-ounce signature "category 15" cocktails with fresh garnishes; rum aficionados will find 34 varieties (flights available). Equally fresh food at bargain prices, including homemade baked goods and ice creams, isn't an afterthought. Chunky velvety conch chowder served in a bread bowl or near-definitive conch fritters are meals in themselves. Hefty sandwiches are slathered with yummy jerk mayo or garlicky aioli. Signature standouts include meltingly moist whole fish escoveitch, curry chicken, popcorn shrimp, and jerk-glazed pork chops. ⊠ *Harbor Dr., George Town* ☎ *345/943–8439* ⊕ *www.breezesbythebay.com* ⊟ *AE, MC, V.*

FREELOADING UP. Competition is fierce between Grand Cayman's many bars and restaurants. In addition to entertainment (from fish feeding to fire eating), even upscale joints host happy hours offering free hors d'oeuvres and/or drinks.

3

$$$– ✕ **Casanova Restaurant by the Sea.** *Italian.* Owner Tony Cres-
$$$$ cente and younger brother–maître d' Carlo offer a genu-
inely simpatico dining experience, practically exhorting
you to *mangia,* and sending you off with a chorus of ciaos
(photos of happy diners cover one wall). There's a bit of
decorative *formaggio*: murals of Calabria, grape clusters,
and chubby cherubs cavorting; paintings of the Amalfi
Coast; UNA FINESTRA SUL MARE ("window to the sea") stenciled
redundantly over arches opening onto the harbor. But the
kitsch doesn't extend to the kitchen, with such sterling Ital-
ian favorites as salmon marinated in citrus, olive oil, and
basil; lovely lemony veal piccata; pappardelle *della brigante*
(with rosemary-scented lamb ragout); or seafood grill in
parsley-garlic-lemon sauce. Enjoy grappa at the marble bar
of La Cantina lounge, which is lined with wooden wine
racks (the impressive selection isn't overly Italian-centric).
The patio juts over the harbor; the moonlight (abetted by
a sound track of Bocelli to Bennett) would transform any
amorous coward into a Casanova. ✉ *65 N. Church St.,
George Town* ☎ *345/949–7633*⊕ *www.casanova.ky* ⌑ *Res-
ervations essential* ▭ *AE, MC, V.*

$$–$$$ ✕ **Champion House II.** *Caribbean.* Ads trumpet this restaurant
as "where the islanders dine." Indeed they have since the
Robinson family started selling takeout from their kitchen
in 1965. This favorite overlooks a garden with a cheery
tropic motif. The West Indies breakfast and themed lunch
buffets are legendary spreads. Local food (curried goat,
oxtail with broad beans, turtle soup, and heavy cake) is
authentic, hearty, and cheap. Pricier global dishes range
from fine Indian vegetarian options like samosas and *masala
dal* (lentils simmered with green chilies) to Eisenhower-era
standards like bacon-wrapped filet mignon in red wine
sauce and scallops braised with sweet peppers in brandy.
✉ *43 Eastern Ave., George Town* ☎ *345/949–7882* ⊕ *www.
championhouse.ky* ▭ *AE, MC, V.*

$$$$ ✕ **Grand Old House.** *Continental.* Built in 1908 as the Petra
Plantation House and transformed into the island's first
upscale establishment decades ago, this grand dame is that
rare restaurant that genuinely transports diners to a gra-
cious era of bygone grandeur sans pretension. The interior
rooms, awash in crystal and mahogany, recall its plantation

house origins. Classical and jazz pianists enhance the period ambience, but outside, hundreds of sparkling lights adorn the gazebos to compete with the starry sky. Rumors of a charming blond ghost trailing white chiffon complete the picture: This is a place to propose or let someone down easily. You'll find such expertly executed classics as seafood thermidor with crème fraîche mashed potatoes and braised beef short ribs with truffle vinaigrette, but the increasingly innovative menu has slowly adopted Asian and even Southwestern influences. Grilled freshwater shrimps float in key lime–garlic sauce on wakame risotto, while spice-crusted rack of lamb is served with gingered vegetables and cardamom jus. The subtle yet complex flavor interactions, stellar service, and encyclopedic if stratospherically priced wine list ensure legendary landmark status. ⊠ *S. Church St., George Town* ☎ *345/949–9333* ⊕ *www.grandoldhouse. com* ⌕ *Reservations essential* ▭ *AE, MC, V* ⊗ *Closed Sept. No lunch weekends.*

$$$–   ✕ **Guy Harvey's Island Grill.** *Seafood.* This stylish, sporty
$$$$ upstairs bistro celebrates the sea, from decor to cuisine. You half expect to find Hemingway regaling fellow barflies in the clubby interior with mahogany furnishings, ship's lanterns, porthole windows, whirring ceiling fans, and Harvey's action-packed marine art. The cool blues echo the sea and sky on display from the inviting balcony. Seafood is carefully chosen to exclude overexploited and threatened species. Seasonally changing dishes are peppered with Caribbean influences but pureed through the French chef's formal training. Hence, silken lobster bisque is served with puff pastry, scallops Rockefeller with spinach and béarnaise sauce, and the signature crab cakes with roasted red pepper aioli. You can select your fish baked, pan-sautéed, or grilled with any of eight sauces. Carnivores needn't despair with rack of lamb in balsamic glaze or an intensely flavored New York strip with fresh herbs (*frites* optional) on offer. Many specialties are cheaper at lunch. ⊠ *Aquaworld Duty-Free Mall, 55 S. Church St., George Town* ☎ *345/946–9000* ⊕ *www.harveysgrill.com* ▭ *AE, D, MC, V.*

$$$–   ✕ **Lobster Pot.** *Seafood.* The nondescript building belies the
$$$$ lovely marine-motif decor and luscious seafood at the intimate second-story restaurant overlooking the harbor. No surprise that fish seem to jump from the plate. Enjoy lobster prepared a dozen ways along with reasonably priced wine, which you can sample by the glass (particularly fine Austrian selections) in the cozy bar. The two musts are the Cayman Trio (lobster tail, grilled mahimahi, and garlic

Farm Fresh

A joint initiative of the Cayman Islands Agricultural Society, the Ministry of Agriculture, the Department of Agriculture, and local vendors-purveyors, the **Market at the Grounds** is a jambalaya of sights, sounds, and smells held every Saturday from 7 AM at the Stacy Watler Agricultural Pavilion in Lower Valley (East End). Local growers, fishers, home gardeners and chefs (dispensing scrumptious, cheap cuisine), and artisans display their wares in a tranquil green setting. To preserve Caymanian flavor, everything must be 100% locally grown. Participating craftspeople and artists, from couturiers to musicians, must use local designs and materials whenever possible. The market fosters a renewed spirit of community, providing literal feedback into the production process, while the interaction with visitors promotes understanding of island culture.

shrimp) and the Pot (lobster, giant prawns, and crab), but the kitchen can happily provide reduced-oil and -fat alternatives to most dishes. The balcony offers a breathtaking view of the sunset tarpon feeding. Lobster is market price and can be as much as $60; other entrées are less expensive. ⊠ *245 N. Church St., George Town* ☎ *345/949–2736* ⊕ *www. lobsterpot.ky* ⊟ *AE, MC, V* ⊗ *No lunch weekends.*

$-$$ ✕ **MacDonald's.** *Caribbean.* One of the locals' favorite burger joints—not a fast-food outlet—MacDonald's does a brisk lunch business in stick-to-your ribs basics like rotisserie chicken and fish escoveitch. Yellows and pinks predominate, with appetizing posters of food, but decor is an afterthought to the politicos, housewives in curlers, and cops flirting shyly with the waitresses. ⊠ *99 Shedden Rd., George Town* ☎ *345/949–4640* ⌂ *No reservations accepted* ⊟ *MC, V.*

SEVEN MILE BEACH

¢-$ ✕ **Al La Kebab.** *Middle Eastern.* Alan and Laura Silverman (he's Canadian, she's German) loved *shawarma* growing up and craved it after moving to Cayman. Their eatery works miracles out of two makeshift lean-tos splashed in vibrant colors and wall-to-wall stainless-steel appliances. They started by serving late-night kebabs and gyros. They remain open until 4 AM weeknights and 2 AM weekends "to keep the roads safe" but now do a brisk lunch trade as construction workers line up with government minis-

Where to Eat in Seven Mile Beach

KEY

◤ Dive Sites
◢ Beaches
1 Restaurants

0 ——— 1 mi
0 ——— 1 km

Conch Point
Conch Point Rd.
Capt. Reg Parson's Rd.
Palmetto Point Rd.
BIRCH TREE HILL
MOUNT PLEASANT
BARKERS
Head of Barkers
Hell
BATABANO
NW Point
CORAL GABLES
Town Hall Rd.
West Bay
Orange Canyon
North West Point Rd.
Trinity Caves
A1
Little Salt Creek
Salt Creek
UPPERLAND
Cemetery Beach
West Bay Rd.
Cemetery Reef
Grand Cayman Yacht Club
Public Beach
A1 **21**
Governors Creek
West Bay
Aquarium
Seven Mile Beach
Trafalgar Place
GOVERNORS HARBOUR
Welch Point
Paradise Reef
20 **19**
The Links at Safehaven Golf Course
18
Falls Plaza
15 **16**
14 **17**
The Strand
13 **11**
Brittania Golf Course
North Sound
12
Galleria Plaza
10
Galleria Loop
Buckingham Square
9
West Shore Center
8
Marquee Plaza
5-**7**
WHITEHALL ESTATES
4
7 Mile Shops
3
E. Tibbets Hwy.
Harquail Byass
2
Eastern Av.
North Sound Rd.
1
George Town
Owen Roberts International Airport
Wreck of the Cali
A1
A2
Eden Rock
A2
Crewe Rd.
Elgin Av.
Smith Rd.
Black Reef Skate Park
A5
Smith's Cove
S. Church St.
Walkers Rd.
South Sound Rd.
A5
South Sound
Caribbean Sea

Al La Kebab, **7**
Blue by Eric Ripert, **16**
Casa Havana, **18**
Chicken! Chicken!, **8**
Cimboco, **6**
Copper Falls, **14**
Eats Cafe, **20**
Hemingway's, **12**
Icoa Fine Foods, **3**
Lone Star Bar & Grill, **10**
Luca, **13**
Mezza, **4**
Neptune, **21**
Ragazzi, **11**
Reef Grill at Royal Pines, **9**
7 Prime Cuts & Sunsets, **15**
Sunshine Grill, **17**
Thai Orchid, **2**
Triple Crown Pub, **5**
The Wharf, **1**
Yoshi Sushi, **19**

Blue by Eric Ripert

ters. Alan calls it a building-block menu, where you can modify the bread and sauce—a dozen varieties including several curries, peanut satay, mango *raita* (yogurt, tomatoes, chutney), tahini, garlic cream, even gravy like Mom used to make. The menu romps from Malaysia through the Mediterranean to Mexico: Spicy chicken tikka, Thai chicken-lemongrass soup, and tzatziki share the stage with unusual salads (try the fabulous Lebanese *fattoush*—toasted bread, mint, and parsley) and creative sides (addictive jalapeño cheddar queso salsa for fries). There's also a George Town outpost. ⊠ *Marquee Plaza, West Bay Rd., Seven Mile Beach* ☎ *345/943–4343* ⊕ *www.kebab.ky* ⚓ *No reservations accepted* ⊟ *D, MC, V.*

★ **Fodor's** Choice ✕ **Blue by Eric Ripert.** *Seafood.* Top Chef judge Eric
$$$$ Ripert consulted on every aspect of the first outpost bearing his name, from decor to dishware. His trademark ethereal seafood (executed by his handpicked brigade), flawless and not fawning service, swish setting, and soothing sophistication sans pretension make this one of the Caribbean's finest restaurants. Choose from a regular three-course or the chef's hedonistic tasting menu (with or without wine pairing). Many dishes are clever improvisational riffs on the mother restaurant (New York's celebrated Le Bernardin), utilizing the island's natural bounty (conch seviche trio recalls the famed fluke version, and the tribute to the great Bernardin tuna foie gras adds Cayman sea salt). The sensuous counterpoint of flavors, textures, even colors

Casa Havana

is unimpeachable, as in sautéed kingklip with avocado-coconut cream, sunflower sprouts, and lime sauce vierge; sautéed ocean yellowtail in bourbon-lime–guajillo-pepper broth with mango-jalapeño salad; or melt-in-your-mouth vanilla-rum panna cotta with caramelized pineapple, lemongrass foam, and cilantro. The vast wine list offers big names but also showcases hot new regions and lesser-known varietals that offer quality and comparative value. The Taste of Blue bar menu is an affordable and admirable way to get a taste of perfection. ⊠ *Ritz-Carlton Grand Cayman, West Bay Rd., Seven Mile Beach* ☎ *345/943–9000* ⚑ *Reservations essential* ▱ *AE, D, MC, V* ⊘ *Closed Sun.–Mon. No lunch.*

★ **Fodor's**Choice ✕ **Casa Havana.** *Eclectic.* This refined eatery
$$$– glamorously channels pre-revolution Cuba with crystal
$$$$ chandeliers, mahogany furnishings, burgundy walls, gold damask curtains, exquisite art naïf and still-life paintings, and picture windows. Jason Koppinger's artfully prepared and presented Asian-Cuban cuisine adds Eastern flair to Floribbean fare, with sophisticated flavor and texture counterpoints. The velvety "Thai" lobster bisque is the gustatory equivalent of a Victoria's Secret silk negligee. Other stunning starters include seared foie gras with caramelized Granny Smith apple salad, cinnamon cider jus and mango essence, and coconut-ginger tuna tartare with avocado mousse, grilled prawns, and lemon olive oil. The must-eat

entrée is macadamia-crusted black cod with spiced shiitake tea and white truffle essence (the crunch and flaky delicacy brilliantly juxtaposed). Standard items are reinvented: goosing polenta with cilantro or soft stilton, or smoking salmon with oolong tea. Incredible island-inspired desserts include key lime cheesecake with island fruit coulis and melba sauce. Wine Master dinners pair several courses with wines (Marchese di Barolo to Gosset Champagne), often introduced by the guest winemakers or owners from as far afield as Tuscany, Australia, Napa, and Chile. Sumptuous Sunday champagne brunches, a longtime local tradition, serve sensational sea views; a raw sushi-seviche bar; cheese selections; and charcuterie, pasta, carving, and dim sum stations. ⊠ *Westin Casuarina, West Bay Rd., Seven Mile Beach* ☎ *345/945–3800 ext. 6017* ⊕ *www.westincasuarina. net* ⌕ *Reservations essential* ⊟ *AE, D, MC, V* ⊙ *No lunch Mon.–Sat.*

$-$$ ✕ **Chicken! Chicken!** *Caribbean.* Devotees would probably award four exclamation points to the marvelously moist chicken, slow-roasted on a hardwood open-hearth rotisserie. Most customers grab takeout, but the decor is appealing for a fast-food joint; the clever interior replicates an old-time Cayman cottage. Bright smiles and home cooking completely from scratch enhance the authentic vibe. Hearty but (mostly) healthy helpings of sides include scrumptious Cayman-style cornbread, honey-rum beans, jicama coleslaw, and spinach-pesto pasta. ⊠ *West Shore Centre, West Bay Rd., Seven Mile Beach* ☎ *345/945–2290* ⊟ *AE, MC, V.*

$$-$$$ ✕ **Cimboco.** *Eclectic.* This animated celebration of all things fun, funky, and Caribbean is saturated in psychedelic colors: orange, lemon, and lavender walls; cobalt glass fixtures; paintings of musicians in fevered Fauvist hues; a mosaic of flames dancing up the exhibition kitchen's huge wood-burning oven. History buffs may be interested to know that the Cimboco was the first motorized sailing ship built in Cayman (in 1927) and for 20 years the main connection/lifeline to the outside world; National Archive photographs and old newspapers invest the space with still more character. Everything from breads (superlative bruschetta and jalapeño corn bread) to ice creams is made from scratch. Artisan pizzas betray a (Wolfgang) Puck-ish sensibility with such toppings as balsamic-roasted eggplant, pine nuts, pesto, and feta; or curried chicken with pineapple and spinach. Signature items include banana-leaf-roasted snapper, fire-roasted bacon-wrapped shrimp, and papaya-chili-glazed pork loin with garlic-lime sautéed cassava, but the daily specials are also inspired. The popular breakfast and brunch are equally creative. Amazingly good desserts start with a moist, intensely rich brownie. The small but well-considered wine list features more than a dozen by the glass. ⊠ *The Marquee, West Bay Rd. at Harquail Bypass, Seven Mile Beach* ☎ *345/947–2782* ⊕ *www.cimboco.com* ⊟ *AE, MC, V.*

$$$–
$$$$ ✕ **Copper Falls.** *Steakhouse.* The restaurant's tagline, "A Rare Steakhouse, Very Well Done," is only a touch hyperbolic. The brashly contemporary look (copper-clad waterfalls and hand-painted metal bas relief contrasting with century-old Douglas fir wainscoting and high-backed suede booths) screams corporate takeover in progress. Hand-cut 28-day aged Angus cuts, from 8-ounce filet mignon to 28-ounce porterhouse, certify its Grade-A status, attracting a demanding business clientele. Lighter options run from pan-fried grouper topped with lobster and mushrooms in sun-dried tomato sauce to Parmesan/Dijon mustard-crusted chicken. There's a choice of five starches (scrumptious garlic mashed potatoes), three vegetables, and six sauces. Best of all, every entrée includes a complimentary beer or cocktail (the martinis would stir 007), helping make Copper Falls pure gold for steak-house purists. ⊠ *43 Canal Point Rd., The Strand, Seven Mile Beach* ☎ *345/945–4755* ⚑ *Reservations essential* ⊟ *AE, D, MC, V* ⊙ *No lunch.*

$$–$$$ ✕ **Eats Cafe.** *Eclectic.* This happy, hopping hangout is more eclectic and stylish than any diner, with dramatic decor (crimson booths and walls, flat-screen TVs lining the counter, pendant steel lamps, an exhibition kitchen, gigantic flower paintings, and Andy Warhol reproductions) and vast menu (Cajun to Chinese), including smashing breakfasts. The 15 burgers alone (Rasta Mon Jerkya to Cajun Peppercorn to I'm Sooo Bleu, as well as fish and veggie versions) could satisfy almost any craving, but you could also get a Caesar salad or sushi, Philly cheese steak or chicken chimichangas. It's noisy, busy, buzzing, and hip—but not aggressively so. ⊠ *Falls Plaza, West Bay Rd., Seven Mile Beach* ☎ *345/943–3287* ⊕ *www.eats.ky* ⊟ *MC, V.*

$$$–
$$$$ ✕ **Hemingway's.** *Eclectic.* Willowy palms, hardwood furnishings, a churchlike profusion of candles and torches, whirring paddle fans, wicker, lacquered bamboo, and picture windows opening onto Seven Mile Beach pay tribute to Hemingway's tropical travels. Specialties are described earnestly with their Hemingway significance: lobster (here

with lemongrass butter sauce) because Papa often feasted on it in Key West, paella because bullfighters fascinated him, rum-and-coconut shrimp with tamarind drizzle since Ernest founded the Royal Order of Shrimp Eaters in Havana. The key lime pie does justice to the restaurant's namesake. ⊠ *Grand Cayman Beach Suites, West Bay Rd., Seven Mile Beach* ☎ *345/945–5700 or 345/949–1234* ⊕ *www.grand-cayman-beach-suites.com* ⚲ *Reservations essential* ⊟ *AE, D, DC, MC, V.*

$$–$$$ ✕ **Icoa Fine Foods.** *Eclectic.* Icoa, the goddess of water worshipped by the indigenous people of Venezuela's Paria peninsula, was renowned for her exceptional beauty and alluring perfume; innovative Dutch chef Jurgen Wevers crafts food that likewise stimulates all the senses, drawing his own adoring acolytes. The minimalist space (Cubist- and Constructivist-inspired art, IKEA-style simple lines, ornate mosaic floor, and lots of stark Starck-like white) allows his cutting-edge cuisine to take center stage. Taste buds tango to such dishes as lump crab cake with marinated melon salad, basil, and yuzu; chicken liver pâté with toasted pistachios, fig compote, puffed cereal crisps, and honey; and braised beef short ribs with gremolata (minced garlic, parsley, and lemon peel), roasted potatoes, and saffron-garlic aioli. Fresh baked breads make a meal in themselves. Desserts are remarkable (you can also buy handcrafted chocolates infused with fresh key limes, passion fruit, pineapple, and Cayman honey). You can sample many of the same or similar dishes at lower lunch prices. ⊠ *9–11 Seven Mile Shops, West Bay Rd., Seven Mile Beach* ☎ *345/945–1915* ⊕ *www.icoacafe.com* ⊟ *MC, V* ⊙ *No dinner Sun.–Thurs.*

$$–$$$ ✕ **Lone Star Bar and Grill.** *Tex-Mex.* This temple to sports and the cowboy lifestyle serves a Texas-size welcome and portions. If it can be barbecued, deep-fried, jerked, pulled, or nacho-ized it's probably on the menu. Many locals swear the burgers are Cayman's best (the Death Burger topped with jalapeño peppers, guacamole, and Swiss cheese should jolt your taste buds). Such Tex-Mex standards as shrimp fajitas are appropriately mouth- and eye-watering, and regulars lick their chops at the reasonable prices, especially on theme nights like Monday, when you can get all-you-can-eat fajitas. ⊠ *686 West Bay Rd., Seven Mile Beach* ☎ *345/945–5175* ⊕ *www.caymanlonestar.com* ⊟ *AE, MC, V.*

$$$–$$$$ ✕ **Luca.** *Italian.* Owners Paolo Polloni and Andi Marcher spared no expense in realizing their vision of a smart (in every sense) beachfront trattoria that wouldn't be out of place in L.A. Everything was painstakingly hand-picked, from the wine "wall" dramatically displaying more than 3,000 bottles from around the globe to the Murano glass fixtures, blown-up photographs in glossy glassy frames, leather banquettes, and a curving onyx-top bar. Chef Frederico Destro delights in unorthodox pairings, all gorgeously presented. Spicy tuna tartare is served with satiny pepper sauce and crunchy alfalfa sprouts. Hudson Valley foie gras knits spinach sauce with Anjou pear. His homemade pastas shine, particularly the pumpkin ravioli in drawn thyme butter and fantastically fluffy spinach gnocchi in Taleggio cream. Entrées are invariably solid, if uneven; the standout is whole Mediterranean striped bass baked in salt crust with a semolina pancake and eggplant soufflé, a superb example of textural counterpoint. His wit and whimsy truly inform the desserts, which are more ambitious and intellectual than successful (chocolate-aubergine mousse or chocolate pappardelle in coriander sauce with pistachio ice cream), yet stimulate the palate and conversation. ⊠ *Caribbean Club, 871 West Bay Rd., Seven Mile Beach* ☎ *345/923–4550* ⌂ *Reservations essential* ▭ *AE, D, MC, V.*

$$$–   ✕ **Mezza.** *Eclectic.* This elegant earth-toned eatery takes
$$$$ its name from the Middle Eastern term for tapas. Just as striking splashes of color (scarlet and lime pillows, vibrant abstract artworks) play off each other, so do the intricate flavors. Witness such appetizers as flash-fried, wakame-rolled tuna roulade encrusted with Japanese breadcrumbs, served with a sesame-infused soy sauce and honeyed wasabi, or hazelnut-thyme-encrusted Brie with strawberry-balsamic glaze. Splendid main courses range from pan-seared scallops served over Parmesan risotto with lemongrass foam to braised lamb shank in anise demi-glace. Many items are available for both lunch and dinner, though the former includes its own cheaper, equally creative lineup of wraps, salads, and more substantial fare. There's an extensive, smartly priced list of wines by the glass, and mellow live music most nights. ⊠ *233 West Bay Rd., Seven Mile Beach* ☎ *345/946–3992* ⌂ *Reservations essential* ▭ *AE, MC, V* ⊘ *No lunch Sat.*

$$$–   ✕ **Neptune.** *Italian.* Despite pretensions toward decorative
$$$$ dash (faux stone arches to mermaid murals), Neptune thrives precisely because the food eschews fancy frills, stressing tried-and-true preparations that incorporate fresh (and easily obtained) ingredients. The greatest Italian hits menu ranges from *insalata Caprese* to carpaccio, lasagna to linguine *fra diavolo*. While seafood reigns supreme, you'll

find standout steaks as well. There's a bias toward cream in the sauces, which some find heavenly, others merely heavy. But personable co-owner–chef Raj Kumar gladly accommodates special dietary requirements, including oil- and salt-free options, as well as such off-the-menu items as salmon Provençal. The likes of Ramazzotti and Rossini provide soothing background music, but avoid Saturday, when karaoke takes over. ⊠ *Trafalgar Place, West Bay Rd., Seven Mile Beach* ☎ *345/946–8709* ▭ *AE, D, MC, V.*

$$–$$$ ✕**Ragazzi.** *Italian.* The title means "good buddies," and this strip-mall jewel offers simpatico ambience indeed, always percolating with conversation and good strong espresso. The airy space is convivial: blond woods, periwinkle walls and columns, and handsome artworks of beach scenes, sailboats, and palm trees (against a striking yellow sky) with the scenes extended onto the frame. Chef Adriano Usini turns out magnificent, meticulously prepared standards (the antipasto alone is worth a visit, as are the homemade breadsticks and focaccia, and definitive carpaccio and Caprese). The shellfish linguine (shrimp, scallops, mussels in a light silken tomato sauce, with cherry tomato skins pulled back and crisped) and gnocchi in four-cheese sauce with brandy and pistachios will please any pasta perfectionist. Two dozen first-rate pizzas emerge from the wood-burning oven, and meat and seafood mains are beautifully done, never overcooked. The wine list is notable (400-odd choices) for a casual eatery, showcasing great range and affordability even on high-ticket, hard-to-find heavy hitters like Biondi Santi Brunello, Jermann Pinot Grigio, and Giacosa Barbaresco; the affable, knowledgeable staff will gladly suggest pairings, including unusual finds. ⊠ *Buckingham Sq., West Bay Rd., Seven Mile Beach* ☎ *345/945–3484* ⊕ *www.eragazzi. com* ▭ *AE, MC, V.*

$$$– ✕**Reef Grill at Royal Palms.** *Seafood.* This class act appeals
$$$$ to a casually suave crowd, many of them regulars, who appreciate its consistent quality, attentive yet unobtrusive service, soothing seaside setting, top-notch entertainment, and surprisingly reasonable prices. The space is cannily divided into four areas, each with its own look and feel. Co-owner–chef George Dahlstrom gives his perfectly prepared, familiar items just enough twist to satisfy jaded palates: calamari is fried in arborio rice batter with lemon aioli; the tuna spring roll kicks with wasabi and ponzu dipping sauce; melt-in-your-mouth braised short ribs have a caramelized onion demi-glace; and sea scallops are pan-seared with corn, smoked bacon cream sauce, and lobster mash. Dance

the calories off to the estimable reggae, calypso, and soca sounds of Coco Red, then adjourn to the cozy lounge for an aged rum or single malt. It's equally enticing at lunch when it exudes a soigné beach-bar ambience. ✉ *537 West Bay Rd., Seven Mile Beach* ☎ *345/945–6358* ⊕ *www.reefgrill. com* ⊟ *AE, MC, V* ⊗ *No dinner Sun. May–Nov.*

$$$– ✕ **7 Prime Cuts/Sunsets.** *Steakhouse.* The Ritz-Carlton's all-
$$$$ purpose dining room transforms from a bustling breakfast buffet (and appealing lunch spot with simpler menus) into an elegant eatery come evening. Tall potted palms, terrazzo floors, red and black columns, and the tiered pool just outside are lit to strategically stylish effect. Sinatra and Ella keep the sultry beat, while the kitchen jazzes standard meat-and-potatoes dishes with inventive seasonings and eye-catching presentations. Splendid aged steaks come with five sauces, from Madagascar-green-peppercorn jus to champagne-tarragon béarnaise. The Kobe beef and foie gras burger and such sides as truffled mac-and-cheese redefine divine decadence. The calorie- and cholesterol-conscious can savor melt-in-your-mouth tuna tartare with soy-spice-ponzu-lime-zest emulsion or impeccably cooked catch-of-the-day with lime beurre blanc, Mojito butter, sweet chili tropical fruit salsa, or Scotch bonnet tartar sauce. Then just surrender to such confections as Volcano chocolate cake with malted milk ice cream and strawberry sauce *dulce de leche*. ✉ *Ritz-Carlton Grand Cayman, West Bay Rd., Seven Mile Beach* ☎ *345/943–9000* ⊕ *www.ritzcarlton.com* ⊟ *AE, D, DC, MC, V.*

$–$$ ✕ **Sunshine Grill.** *Caribbean.* This cheerful, cherished locals'
☾ secret serves haute comfort food at bargain-basement prices. Even the chattel-style poolside building, painted a delectable lemon with lime shutters, whets the appetite. Sunshine ranks high in the island's greatest burger debate, while the jerk-chicken egg rolls and fabulous fish tacos elevate pub grub to an art form. Wash it down with one of the many signature libations, like the Painkiller. Take advantage of affordably priced nightly dinner specials like Thai chili salmon, red snapper amandine, and Cuban pork loin with *sofrito* (a dip of cilantro, garlic, onions, and oregano). Don't miss Thursday's all-you-can-eat Caribbean BBQ buffet. ✉ *Sunshine Suites, West Bay Rd., Seven Mile Beach* ☎ *345/949–3000* ⊟ *AE, MC, V.*

$$$– ✕ **Thai Orchid.** *Thai.* East meets West at this elegant eatery,
$$$$ and the combination makes for a tasty meal. The look jux-taposes some Thai crafts and black-lacquer accents with track lighting, pomegranate and mango sponge-painted

walls, and bold artworks of semi-abstract beach scenes and decidedly Western cupids. The Thai chefs turn out splendid classics like *yum nuer* (sliced char-grilled strip loin tossed with green salad in lime dressing); the standout signature entrée is boneless duck sautéed with basil and bell peppers in chili sauce. Seafood lovers can opt for the fresh sushi, and plentiful vegetarian options include curries perfumed with lemongrass. Sunday's Thai/sushi buffet (just CI$13.95) is a superb bargain. Desserts return West, besting most Asian restaurants: Dark-and-white chocolate mousse cake with *crème anglaise* and raspberry coulis is a standout. ⊠ *Queens Court, West Bay Rd., Seven Mile Beach* ☎ *345/949–7955* ⊕ *www.thaiorchid.ky* ⊟ *AE, MC, V.*

$–$$ ✕ **Triple Crown Pub.** *British.* This mate-y pub lures lonely London-to-Limerick lads and lasses with a lengthy list of draft beers and fittings and furnishings sourced throughout the United Kingdom. Popular British standbys range from Lancashire hot pot (baked lamb stew topped with sliced potatoes) to a beef-and-ale pie that should be packaged for supermarkets, as well as the odd fancy effort, such as cider-steamed mussels finished with parsley cream sauce. Smoke-eating machines efficiently minimize haze; big-screen TVs blast major British and occasionally even U.S. sporting events. The bar menu is served until midnight. Prices are generally low—the Sunday all-you-can-eat carvery is only CI$16.25, and two-for-one steak dinner nights CI$17.95. Entertainment encompasses raucous trivia and bingo competitions, karaoke, DJ Fridays, and occasional live bands. ⊠ *Marquee Plaza, Seven Mile Rd., Seven Mile Beach* ☎ *345/943–7821* ⊟ *AE, MC, V.*

$$$– ✕ **The Wharf.** *Seafood.* The popularity of this large restaurant
$$$$ often leads to impersonal service and mediocre food. But the location, a series of elevated decks and Victorian-style gazebos hugging the sea, is enviable and helps to explain its enduring appeal (wedding parties have their own pavilion, but celebrations of all sorts can overrun the place, including Boogie Nights Fridays). The Ports of Call bar is a splendid place for sunset fanciers, and tarpon feeding off the deck is a nightly (9 PM) spectacle. Stick to simpler fare (Creole-style marinated conch, the signature basil-and-pistachio-crusted sea bass in champagne cream) and avoid anything sounding too pretentious. Chef Christian Reiter is Austrian and patriotic, so save room for dessert: Granny Smith apple tarte tatin with vanilla anglaise and rum-raisin ice cream or pear cheesecake on chilled sabayon with red-wine-poached pears don't disappoint. ⊠ *43 West Bay Rd., Seven Mile*

Beach ☎ *345/949–2231* ⊕ *www.wharf.ky* ⌣ *Reservations essential* ▭ *AE, MC, V* ⊙ *No lunch.*

$$–$$$ ✕ **Yoshi Sushi.** *Japanese.* The superlative sushi's fresh—and the clientele sometimes even fresher—at this modish, modern locals' lair. Scarlet cushions, cherry pendant blown-glass lamps, leather and bamboo accents, and maroon walls help create a sensuous, even charged vibe in the main room. The backlit bar sees its share of carefree customers trying to manipulate their chopsticks after a few kamikaze sake bomber missions (plunging hot cups of sake into frosty Kirin beer). Savvy diners literally leave themselves in Yoshi's hands (the rolls and sushi "pizzas" are particularly creative), while the raw-phobic can choose from fine cooked items, from beef tataki to tempura to teriyaki. The congenial staff recommends intriguing sake and beer pairings, though the wine list and martini selection are also admirable for an Asian eatery. ✉ *Falls Plaza, West Bay Rd., Seven Mile Beach* ☎ *345/943–9674* ⊕ *www.eats.ky* ⌣ *Reservations essential* ▭ *AE, MC, V.*

WEST BAY

$–$$ ✕ **Alfresco.** *Caribbean.* This ultra-friendly locals' insider spot, straddling the unofficial "border" between Seven Mile Beach and West Bay, resembles a little neighborhood diner transported to the ocean. Enjoy equally fresh sea breezes and food on the waterfront wood deck (built over a former parking lot), under one of the mismatched umbrellas. The co-owner is a longtime fisherman, and the fish-and-chips would make any Londoner proud. Other savvy seafood selections run from fiery Scotch bonnet shrimp to lobster ravioli in gossamer pumpkin cream sauce. Indeed, the menu is as much Capri as Cayman, with yummy pizzas and fried calamari served with both jerk mayo and marinara sauce. ✉ *53 Town Hall Rd., West Bay* ☎ *345/947–2525* ▭ *D, MC, V.*

$$$$ ✕ **Calypso Grill.** *Eclectic.* Shack chic describes this inviting split-level space splashed in Dr. Seuss primary colors that contrast with brick walls, hardwood furnishings, terra-cotta floors, trompe l'oeil shutters, and (real) French doors opening onto sweeping North Sound views. If the interior is like stepping into a Caribbean painting, the outdoor deck serenely surveying frigate birds watchfully circling fishing boats is a Winslow Homer canvas brought to life. George Fowler's menu rightly emphasizes fish hauled in at the adjacent dock, so fresh (and never overcooked)

Where to Eat in West Bay

KEY

⬥ Dive Sites

⛱ Beach

1 Restaurants

0	2 mi
0	2 km

Conch Point

Palmetto Point Rd.

Conch Point Rd.

3

Capt. Reg Parson's Rd.

BIRCH TREE HILL

MOUNT PLEASANT

BARKERS

Boatswain's Beach

2

Hell

Head of Barkers

NW Point

CORAL GABLES

Town Hall Rd.

4 BATABANO

5–**7**

West Bay

Orange Canyon

1 Old Homestead

North West Point Rd.

West Bay Public Beach

Little Salt Creek

UPPERLAND

Salt Creek

Boat Launch

Trinity Caves

Cemetery Reef

West Bay Rd.

Grand Cayman Yacht Club

Governors Creek

A1

GOVERNORS HARBOUR

Welch Point

Alfresco, **1**
Calypso Grill, **5**
Cracked Conch, **2**
Liberty's, **4**
Morgan's Harbour, **6**
Osetra Bay, **7**
Pappagallo, **3**

that it almost literally jumps from the plate. You'll never go wrong with the unvarnished catch-of-the-day grilled, blackened, or sautéed. Though this is seafood's turf, land-lubbers can savor a veal chop with morel-marsala sauce or a proper rack of lamb. End with the sticky toffee pudding. ⊠ *Morgan's Harbour, West Bay* ☎ *345/949–3948* ⊕ *www.calypsogrillcayman.com* ⌕ *Reservations essential* ⊟ *AE, D, MC, V* ⊘ *Closed Mon.*

WORD OF MOUTH. "We had dinner at Calypso Grill—my wife had the grilled tiger shrimp—a bit overpriced but good nonetheless. I had the blackened tuna and crab cakes as an appetizer. This was probably the best meal we had on the island. . . . Both my wife's shrimp and my blackened tuna came with the same (great) micro shoestring fries and grilled asparagus."   —DKG50

$$$–
$$$$
✕ **Cracked Conch.** *Eclectic.* This longtime institution rebuilt after Hurricane Ivan, effortlessly blends upscale and down-home. The interior gleams from the elaborate light-and-water sculpture at the gorgeous mosaic-and-mahogany entrance bar to the plush booths with subtly embedded lighting. You can drink in the remarkable water views

through large shutters, but for maximum impact, dine on the multi-tiered patio. Newfangled variations on old-fashioned cuisine include honey-jerk-glazed tuna with cucumber relish, crispy calamari with cardamom-marinated carrots and chipotle sauce, and braised turtle in coffee cream. Sample stellar signature items which include the definitive conch chowder or seviche, short-rib ravioli with truffles and Parmesan foam, and mahimahi poached with dark rum butter sauce, turmeric wilted spinach, and tomato chutney. Desserts delight from a gossamer vanilla crème brûlée with pineapple-bergamot salsa to a miraculously moist guava-glazed bread-and-butter-pudding. Locals flock to Sunday brunch or Monday's DJ-fueled all-you-can-eat barbecue bash, or they just hang out at the wildly decorated dockside Macabuca tiki bar (fab sunsets, sunset-hued libations), which lives up to its mellow name, indigenous Taíno for "What does it matter?" ✉ *Northwest Point Rd., West Bay* ☎ *345/945–5217* ⊕ *www.crackedconch.com.ky* ▭ *AE, MC, V* ⊘ *No dinner Sun.*

$$–$$$ ✕ **Liberty's.** *Caribbean.* Just follow the boisterous laughter and pulsating Caribbean tunes to this hard-to-find mint-green Caymanian cottage where you feel like you've been invited to a family reunion. The Sunday Caribbean buffet attracts hordes of hungry churchgoers, but every day offers authentic turtle steak, oxtail, jerk, and delectable fried snapper with sassy salsas that liberate your taste buds from the humdrum. ✉ *140 Reverend Blackman Rd., West Bay* ☎ *345/949–3226* ▭ *MC, V.*

$$$ ✕ **Morgan's Harbour.** *Eclectic.* Energetic, effervescent Janie Schweiger patrols the front while husband Richard rules the kitchen at this simpatico seaside spot with smashing North Sound views. Locals (and fishers) cruise into the adjacent dock for refueling of all sorts. You can sit in one of the cozy buildings decorated with Depression-era chandeliers and vivid aquatic artworks ("It's the House of Doors," Janie quips, "25 ways in but of course we don't want you to leave") or admire the dexterous marine maneuverings from the interlocking decks. Richard's menu dances just as deftly from Asia to his Austrian home. Nifty, nimbly prepared nibbles include the wildly popular 10-ounce Brie-topped jerk burger and seviche, but everything from chicken schnitzel to seafood risotto is expertly cooked to order, often with a creative twist. ✉ *Morgan's Harbour, West Bay* ☎ *345/946–7049* ⊕ *www.morgansharbour.net* ▭ *AE, MC, V.*

$$$$ ✕ **Osetra Bay.** *Eclectic.* Whether by day (when fishing boats as brightly colored as a child's fingerpainting trawl the tourmaline North Sound) or by night (when Cayman Kai's lights twinkle as the moon dapples the water with a thousand gold doubloons), the view alone guarantees a memorable meal. The design is almost as appetizing, from glowing columns strategically placed to flatter diners to the intimate billowing-draped dining cabanas to the stark Starck-ish white-on-white ultra-lounges. Every element infuses the casual Caribbean underpinnings with a chic South Beach sensibility, bringing literal caviar to Cayman. The everchanging sophisticated seasonal menu emphasizes seafood (pan-seared tuna with foie gras in vanilla-apple butter, jumbo scallops swimming in sweet-pea mousse, roasted sea bass with Scotch bonnet miso and shaved ackee), though vegetarians will delight in the pastas, and carnivores can stake out dishes like the dry-aged truffled rib eye. ✉ *Morgan's Harbour, West Bay* ☎ *345/325–5000* ⌂ *Reservations essential* ═ *AE, MC, V* ☉ *No lunch weekdays.*

$$$– $$$$ ✕ **Pappagallo.** *Italian.* Pappagallo, Italian for "parrot," hauntingly perches on the edge of a lagoon in a 14-acre bird sanctuary. Inside, riotously colored macaws, cockatoos, and parrots perch on swings behind plate glass, primping, preening, and practically commenting on the billing and cooing clientele. You feel like hacking through the luxuriant vegetation inside and out; the lost-in-the-jungle exoticism is enhanced by locally hewn stones, bamboo, homemade rope, and thatched palapas for outdoor seating. Yet the sleek deco-inspired black-marble and polished-brass accents bespeak the underlying seriousness. Chef Steve Wagner's food is definitely not for the birds. Chunky yet silken seafood chowder is enlivened by jalapeño-cured bacon. The kick of a jerk Kurobuto pork chop flamed with Jack Daniel's and accompanied by mango-lime salsa is softened by downy sour-cream-scallion mashed potatoes, each element providing sterling textural counterpoints. Be sure to thank Bogie, the African gray parrot, who really rules the roost. ✉ *Barkers, Conch Point, West Bay* ☎ *345/949–1119* ⊕ *www.pappagallo.ky* ⌂ *Reservations essential* ═ *AE, MC, V* ☉ *No lunch.*

Where to Eat Elsewhere on the Island

Grand Old House, **1**
Kaibo Beach Bar
& Grill, **8**
The Lighthouse, **2**
Over the Edge, **7**

Pelican's Reef, **6**
Portofino Wreck View, **5**
Roland's Garden, **3**
Vivine's Kitchen, **4**

Food Fêtes

Gastronomy is big business on Grand Cayman, as upmarket eateries bank on the tourist dollar. Increasingly popular culinary events introduce visitors to local culture while beefing up biz, especially off-season. January's "A Taste of Cayman" has titillated taste buds for more than two decades, thanks to more than 30 participating restaurants, raffles, entertainment, and cook-offs. Celeb chef Eric Ripert debuted "Caribbean Rundown" weekend in October 2007 at his Blue by Eric Ripert in the Ritz-Carlton, including cooking classes, fishing trips, and gala dinners, *Top Chef* competitor Dale Levitzki in tow. It was such a success that *Food & Wine* co-sponsors the subsequent editions—now called Cayman Cookout—every January, with even more top toques stirring the broth: a recipe for success in this case. Both fests benefit local charities.

3

EAST END

$$$– $$$$ ×**The Lighthouse.** *Seafood*. The nonworking, conical white stucco lighthouse surrounded by fluttering flags serves as a beacon for hungry East End explorers. The interior replicates a yacht: polished hardwood floors, ships' lanterns, mosaic hurricane lamps, steering wheels, marine artworks, portholes, and waiters in crew's garb with chevrons. Most tables afford sweeping sea vistas, but prize romantic seating is on the little deck. Shipshape starters include Miss Nell's red conch chowder (she lives in the pink house behind the restaurant) and flash-fried calamari with shaved onions and sweet chili dip. Photo-shoot-worthy entrées (such as spice-rubbed barramundi with strawberry-kiwi salsa and plantains drizzled with red pepper coulis) sing with color and flavor. Carnivores can devour braised veal shank with almond polenta or chicken breast with cranberry-Dijon cream. Vegetarians will delight in the curries, tofu stir-fries, and pastas. Save room for desserts, including the tropical cheesecake. The comprehensive wine list extends to a superb postprandial selection of liqueurs, aged rums, Ports, and grappas. The gift shop offers lovely jewelry and handmade ceramic lighthouses. ✉ *Oceanside, Breakers, East End* ☎ *345/947–2047* ⊕ *www.lighthouse.ky* ▭ AE, D, MC, V.

$$$– $$$$ ×**Pelican's Reef.** *Eclectic*. The Reef Resort's all-purpose dining room converts into a refined space come evening, its marine murals illuminated by candles, with clever partition-

ing by framed sails to enhance its intimacy. Chef Robert hails from Jamaica, but even his buffets merrily marry culinary influences: He'll infuse hummus with saffron, spike avocado rolls with corn salsa, flambé jerk chicken in creamy Grand Marnier sauce. Standouts include conch sausage with caramelized onions and potato cakes, and blackened tuna with mango salsa. Everything utilizes the freshest produce. Occasional limbo contests and the iconic Barefoot Man's inimitable song stylings can alter the ambience from romantic to raucous. ⊠ *Reef Resort, Colliers, East End* ☎ *345/947–3100* ⊕ *www.thereef.com.ky* ⚓ *Reservations essential* ⊟ *AE, D, MC, V.*

$$$– $$$$ ✕ **Portofino Wreck View.** *Italian.* Like many a restaurant marketing its view, Portofino delivers on that promise, and fortunately the food isn't a wreck. Though the breezy turquoise-and-coral deck is in demand, the darling interior (chartreuse and aqua color scheme with frescoes of grape arbors) is just as romantic in the evening. Though billed as an Italian and local restaurant, Portofino is Indian-owned, and the killer (in more ways than one) curries are the top choice. The menu gallops from coconut shrimp in mango-apricot chutney to spaghetti carbonara to chicken Kiev with varying success. Sunday brunch with carving station is a popular local draw (and bargain at CI$20.95). ⊠ *Colliers Bay, East End* ☎ *345/947–2700* ⚓ *Reservations essential* ⊟ *AE, MC, V.*

$–$$ ✕ **Roland's Garden.** *Eclectic.* Foodies seeking the quirky and unexpected will revel in this secret garden. Chef Roland Schoefer arrived in Cayman a quarter century ago after running top-notch restaurants in Heidelberg, Germany. His idiosyncratic touch engendered a series of successes, but this free spirit abandoned the corporate cooker. Now Roland advertises, "No menu, no liquor (B.Y.O.B.), no invoice, no restaurant." He cooks to order for the evening's exact number of reservations (up to 18 guests); he'll try to accommodate dietary and allergic restrictions, but don't dare tell him your dislikes. There's no menu: What he prepares is what you get, generally a five-course meal incorporating whatever's fresh from the market and his fishing buddies. He'll sit at your table, a Yankees cap replacing the typical toque, explaining each dish in delectable detail. Perhaps it's tuna carpaccio with pesto and feta, followed by homemade sausage, segueing into classic Wiener schnitzel with spaetzle, climaxing with a to-die-for strudel. The setting is equally eclectic: a virtual jungle filled with parrots, anchors, ships' lanterns, rigging, beach umbrellas, rotat-

Eating at a Home Kitchen

Aspiring Anthony Bourdains on Grand Cayman should seek out roadside vans, huts, kiosks, and stalls dishing out unfamiliar grub that might unnerve wannabe *Survivor* contestants. These casual spots offer authentic fare at very fair prices, with main dishes and heaping helpings of sides costing under CI$10. If you thought Mickey D's special sauce or Coke was a secret formula, try prying prized recipes handed down for generations from these islanders.

Bodden Town's jerk emporia are generally considered the best. **Biggie's Jerk Stand** (⊠ *Bodden Town* ☎ *345/947–3155*) qualifies as upscale (it has a real oven); ask if he's doing a whole pig roast on weekends. A faux cow and pig greet you at **Rankin's Jerk Centre** (⊠ *3032 Shamrock Rd., Bodden Town* ☎ *345/947–3155*), where you can savor Miss Rankin's scrumptious turtle stew and jerk dishes in her alluring garden. **Chester's Fish Fry** (⊠ *Bodden Town*

☎ *345/939–3474*) has a devoted following for his jerk pork, fried fish, and downy fritters.

Two of these most casual eateries on the island are George Town institutions. Even politicos stand in line at **Tony's Jerk Foods** (⊠ *193 School Rd., George Town* ☎ *345/916–6860*), which serves everything from cow foot to conch stew (you can't miss the exterior's beach mural). **Seymour's Jerk Centre** (⊠ *Shedden Rd., George Town* ☎ *345/916–8531 or 345/916–5418*), in the parking lot of Roy's Boutique, is where island icon Seymour Silburn dishes out succulent slow-cooked smoky jerk (regulars have gotten their fix for more than two decades).

West Bay's popular family-run **Heritage Kitchen** (⊠ *Just off Boggy Sand Rd., West Bay*) serves up legendary raconteur Tunny Powell's fish tea, barbecue ribs, and fish fry—with a generous portion of local lore.

---

ing imaginatively hung artworks, and giant standing fan to blow away mosquitoes. The pièce de résistance? "Pay me whatever you think it's worth," winks Roland, passing around a carved driftwood bowl, and he's serious. ⊠ *"Cottage," Frank Sound Rd., East End* ☎ *345/926–7670* ⊕ *www. chefroland.com* ⌔ *Reservations essential* ⊟ *No credit cards* ⊗ *No lunch; no dinner some nights.*

$–$$ ✕ **Vivine's Kitchen.** *Caribbean.* Cars practically block the road at this unprepossessing hot spot for classic Caymanian food. You're actually eating in Vivine and Ray Watler's home;

the prime seating is actually in the waterfront courtyard, where you will be serenaded by rustling sea-grape leaves, crashing surf, and screeching gulls dive-bombing for their lunch. Daily changing menu items, all sourced locally to guarantee freshness, are scrawled on a blackboard: perhaps stewed turtle, curried goat, barbecued chicken, and snapper made to order, with cassava and sweet-potato cake sides. Burgers, dogs, and chicken and chips make a concession to more timid taste buds. Alcohol isn't served, but fresh tamarind, mango, and sorrel juices pack a flavorful punch. Vivine generally closes early (and occasionally on Monday nights) but stays open if there's demand—and any food left. ⊠ *Austin Dr., Gun Bay, East End* ☎ *345/947–7435* ⊟ *No credit cards.*

NORTH SIDE

$$$– $$$$ ✕**Kaibo Beach Bar and Grill.** *Caribbean.* Spectacularly overlooking the North Sound, this quintessential beach hangout rocks days (fantastic lunches that cost half the price of dinner, festive atmosphere including impromptu volleyball tourneys, and free Wi-Fi) but serves murderous margaritas and mudslides well into the evening to a boisterous bevy of yachties, locals, sports buffs, and expats. Enjoy New England–style conch chowder with a hint of heat, spinach-artichoke dip, baked Brie, hefty burgers, and wondrous wraps (seared tuna in wasabi mayo, grilled spice-marinated chicken with jerk mayo), either on the multi-tiered deck garlanded with ships' rope and Christmas lights or in hammocks and thatched cabanas amid the palms. The three-course dinner with glass of wine for CI$39 is quite a bargain. The handsome, nautically themed second-floor dining room, open weekend nights, serves more creative fare (specialties include Dover sole with dill-caper velouté, honeycomb, and beetroot puree), but the ultimate in romance is the catered "Luna del Mar" evening hosted every Friday closest to the full moon. ⊠ *585 Water Cay Rd., Cayman Kai, North Side* ☎ *345/947–9975* ⊕ *www.kaibo.ky* ⊟ *AE, MC, V.*

$$–$$$ ✕**Over the Edge.** *Caribbean.* This fun, funky seaside spot brims with character and characters (a soused regular might welcome you by reciting "the daily lunch special: chilled barley soup . . . that's beer"). The nutty nautical decor (brass ships' lanterns dangle from the ceiling, while steering wheels, lacquered turtle shells, and fishing photos adorn the walls) contrasts with cool mirrored ads for Gitanes

Culinary Quality Control

In more than a decade at the helm of New York's Le Bernardin, sometime *Top Chef* panelist Eric Ripert has garnered every gastronomic accolade. Born in Antibes on the French Riviera, Ripert apprenticed at Parisian institution La Tour d'Argent and Joël Robuchon's Jamin, then worked stateside with Jean-Louis Palladin and David Bouley before Le Bernardin reeled him in. He opened his first "name" restaurant, Blue by Eric Ripert, at the Ritz-Carlton Grand Cayman in 2005. Others have since followed.

The Caribbean wasn't on Ripert's radar, as he has told us, but "the resort owner, Michael Ryan, was in New York for dinner at Le Bernardin. He wanted to discuss the Ritz and me opening its signature restaurant. When I came down, he picked me up, put me on a boat to swim at Stingray City, loaded me with champagne, then came straight here to discuss business.... I loved it, felt confident because of his commitment to quality and service."

The greatest challenge was "the quality of the seafood, which sounds illogical, but most fish here comes frozen from the United States. We visited fishermen, created a network, to get fresh catch regularly. It's the only item the hotel allows cash for, so Richard [Brower, now the executive chef] carries a big wad! We fought passionately for the quality of the seafood, since that's one of my trademarks. And with so few farmers and growers on island...produce was even more challenging, but we found squash, salad greens, herbs."

"Trying to use what's already here inspires me," says Brower. "It's cooking in the landscape.... I can now get lemongrass, thyme, mint, basil, papaya, mango, callaloo, sweet potatoes, good stew tomatoes, Scotch bonnet, and other peppers. I'm a big advocate of the locally produced Cayman sea salt." He encourages local purveyors, but paramount was persuading management to commit the funds for specialty products worth the price. "We work with a couple of commercial fishing boats that bring huge wahoo, ocean yellowtail, deep-water snapper from as far afield as Mexico.... So fresh and so beautiful, a pleasure to work with."

Ripert draws parallels to his Mediterranean upbringing. "It's a different feel and look, of course, as are the cooking ingredients and preparations. But both cultures place great emphasis on food as a key part of their lives and borrow from many heritages. And both cultures know how to relax and enjoy themselves!"

and Mumm Cordon Rouge and trendily semi-open kitchen with fresh fish prominently displayed. The jukebox jumps (country music rules the roost), and the tiki-lit terrace offers stunning views and fresh breezes. Expertly prepared local fare (curried chicken to conch steak to Cayman rock lobster escoveitch, served with rice and beans, plantains, and festival bread) is a bargain, especially at lunch, though the chef also surprises with such gussied-up fare as shrimp in Pernod sauce and turtle steak in port. ⊠ *Old Man Bay, North Side* ☎ *345/947–9568* ⊟ *AE, D, MC, V.*

Where to Stay in Grand Cayman

WORD OF MOUTH

"The nicest beach in Cayman is where the Westin is. Have stayed there and enjoyed it. . . . You may want to stay in a condo to cut food costs, which are very high in Cayman."

—summer04

By Jordan
Simon

DESPITE ITS SMALL SIZE, Grand Cayman offers a surprising range of accommodations: large luxury resorts, medium-size chain hotels, cozy condo enclaves, locally owned guesthouses—from boutique-y to budget, not to mention private villas.

The massive Ritz-Carlton resort on Seven Mile Beach was the first of several larger developments constructed under new laws allowing seven-story buildings. It was followed by the classy Caribbean Club Condominiums and the new, rebuilt upscale Beachcomber. Now high-rises sprout like fungi along Seven Mile Beach, each vowing and vying to be better—or at least grander—than the last.

Some of the acceptance of ever grander development can be attributed to the lingering devastation of 2004's Hurricane Ivan, which totaled the island. The 230-room Hyatt Regency hotel, long the island standard-bearer, never recovered from the damage; Hyatt eventually withdrew from its last management responsibilities. For good or bad, Ivan provided many complexes with an excuse to renovate, even rebuild from the ground up and go ever higher. While the tacky, dilapidated condo enclaves were swept away, now practically every sizable lot of Seven Mile Beach is in various stages of development.

Brace yourself for resort prices—there are few accommodations in the lower-cost ranges in Grand Cayman. You'll also find no big all-inclusive resorts on Grand Cayman, and very few offer a meal plan of any kind. Happily, parking, at least, is always free at island hotels and resorts.

WHERE TO STAY

Seven Mile Beach is Boardwalk and Park Place for most vacationers. In a quirk of development, however, most of the hotels sit across the street from the beach (though they usually have beach clubs, bars, water-sports concessions, and other facilities directly on the sand). Most of Grand Cayman's condo resorts offer direct access to Grand Cayman's prime sandy real estate. Snorkelers should note that only the northern and southern ends of SMB feature spectacular reef development; the northern end is much quieter, so if you're looking for action, stay anywhere from the Westin Casuarina south, where all manner of restaurants and bars are walkable.

BEST BETS

Fodor's Choice ★
Caribbean Club, Lighthouse
Point, Reef Resort, Ritz-Carlton
Grand Cayman, Coral Reef
Villa.

BEST BEACHFRONT
Coral Stone Club, Lacovia
Condominiums, Reef Resort,
Southern Cross Club, Westin
Casuarina

**BEST FOR AN
ECOFRIENDLY TRIP**
Cobalt Coast, Compass Point,
Lighthouse Point

BEST FOR FAMILIES
The Meridian, Ritz-Carlton
Grand Cayman, Great Escapes,
Pease Bay House, Scuba
Shack

BEST SERVICE
The Alexander, Reef Resort,
Ritz-Carlton Grand Cayman,
Westin Casuarina

BEST FOR ROMANCE
Caribbean Club, Cotton Tree,
Shangri-La B&B, Turtle Nest
Inn, Fishbones, Venezia, Villa
Habana

Tranquil **West Bay** retains the feel of an old-time fishing village; diving is magnificent in this area, but lodging options are limited, especially now that the long-promised Mandarin Oriental remains on indefinite hold.

Those who want to get away from it all should head to the bucolic **East End** and **North Side,** dotted with condo resorts and villas. The dive sites here are particularly pristine.

The **Cayman Kai/Rum Point,** starting at West Bay across the North Sound, offers the single largest concentration of villas and condo resorts, stressing barefoot elegance.

PRICES

Assume that hotels operate on the European Plan (EP, with no meals) unless we specify that they use either the Continental Plan (CP, with a Continental breakfast), Breakfast Plan (BP, with full breakfast), or the Modified American Plan (MAP, with breakfast and dinner). Other hotels may offer the Full American Plan (FAP, including all meals but no drinks) or may be All-Inclusive (AI, with all meals, drinks, and most activities).

WHAT IT COSTS IN U.S. DOLLARS					
	¢	$	$$	$$$	$$$$
Hotels*	under $80	$80–$150	$150–$250	$250–$350	over $350
Hotels**	under $125	$125–$250	$250–$350	$350–$450	over $450

*EP, BP, CP; **AI, FAP, MAP; hotel prices are per night for a double room in high season, excluding 10% tax, 10%–15% service charges, and meals (except at all-inclusives).

HOTELS AND RESORTS

Grand Cayman offers something for every traveler, with well-known chain properties in every price range and style. Accommodations run the gamut from outrageously deluxe to all-suites to glorified motor lodges. Add to that locally run hostelries that often offer better bang for the buck. Still, in a Caymanian quirk, condo resorts take up most of the prime beach real estate. And, with a couple of exceptions, hotels along Seven Mile Beach actually sit across the road from the beach (though they usually have beachfront eateries, bars, "private" beach clubs, and water-sports concessions directly on the sand).

B&BS, INNS, AND GUESTHOUSES

They may be some distance from the beach and short on style and facilities—or they may be surprisingly elegant, but all these lodgings offer a friendly atmosphere, equally friendly prices, and your best shot at getting to know the locals. Rooms are clean and simple at the very least, and most have private baths.

CONDOMINIUMS AND PRIVATE VILLAS

On Grand Cayman the number of available condos and villas greatly outnumbers hotel rooms. Most condos are very similar, with telephones, satellite TV, air-conditioning, living and dining areas, patios, and parking. Differences are the quality of in-condo amenities, facilities within their individual complexes (though pools, hot tubs, and barbecue grills are usually standard), proximity to town and the beach, and views. Some condos are privately owned and rented out directly by the owners; other complexes are made up solely of short-term rentals.

Grand Cayman's private villa rentals range from cozy one-bedroom bungalows to grand five-bedroom manses. Some stand completely independent; others may be located in a larger complex or enclave. While at first glance rental fees for villas may seem high, larger units can offer significant savings over hotels for families or couples traveling together. For example, if the cost of a three-bedroom villa is divided among three couples, the seemingly high nightly rental cost of $900 per night would only be $150 per person ($300 per couple); few hotels on Grand Cayman are so moderately priced. And as in a condo, a full kitchen helps reduce the stratospheric price of dining out; a laundry room helps with clean-up, especially for families. Unless otherwise noted, all villas have landline phones, and local calls are usually free; phones are generally locked for international calls, though Internet phone service could be included. Villa agents can usually help you rent a cell phone.

4

Rates are highest during the winter season from mid-December through mid-April. Most condo and villa rentals require a minimum stay, often five to seven nights in high season (during the Christmas holiday season the minimum will be at least one week and is sometimes two weeks, plus there are exorbitant fees). Off-season minimums are usually three to five nights.

Several of the condo- and villa-rental companies have Web sites where you can see pictures of the privately owned units and villas they represent; many properties are represented exclusively, others handled by several agents. In general, the farther north you go on Seven Mile Beach, the older and more affordable the property. Note also that many offices close on Sunday; if that's your date of arrival, they'll usually make arrangements for your arrival. There's often no maid service on Sunday either, as the island practically shuts down.

VILLA AND CONDO RENTAL AGENTS

The **Cayman Islands Department of Tourism** (⊕ *www.caymanislands.ky*) provides a list of condominiums and small rental apartments. There are several condo and villa enclaves available on the beach, especially on the North Side near Cayman Kai, away from bustling Seven Mile Beach.

Quoted prices for villa and private condo rentals usually include government tax and often service fees (be sure to verify this). As a general rule of thumb, Seven Mile Beach properties receive daily maid service except on Sunday, but at villas and condos elsewhere on the island, extra services such as cleaning must be prearranged for an extra charge.

Blue Escapes (☎ *512/472–8832 or 800/556–4801* ⊕ *www. blueescapes.com*) is an up-and-coming international broker that also works with top-notch on-island realtors.

Cayman Island Vacations (☎ *813/854–1201 or 888/208–8935* ⊕ *www.caymanvacation.com*) was started by the affable couple Don and Linda Martin in 1989. Longtime Cayman homeowners, they represent more than 50 villas and condos (including their own). Extremely helpful with island suggestions, they can make arrangements for a rental car and extras. They arrange diving discounts, and Linda is one of Cayman's leading wedding coordinators.

Cayman Villas (☎ *800/235–5888 or 345/945–4144* ⊕ *www. caymanvillas.com*) represents villas and condos on Grand Cayman and Little Cayman; from studios to six-bedrooms with private pool. They'll gladly facilitate connections with potential staff from chefs to chauffeurs, recommend restaurants and tour operators, and even put you in touch with wedding coordinators. A great selling point: Every property has a manager, available 24/7 via cell phone, who lives on-site or nearby. They work with industry leader WIMCO and the up-and-coming international villa broker Blue Escapes.

Grand Cayman Villas (☎ *877/426–8455* ⊕ *www.grandcayman-villas.net*) was started by Virginia resident Jim Leavitt to help his fellow second-homeowner friends on Grand Cayman advertise their villas at a better rate; he now carries listings for 250 fine properties island-wide.

Island Hideaways (☎ *800/832–2302* ⊕ *www.islandhideaways. com*) rents villas all over the Caribbean, including some in the Cayman Islands.

WIMCO (☎ *866/850–6140* ⊕ *www.wimco.com*), or the West Indies Management Company, is synonymous with quality throughout the world, especially the Caribbean.

EAST END

$$–$$$ ⊡ **Compass Point Dive Resort.** *Condo Resort.* This tranquil, congenial little getaway run by the admirable Ocean Frontiers scuba operation would steer even non-divers in the right direction. The eco-centric waterfront property is most attractive, from the powder-blue buildings elevated on stilts with white columns and trim to the interiors contrasting sparkling white-tile floors with luscious lemon, tomato, and peach walls. Smallish but spotless units contain nearly every

Market Watch

Most condo and villa rentals start on Saturday. Since all the island's major supermarkets (and most other stores) close on Sunday, condo and villa renters may want to stop off for essentials right after they pick up their rental car. There are several American-style supermarkets near the airport, along West Bay Road parallel to Seven Mile Beach, and elsewhere in the island; *for specific listings, see ⇨ Foodstuffs in Exploring Grand Cayman (with Shopping)*. All stock fresh produce, poultry, and seafood; meats; baked goods; cold cuts and cheeses; hot and cold ready-made dishes at deli counters; and anything canned, frozen, and boxed. Just don't get sticker shock: Prices average 25%–30% more than at home.

If you expect to arrive on a Sunday or holiday when the supermarkets are closed, ask the condo resort or rental agent to arrange a starter kit. **Cayman Vacation Shoppers** (☎ *345/916–2978 ⊕ www. caymanshoppers.com*) is a godsend for advance provisioning; it's also the only outfit on the island permitted to deliver wine and spirits on Sunday.

4

---

modern comfort: a full kitchen with dishwasher, free Wi-Fi, flat-screen TV (with DVD player), jetted tub, and washer/dryer. The emphasis is on activity and the environment. Aside from the dive boats and superior snorkeling around the dock, bikes, kayaks, paddleboats, and kite boards are available, as are tours and instruction; the owners are developing an eco-lodge annex across the road. The biggest drawback is the lack of a nearby restaurant or even bar, though there's a barbecue grill (and nightly events) by the pool and a grocery–pizza parlor just down the road. **Pros:** top-notch dive operation; good value especially with packages; affable international staff and clientele. **Cons:** no restaurant or bar; isolated location requires a car. ⊠ *Austin Conolly Dr., Box 200, East End* ☎ *345/947–7500 or 800/348–6096* ⊕ *www.compasspoint.ky* ⬃ *21 1-bedroom and 9 2-bedroom condos* ⬙ *In-room: kitchen, DVD, Wi-Fi. In-hotel: pool, diving, water sports, beachfront, bicycles, laundry facilities, Wi-Fi hotspot* ⊟ *AE, MC, V* ⥾ *EP.*

$$$$ ⛲ **Pease Bay House.** *Private Villa.* Political pooh-bahs (like the late senator Ted Kennedy) and tycoons toting tykes should find sufficient space for their entourages in this wallow-worthy mini-compound just 20 minutes yet worlds away from George Town. From the imposing gated entrance

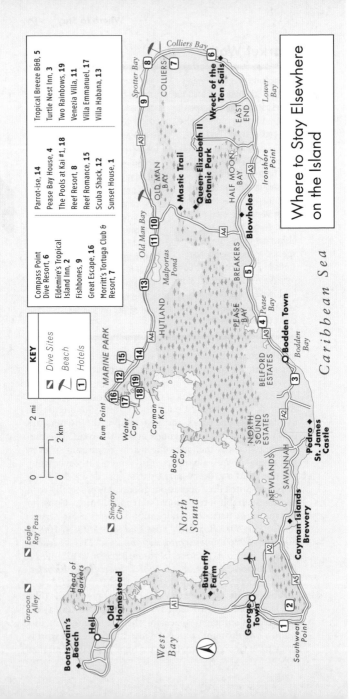

Where to Stay Elsewhere on the Island

KEY

■ Dive Sites
🏖 Beach
[1] Hotels

Compass Point Dive Resort, **6**
Eldemire's Tropical Island Inn, **2**
Fishbones, **9**
Great Escape, **16**
Morritt's Tortuga Club & Resort, **7**

Parrot-ise, **14**
Pease Bay House, **4**
The Pools at Kai #1, **18**
Reef Resort, **8**
Reef Romance, **15**
Scuba Shack, **12**
Sunset House, **1**

Tropical Breeze B&B, **5**
Turtle Nest Inn, **3**
Two Rainbows, **19**
Venezia Villa, **11**
Villa Emmanuel, **17**
Villa Habana, **13**

CLOSE UP

Other Lodgings to Consider

Obviously, we can't include every property deserving mention without creating an encyclopedia. Our favorites receive full reviews, but you might consider the following accommodations, many of them equally meritorious.

Beachcomber (⊠ *West Bay Rd., Seven Mile Beach* ☎ *345/943–6500* ⊕ *www. beachcomber.ky*) rose phoenix-like post-Ivan as a glam high-rise with 40 spacious 2- to 4-bedroom condos (roughly 24 in the rental pool). The decor is high-end, the amenities and appliances high-tech, and there's free underground parking, long distance calls to North America, and Wi-Fi; HDTV with DVD, a washer/dryer, and a dishwasher. The beach is gorgeous, and the location is ideal (walking distance to groceries and restaurants). It compares favorably to neighbors Caribbean Club and Meridian.

Morritt's Tortuga Club and Resort (⊠ *East End* ☎ *345/947–7449 or 800/447–0309* ⊕ *www.morritts.com*) offers 146 well-maintained, fully equipped, mostly time-share units, albeit many lacking beach views and/or access (the

best and priciest are branded "Grand Resort"). The more than adequate activities and amenities include the respected Tortuga Divers outfit. It's right next door to the Reef Resort.

Plantana (⊠ *1293 West Bay Rd., Seven Mile Beach* ☎ *345/945–4430* ⊕ *www.plantanacayman.com*) is exceedingly lush, set on a stunning stretch of sand with smashing views of the leviathan ships lumbering into George Town and permeated with the sounds of surf and birdsong. The 49 individually decorated one- to three-bedroom units are fully outfitted (including washer/dryers) and handsomely appointed, with designs running from contemporary to colonial, even Asian-inspired.

Silver Sands (⊠ *West Bay Rd., Seven Mile Beach* ☎ *345/949–3343* ⊕ *www.silversandscondos.com*) is an older compound that anchors the quieter northernmost end of Seven Mile Beach, with terrific snorkeling off the spectacular sweep of glittering sand. Most of the 42 cramped units have balconies with fabulous views; second-floor units with vaulted ceilings are preferable.

4

and lavishly landscaped drive to old-world decor (19th-century art, antique armoires and four-posters, Persian throw rugs, pilasters, piano, crystal chandeliers, coffered ceilings, gold gilt trim, mahogany moldings, marble bath columns) to newfangled gadgetry (Wi-Fi, intercom system,

The Reef Resort

Wolf kitchen appliances, SubZero wine cooler), it oozes cash and cachet. Thoughtful extras include tennis court, three-car garage, and whimsical kids' rooms with hand-painted animals, cartoon characters, and smiling choo-choo tracery. The 250-foot beach includes a cozy palapa with hammocks, fascinating tidal pools, and a protective encircling reef for safe swimming. **Pros:** sumptuously outfitted and appointed yet family-friendly, remote and tranquil, high-tech. **Cons:** may strike some as pretentious and intimidating; remote, incongruous art from lascivious nudes to religious icons could offend guests at either extreme. ⊠ *Pease Bay, between Bodden Town and Colliers* ⊕ *www. caymanvillas.com* ⬟ *5 bedrooms, 5½ baths* ⬠ *Dishwasher, DVD, Wi-Fi, daily maid service, pool, beachfront, tennis court, laundry facilities* ▭ *AE, D, MC, V* ⦿ *EP* ⬡ *7-night minimum, 5-night minimum off-season.*

★ **Fodor'sChoice** ⊠ **Reef Resort.** *Condo Resort.* This exceedingly
$$$– well run time-share property (don't worry: no aggressive
$$$$ hawking!) seductively straddles a 600-foot beach on the less hectic East End. Casual elegance prevails throughout, from granite accents to four-poster beds in the newer units. Each villa has a roomy terrace facing the sea; two-bedroom units can be partitioned, but even the studio has a microwave and fridge. Every year brings improvements (advance online check-in, hurricane-guarantee policy, spa and gym since 2008, and the only place offering power-assisted snorkeling on DPVs—Dive Propulsion Vehicles).

The resort is almost obsessively maintained. You always see a smiling staffer with a paintbrush or hedge clippers; there's even a relaxation guru, Jake Wheeler, to help you de-stress. This cordial, mellow, yet efficient service is a major selling point. Kids love when concierges conduct regular fish feedings at the dock or local artisans demonstrate techniques. The famous "Barefoot Man" performs his lighthearted country-calypso songs on Caribbean life at Pelican Reef on Tuesday and Thursday, luring lively locals. The food here (and killer cocktails at the bar) would tempt anyone; an all-inclusive plan is now an option. **Pros:** romantically remote; glorious beach; enthusiastic staff (including a crackerjack wedding coordinator); great packages. **Cons:** remote; few dining options within easy driving distance; sprawling layout. ⊠ *Queen's Hwy., Box 20865 SMB, East End* ☎ *345/947–3100 or 888/232–0541* ⊕ *www.thereef.com.ky* ⤺ *152 suites* ⌂ *In-room: safe, kitchen (some), refrigerator, DVD, Wi-Fi. In-hotel: 2 restaurants, bar, tennis court, pools, gym, spa, beachfront, diving, water sports, bicycles, laundry facilities, Internet terminal, Wi-Fi hotspot, parking (free)* ⊟ *AE, MC, V* ⫯⚬⫯ *EP.*

$–$$ ☆ **Turtle Nest Inn and Condos.** *Vacation Condos.* This affordable, intimate, Mediterranean-style seaside inn has roomy one-bedroom apartments and a pool overlooking a narrow beach with good snorkeling. You can find basic supplies some 10 minutes west at a shopping center in Savannah, but you'll still need to rent a car to get around. The apartments enchant, with arcaded balconies, beamed ceilings, black iron grillwork, vivid throw rugs, and stylish artworks. The two-bedroom condos have washer/dryers and dishwasher. The meticulous attention to detail is exceptional, from the high-thread-count sheets to the basket of suntan lotions in the lobby for forgetful guests. Other nice touches include World Phones with cheap fixed rates for rent; complimentary use of kayaks, rafts, and snorkeling gear; and fantastic packages including a rental car for weeklong stays. **Pros:** wonderful snorkeling; thoughtful extras; caring staff; free Wi-Fi. **Cons:** car necessary; occasional rocks and debris on beach; ground-floor room views slightly obscured by palms; road noise in back rooms. ⊠ *166 Bodden Town Rd., Box 187, Bodden Town* ☎ *345/947–8665* ⊕ *www. turtlenestinn.net* ⤺ *8 apartments, 10 2-bedroom condos* ⌂ *In-room: kitchen, DVD, Wi-Fi. In-hotel: pool, beachfront, water sports, laundry facilities, Wi-Fi hotspot* ⊟ *AE, D, MC, V* ⫯⚬⫯ *EP.*

$ ⊞ **Tropical Breeze B&B**. *B&B*. This serene hideaway tucked away amid splendiferous gardens allows you to get back to nature but not to basics. Owner Lisa Powell-Ebanks, a dedicated conservationist, has carefully replanted and pre-served indigenous Cayman flora (bougainvillea to banana orchids, Christmas palms to papaya), leaving it untouched wherever possible and creating an almost tree-house feel. The five rooms and separate two-bedroom cottage have botanical names; you'll receive fascinating information on "your" plant. As if the colors and aromas weren't stimulating enough, you'll fall asleep to the soothing sounds of surf and awaken to birdcall. The verandas command sensational views of the water, plied by vividly colored fishing boats (bonefishing here is particularly good). A small private beach with excellent snorkeling sits across the road. The Royal Palm Cottage and main house's Periwinkle and Sea Grape rooms also soak in the views. The one worm in paradise: As the rooms only have fridges, those who need more than juice and cereal in the morning must either drive 10 minutes or accept the steep surcharge for breakfast and maid service ($50 per night on top of the room rate). **Pros:** beautiful landscaping with nature trails and gar-den cabanas; remote yet nicely equipped. **Cons:** expensive maid service/breakfast surcharge; car necessary; petite pool; smallish pebbly beach is across the road. ⊠ *1669 Bodden Town Rd. between Midland Acres and Breakers, East End* ☎ *345/916–0318 or 866/978–5908* ⊕ *www.caymanseasidev-illas.com* ⌂ *5 rooms, 1 2-bedroom cottage* ⌂ *In-room: refrigerator, Wi-Fi. In-hotel: pool* ⊟ *MC, V* ⓄⓁ *EP.*

GEORGE TOWN AND ENVIRONS

$ ⊞ **Eldemire's Tropical Island Inn**. *B&B*. You're about 15 minutes from Seven Mile Beach at this guesthouse south of George Town, but less than 1 mi (1½ km) north of Smith Cove Beach. Eldemire's daughter and granddaugh-ter maintain both her tradition of warm welcomes and her extravagant gardens, which threaten to spill into the rooms. The homey feel is accentuated by chickens running around the property, a Gospel Shop and Video Club on-site (where you can get refreshments, terrific reggae CDs—and "faith" men's ties and prayer shawls), and invitations to the family's private North Side beach. The units, which have cheery walls (powder blue, magenta, lime green) and basic furniture with some flourishes like hand-painted cabi-nets, are cute and cozy. You only get breakfast with the

Buildings in George Town

regular rooms, but everyone has kitchen access. Eldemire's attracts a fascinating mix of locals, visitors from around the Caribbean (such as rugby and soccer tournament teams), and international backpackers. **Pros:** authentic Cayman hospitality and feel; inexpensive (with constant deals and discounts for paying cash); great dive packages arranged. **Cons:** hard to find; slightly rundown; not on the beach. ⊠ *18 Pebbles Way, off S. Church St., Box 482, George Town* ☎ *345/916–2022 or 345/916–8369* ⊕ *www.eldemire.com* ⤏ *4 rooms, 2 studios, 2 apartments* ⚘ *In-room: no phone, kitchen (some). In-hotel: pool, laundry facilities, Wi-Fi hotspot, bicycles* ═ *MC, V* ⦿ *EP.*

$$–$$$ ⊠ **Sunset House.** *Hotel.* This amiable seaside dive-oriented resort is on the ironshore south of George Town, close enough for a short trip to stores and restaurants yet far enough to feel secluded. The rooms are simple and in dire need of sprucing up (decor and condition vary wildly; the 500 block received a slight refurbishment in early 2008, while the 400 block offers some of the best views), but good diving and a homey atmosphere are the main attractions. A terrific reef is just steps from the rooms. The thatch-roof My Bar is tremendously popular, especially at sunset, and the world-famous Cathy Church's Underwater Photo Centre and Gallery is based here to round out the island's most comprehensive diving services. **Pros:** great shore diving and dive shop; lively bar scene; fun international clientele. **Cons:** often indifferent service; somewhat run-down; no real swimming beach. ✉ *390 S. Church St., Box 479GT, George Town* ☎ *345/949–7111 or 800/854–4767* ⊕ *www. sunsethouse.com* ⌖ *58 rooms, 2 suites* ⚷ *In-room: kitchen (some). In-hotel: restaurant, bar, pool, diving, laundry facilities, Internet terminal, Wi-Fi hotspot* ⊟ *AE, D, MC, V* ⎮⦿⎮ *EP.*

NORTH SIDE/CAYMAN KAI/RUM POINT

$$$$ 🏠 **Fishbones.** *Private Villa.* The setting may be unsurpassed, atop an ironshore cliff (with natural coral steps carved from the bluff leading first to a sundeck, then to the Caribbean and a sublime reef). Two tiny, romantic private coves are within wading distance. A unique third-story lookout, decked out in red, white, and blue, affords 360-degree vistas of sea and land. A screened lanai overlooks the water and large pool; the open deck contains a colonnaded gazebo perfect for reading in the shade. The interior design is equally thoughtful, with a two-story open living room decorated with refined hardwood and rattan furnishings, Morris-style rugs, and sunset photos. The kitchen contains state-of-the-art Viking appliances. All three bedrooms (master on the ground floor with jetted tub and walk-in shower) offer ocean views; the upstairs bedrooms are divided by a foyer with home office and nursery. Appealing touches include gingerbread-trim white-wood headboards. **Pros:** magnificent setting and views; complimentary Wi-Fi; splendid oceanfront pool; fantastic snorkeling. **Cons:** car necessary; no beach but a quick swim or wade (bring reef walkers) to the private coves on property. ✉ *Just off Queen's Hwy., North Side* ⊕ *www.caymanvacation.com* ⌖ *3 bedrooms, 3 baths* ⚷ *Dishwasher, DVD, Internet, Wi-Fi, laundry facilities* ⊟ *AE, MC, V* ⌖ *7-night minimum, 5-night minimum off-season.*

$$$$ 🏠 **Great Escape.** *Private Villa.* The peripatetic French owners of this très chic, *charmant* cottage filled the rooms with objets d'art from their travels. The living room goes native with thatch lamps, hand-painted African woodcarvings, bold jungle scenes, and even brighter fabric accents in cherry and aquamarine. The master bedroom is somewhat more subdued, with muted earth tones, swirling acrylic lamps, a ceremonial sword, coyly curvaceous window seat, and huge earthenware urns—all reflected in mirrors (you can watch yourself exercising in the small home gym). There are plush leather loungers and a sports-bar-worthy flat-screen TV. The screened patio overlooks an L-shaped

pool with wonderful mosaics and a table and chairs built into the shallow end. Hammocks swing on a sandy patch, though there's too much turtle grass in the otherwise clear water for swimming. Kids, nonetheless, will enjoy watching angelfish congregate at the private dock, as well as the Ping-Pong table and grill. An adjacent fully equipped guest cottage with kitchen, bathroom, four-poster bed, French doors, and sunshine-yellow walls is ideal for a second couple but adds almost $200 to the nightly charge. **Pros:** artsy; walk to Kaibo Yacht Club and Rum Point; good value. **Cons:** not on swimming beach; mosquitoes and no-see-ums can be problematic on still days. ⊠ *127 Sand Point Rd., Cayman Kai* ⊕ *www.caymanvillas.com* ⇱ *4 bedrooms, 3 baths* ⚄ *Dishwasher, DVD, pool, gym, beachfront, laundry facilities, Wi-Fi* ⊟ *AE, D, MC, V* ⚲ *5-night minimum, 3-night minimum off-season.*

$$$$ 🖭 **Parrot-ise.** *Private Villa.* The biggest selling points of this roomy photo-shoot-worthy property are its two master oceanfront bedrooms, which eliminate squabbling between two couples traveling together or families with older kids. The third bedroom is cramped by comparison but has the same vibrant color scheme and 25-inch TV as the others. The newly added second-floor owner's suite is larger than many apartments and has its own private ocean-view balcony. Throughout, a tropical motif predominates, with the living room highlighted by an enormous canvas of parrots playing peekaboo in a jungle. But nature provides the real artistry, an ever-changing canvas of sea and sky. The rear accesses a gentle incline with steps leading to a dazzling, secluded beach framed by sea grapes; as at all the residences along the north shore, the offshore reef explodes with color. A top-of-the-line kitchen, sizable kidney-shaped pool, large screened patio with Weber grill, two-person hammock, and complimentary Wi-Fi and unlimited U.S. Internet calling complete the worthy amenities. **Pros:** close to Rum Point and Cayman Kai but far enough for privacy; pretty beach with fine reef for snorkeling; two master bedrooms obviate competition. **Cons:** car required; water can get rough here. ⊠ *Off Rum Point Dr., 1 mi (1½ km) east of Rum Point, North Side* ⊕ *www.caymanvacation.com* ⇱ *4 bedrooms, 3½ baths* ⚄ *Dishwasher, DVD, Internet, Wi-Fi, pool* ⊟ *AE, MC, V* ⚲ *7-night minimum, 5-night minimum off-season.*

$$$ 🖭 **The Pools at Kai #1.** *Private Villa.* This series of old-fashioned yet futuristic-looking concrete beach houses have enormous picture windows, high ceilings (others in the complex are duplex), and a leviathan lanai with an indoor

pool—a favorite with kids and couples alike, it can be accessed from both the living room and bedroom. Unit 1 has a smartly Starck-ish look: White walls and tile floors are offset by chrome and black tables and lamps, a charcoal sleeper sofa with yellow throw pillows and crimson antimacassar, and striking still-life paintings of fruit against a black background. Whimsical touches abound, such as a beach mural in the bathroom. The end unit offers the best views and most privacy in the enclave; a private dock enables boats to pick you up for sunset sails and Stingray City jaunts. The villa is suitable for honeymooners, but a larger (more expensive) adjoining unit could accommodate a family. The one-bedroom #5 and #12 and two-bedroom #10 units are also recommended. **Pros:** complimentary Wi-Fi; near Cayman Kai activity; great views and beach. **Cons:** on holidays the beach becomes crowded with barbecues; privacy potentially compromised by curious beachcombers; maid service costs extra. ⊠ *Kaibo Crescent, Water Cay Rd., Cayman Kai* ⊕ *www.caymanvillas.com* ⊅ *1 bedroom, 1 bath* ♨ *Dishwasher, DVD, Internet, Wi-Fi, pool, beachfront, water toys, laundry facilities, no smoking* ⊟ *AE, D, MC, V* ☞ *5-night minimum, 3-night minimum off-season.*

$$$$ ⊡ **Reef Romance.** *Private Villa.* Despite the apt name, this attractive two-story building is splendidly appointed, with a sunken living room, stained-glass windows and wall hangings, and burled-wood furnishings (not to mention a magnificent mahogany and wrought-iron four-poster in the master bedroom, which can be locked off for a four-bedroom rental). The size is ideal for larger families or small corporate retreats. Though the kitchen is cramped, walk-in closets provide plentiful storage space. For competing couples or kids, all guest bedrooms (two on either side) have sublime water views. The British owners live in Dubai and own a garden-furnishings business; beautiful examples of their work grace the pool area (which also has a grill). The private beach is lovely, with marvelous snorkeling, and the owners usually leave their kayak out. **Pros:** fabulous views; well equipped; superlative snorkeling. **Cons:** turtle grass in shallow water; smallish pool and kitchen. ⊠ *Off Rum Point Dr., 1 mi (2 km) east of Rum Point, Cayman Kai* ⊕ *www. caymanvillas.com* ⊅ *5 bedrooms, 5 baths* ♨ *Dishwasher, DVD, Internet, Wi-Fi, pool, beachfront, laundry facilities, no smoking* ⊟ *AE, D, MC, V* ☞ *7-night minimum, 5-night minimum off-season.*

$$$$ ⊡ **Scuba Shack.** *Private Villa.* Ignore the unassuming, even ugly, exterior: Entering the abode of Connie Sun Ritchie, a

certified PADI dive instructor, is like walking into an artist-designed aquarium. Her bubbly personality informs every aspect of Connie Kai. The fanciful decor includes painted driftwood sculptures, an amazing rug illustrating sea life, tables with hand-painted aquatic scenes, shell-filled lamps, underwater photography, vivid beach paintings, a "coral" dining room with faux limestone wall and turquoise chairs, and of course the shower curtain depicting denizens of the deep. The real selling point may be the sporty extras: complimentary snorkeling equipment; filled scuba tanks upon request (fine shore diving, weather permitting); kayaks; john boat; floats and other toys. There's great diving right from the gorgeous beach. Connie's 24-foot Proline is available for rent with captain (charter in advance for diving, fishing, private Stingray City trips, and more); Red Sail Sports at Rum Point will offer a discount to guests. But you can just loll in hammocks in a big breeze-swept cabana on the 200-foot beach, by the kidney-shaped pool as you grill some fresh seafood, or in heavenly reclining leather chairs should you prefer your sports on TV. **Pros:** snorkelers' and divers' delight; includes free diving and water-sports equipment; complimentary Wi-Fi and Vonage. **Cons:** isolated location makes a car necessary; beach is gorgeous but not maintained. ✉ *69 Old Robin Rd., Old Man Bay, North Side* ⊕ *www.caymanvacation.com* ⤳ *3 bedrooms, 2 baths* ⌂ *Dishwasher, DVD, Wi-Fi, pool, beachfront, water toys, laundry facilities* ▤ *AE, MC, V* ⟲ *7-day minimum, 5-day minimum off-season.*

$$$$ ▣ **Two Rainbows.** *Private Villa.* Located at the very tip of Cayman Kai, this mellow mansion with Victorian flourishes offers unimpeded vistas of the entire North Sound from virtually every angle, including all five bedrooms. Huge glass doors open to the powdery beach and private dock. The interiors define sunny and airy, emphasizing pastels from canary yellow to robin's-egg blue, charming quilts, adorable prints of festive monkeys, painted crabs and geckos "climbing" the walls, and plentiful plants contrasting with immaculate white tile floors. Hammocks and rocking chairs on the colorful screened-in porch complete the laidback picture. **Pros:** easy walk to beach bar and water sports; superb views; very comfortable. **Cons:** small pool; slightly worn albeit well maintained; dangerous step between kitchen and living-dining area. ✉ *Cayman Kai* ⊕ *www.caymanvillas.com* ⤳ *5 bedrooms, 4½ baths* ⌂ *Dishwasher, DVD, Internet, pool, beachfront, laundry facilities.* ▤ *AE, MC, V* ⧍ *EP.* ⟲ *7-night minimum, 3-night minimum off-season.*

$$$$ ⊞ **Venezia Villa.** *Private Villa.* This Venice-inspired stunner could grace the pages of *Architectural Digest* even without its smashing ocean views. Exquisite Doge-worthy interiors reflect not only the professional design but the South African owner's world travels. The living room's black-lacquer table and leather sofa contrast with ornate draperies, a circular inlaid-wood table, deep coral and vermilion walls, gold gilt frames, Murano glass, marble columns, and polished-wood cabinets. The commercial kitchen has marble floors, black-granite counters, elegant wood cabinetry, and high-end appliances. A spiral staircase winds from the dining room (seating 10) to the vast master suite with four-poster canopy bed, telescope, huge sundeck, and dramatic bath awash in crystal and Italian travertine. Rooms are saturated with light and color, their airiness enhanced by floor-to-ceiling windows and 10-foot ceilings. The 325-foot main beach is glorious; even the palm trees scrupulously line up as if in salute. The two-story deck juts 12 feet into the water (where a nearby barrier reef guarantees delightful snorkeling and sheltered swimming). A full gym, complimentary Wi-Fi and Vonage, and Bose sound system complete the picture. **Pros:** decadent luxury; high-tech heaven; beautiful beach and reef. **Cons:** remote location, decor may be too ornate for some, no pool; not child-friendly. ⊠ *Old Man Bay, North Side* ⊕ *www.caymanvacation.com* ⇋ *2 bedrooms, 2 bathrooms* ⚙ *Dishwasher, DVD, Internet, Wi-Fi, gym, beachfront, laundry facilities* ▤ *MC, V* ☞ *7-night minimum, 5-night minimum off-season.*

$$$$ ⊞ **Villa Emmanuel.** *Private Villa.* This grand option is more McMansion than villa, with a sweeping staircase, columns, and beveled-glass door. The interior is huge but oddly configured, with no flow. It also has a "rental" feel, with comfortable but staid grandmotherly furnishings lacking distinction. The huge kitchen with a center island is a plus for family entertaining. The master bedrooms impress with jetted tub and walk-in closet, but the guest bedrooms are cramped. Two upstairs common rooms with independent water-view patios cleverly divide the bedrooms; three TV areas reduce family friction over the remote. As at most villas right on the sound, there's no real beach, though views are delightful. **Pros:** nice views of North Sound; lots of patios for relaxing. **Cons:** steep front steps; shared baths and small secondary bedrooms; not on great beach. ⊠ *378 Water Cay Rd., Cayman Kai* ⊕ *www.caymanvillas.com* or *www.grandcaymanvillas.net* ⇋ *5 bedrooms, 3½ baths*

⌂ *Dishwasher, DVD, Internet, beachfront, laundry facilities, no smoking.* ☱ *AE, D, MC, V* ⌕ *7-night minimum, 5-night minimum off-season.*

$$$$ ⛱ **Villa Habana.** *Private Villa.* The architect-owner designed this charmer with a vaguely New England look and spectacular water views. Good bones show in the careful details like tongue-and-groove joint work, cathedral ceilings, bedroom doors opening to the wonderful wood patio, and smart maximization of available space. The elegant simplicity continues with colonial-style touches (including four-poster beds), comfy cow-skin chairs, homey family sporting photos (golf to crew), and a gorgeous wood kitchen. Downstairs, a spacious track-lit playroom explodes with color from fabrics to vibrant art naïf. It's the ideal cozy, tasteful beach house. **Pros:** pretty interiors; great snorkeling; huge flat-screen TV in playroom; supermarket one block away. **Cons:** no pool; car needed; somewhat cramped bathrooms; narrow, rocky beach could use better maintenance. ⊠ *Between Hutland and Grape Tree Point, North Side* ⊕ *www.caymanvillas.com* ⌕ *2 bedrooms, 2 baths* ⌂ *Dishwasher, DVD, Internet, beachfront, laundry facilities* ☱ *AE, D, MC, V* ⌽ *EP* ⌕ *5-night minimum, 3-night minimum off-season.*

SEVEN MILE BEACH

$$$$ ⛱ **Aqua Bay Club.** *Vacation Condos.* One of the older condo complexes, ABC is scrupulously maintained, quiet, and affordable. Three peach-colored three-story buildings surround lovely landscaping fronting a pristine stretch of sand dotted with inviting palapas and palm trees for shade. Each condo—some split-level—looks smack onto the water from its spacious screened-in patio or balcony. Most have sofa beds, and management will provide cribs; the only downside for families is that the beach can be rocky in spots. Units vary according to individual owners' whims: Some have refined wrought-iron four-poster beds and beveled glass. Unit 7 is exceedingly handsome, with hand-painted shelves and cabinets and antique doors and window frames hung as artwork. **Pros:** great snorkeling very close to Cemetery Reef; friendly staff; free local calls. **Cons:** beach can be rocky; no elevator in complex. ⊠ *West Bay Rd., Box 30091, Seven Mile Beach* ☎ *345/945–4728 or 800/825–8703* ⊕ *www.aquabayclub.com* ⌕ *21 units* ⌂ *In-room: DVD, Wi-Fi. In-hotel: pool, tennis court, laundry facilities* ☱ *AE, MC, V* ⌽ *EP.*

DID YOU KNOW?

Seven Mile Beach is one of the Caribbean's most beautiful, and it's kept free from litter and pesky peddlers.

Caribbean Club

$$$–   🖭 **The Anchorage.** *Vacation Condos.* Don't be deceived by the
$$$$ slightly dilapidated facade: This intimate resort's interiors
were completely gutted and upgraded post-Ivan, and they're
still a great value. The two-bedroom condos are cramped
compared to those at otherwise newer compounds, but
fully equipped, modernized, scrupulously clean, and—
most important—affordable (though the surcharge for
oceanfront/-view units, despite admittedly glorious sweep-
ing panoramas from the third floor, is steep). Many have an
odd, if versatile, L-shaped layout, though owners adapt the
space ingeniously into "dens" with trundle beds, extra TV
rooms, or offices. But the peace and little extras make the
Anchorage a safe port of call for any family. **Pros:** incred-
ible vistas from George Town to West Bay from higher
units; nice beach and snorkeling; great pool at the edge
of the Caribbean. **Cons:** a bit isolated from action; boxy
apartments. ⊠ *1989 West Bay Rd., Box 30986, Seven Mile
Beach* ☎ *345/945–4088* ⊕ *www.theanchoragecayman.com*
⤴ *15 2-bedroom condos* ⚭ *In-room: kitchen, DVD, Wi-Fi,
Internet. In-hotel: tennis court, pool, beachfront, laundry
facilities* ▭ *AE, MC, V* ⎮⊙⎮ *EP.*

★ Fodor's Choice 🖭 **Caribbean Club.** *Vacation Condos.* Sleek but
$$$$ not slick, this gleaming boutique facility completely rein-
vented itself post-Ivan, including a striking lobby filled
with aquariums, a stunning infinity pool, and the aggres-
sively contemporary trattoria, Luca. Enormous individu-
ally owned and decorated units occupy a plantation-style

Where to Stay in Seven Mile Beach

KEY

- Dive Sites
- Beach
- 1 Hotels

Conch Point
Palmetto Point Rd.
Capt. Reg Conch Point Rd.
Parson's Rd.

BARKERS

BIRCH TREE HILL
MOUNT PLEASANT

Head of Barkers

Hell

BATABANO

NW Point

CORAL GABLES
Town Hall Rd.

West Bay

North West Point Rd.

Orange Canyon

Little Salt Creek
Salt Creek

Cemetery Beach

UPPERLAND

Trinity Caves

Grand Cayman Yacht Club

Cemetery Reef

Governors Creek

Aquarium

Trafalgar Place

GOVERNORS HARBOUR
Welch Point

Public Beach

Falls Plaza

Paradise Reef

The Links at Safehaven Golf Course

0   1 mi
0   1 km

The Strand

Brittania Golf Course

Galleria Plaza

Galleria Loop

West Shore Center

Buckingham Square

North Sound

Marquee Plaza

WHITEHALL ESTATES

7 Mile Shops

Harquail Byass

Eastern Av.

North Sound Rd.

Owen Roberts International Airport

Wreck of the Cali

George Town

Eden Rock

Elgin Av. Smith Rd.

Crewe Rd.

Black Reef Skate Park

Smith's Cove

S. Church St.

Walkers Rd.

South Sound Rd.

South Sound

Caribbean Sea

The Anchorage, **17**

Aqua Bay Club, **20**

Beachcomber, **8**

Caribbean Club, **7**

Christopher Columbus, **18**

Comfort Suites Grand Cayman, **3**

Coral Reef Villa, **16**

Coral Stone Club, **11**

Discovery Point Club, **19**

Grand Cayman Beach Suites, **6**

Grand Cayman Marriott Beach Resort, **4**

The Grandview, **2**

Harbour View Apartments, **1**

Lacovia Condominiums, **5**

The Meridian, **9**

Plantana, **15**

Ritz-Carlton, **12**

Silver Sands, **21**

Sunshine Suites Resort, **10**

Villas of the Galleon, **13**

Westin Casuarina Resort & Spa, **14**

seven-story "tower," offering beach views flanked by two three-story buildings with oceanfront units. No expense was spared to appeal to the style-conscious: The usual luxury brand players are represented from Villeroy & Boch china to Gilchrist & Soames toiletries. Kitchens have curved granite bars and stainless-steel appliances, including both regular and convection ovens. The decor seamlessly fuses classic (coffered ceilings, polished hardwood furnishings, glass-and-iron tables, Italian marble accents throughout) with contemporary convenience (iPod stations, plasma TV/DVD, washer/dryer). Nice touches include wraparound balconies in many units, oversize jetted tubs, and walk-in his and hers closets. Personal assistants, trainers, chefs, nannies, and the like can of course be arranged. **Pros:** luxurious, high-tech facilities beyond the typical apartment complex; trendy Italian restaurant on-site. **Cons:** stratospheric prices; though families are welcome, they may find it rather imposing; smaller balconies on top floor (albeit amazing views). ⊠ *871 West Bay Rd., Box 30135, Seven Mile Beach* ☎ *345/623–4500 or 800/941–1126* ⊕ *www.caribclub.com* ↘ *37 3-bedroom condos* ⚠ *In-room: kitchen, Wi-Fi. In-hotel: restaurant, room service, bar, pool, gym, beachfront, laundry facilities* ⊟ *AE, D, DC, MC, V* ⊖*EP.*

$$$ ⚟ **Christopher Columbus.** *Vacation Condos.* This enduring
ℭ favorite is quite a discovery for families, sitting on the peaceful northern end of Seven Mile Beach. Though snorkeling is superb right offshore, the CC's beach is free of rocks; the parrot-green lawn fronting the sand is so perfectly maintained you could play croquet. Thatched cabanas and a gazebo offer shade aplenty. Living rooms and kitchens are enormous; the decor generally favors soft seashell and sunrise colors of pink, mint, and baby blue, with nautical artworks aplenty. Although this is hardly party central, the north-building units are quietest. Units 8 and 10 (the latter a particularly good value for families, as its "den" has two twin beds) are among the stunners opening onto the beach; however, only the pricier three-bedroom units offer beach views. **Pros:** excellent snorkeling from a fine stretch of beach; great value; free Wi-Fi. **Cons:** car really needed; often overrun by families during holiday seasons and summer; top floors feature splendid vistas but difficult access for physically challenged. ⊠ *2013 West Bay Rd., Seven Mile Beach* ☎ *345/945–4354 or 866/311–5231* ⊕*www. christophercolumbuscondos.com* ↘ *30 2- and 3-bedroom condos* ⚠ *In-room: kitchen, Internet, Wi-Fi. In-hotel: tennis*

courts, pool, beachfront, laundry facilities, Wi-Fi hotspot ⊟ *AE, D, MC, V* ⊙*EP.*

$$–$$$ ⚓**Comfort Suites Grand Cayman.** *Hotel.* This no-frills, all-suites hotel has an ideal location on West Bay Road, next door to the Marriott and near numerous shops, restaurants, and bars. Studios (kitchenettes, shower-only bathrooms) as well as one- and two-bedroom suites (full kitchens, full bathtubs) are a tad run-down and musty, resembling oversized office cubicles, but they have the comforts and conveniences of home as well as complimentary Continental breakfast and free Wi-Fi. Regrettably, it looks like a mid-price chain hotel transplanted from the Midwest with little Caribbean flair aside from splendid underwater photos and a marine-theme mosaic bar. The sea is a short walk from the property, but this isn't the nicest part of Seven Mile Beach. Still, it should please families (all units contain sleeper sofas) or groups who want to save a bit on meals. **Pros:** affordable; nice complimentary extras like Continental breakfast and Wi-Fi; fun, youngish crowd. **Cons:** nearly a block from the beach; new condominium blocks sea views; no balconies; bar closes early. ⊠ *West Bay Rd., Seven Mile Beach* ☎*345/945–7300 or 800/517–4000* ⊕ *www.caymancomfort.com* ⌁ *108 suites* ⚂ *In-room: safe, kitchen, Internet, Wi-Fi. In-hotel: restaurant, room service, bar, pool, gym, diving, bicycles, laundry facilities, Wi-Fi hotspot, parking (free)* ⊟ *AE, D, MC, V* ⊙*CP.*

★ **Fodor's**Choice⚓**Coral Reef Villa.** *Private Villa.* One of only
$$$$ six private villas on Seven Mile Beach, this peach stucco, white colonnaded beauty offers gazillion-dollar views; the sun seems to plunge into the sea right in front of the villa. The front door opens onto the spare sparkling living room and a huge picture window onto the beach (where a canopy bed awaits loungers) beyond the pool. Everything displays impeccable taste without ostentation, down to the smallest detail: frosted glass panels of marine life, a grand spiral staircase, huge open kitchen including a grill, jetted tub in the master bedroom, spacious railed second-floor balcony overseeing the action, covered patio pool that can be curtained off for privacy. The decor favors pristine white, peppermint pink, and powder blue, accentuating the airy, sun-drenched feel. Bunk beds and a trundle accommodate families nicely; a one-bedroom apartment brings the total to five bedrooms if desired. It's a five-minute walk to Cemetery Reef snorkeling, and the affable owner lives on property so he can answer any questions or resolve any problems. **Pros:** superlative views; stylishly understated; magnificent

snorkeling nearby. **Cons:** wildly expensive; car needed for most Seven Mile Beach and George Town attractions; kids from nearby resorts may wander onto beach. ⊠ *West Bay Rd., Seven Mile Beach* ⊕ *www.caymanvillas.com* ⟲ *4 bedrooms, 3½ baths, 1 1-bedroom apartment* ⚷ *Dishwasher, DVD, Wi-Fi, daily maid service, pool, beachfront, laundry facilities* ⊟ *MC, V* ⟲ *7-night minimum.*

$$$$ ▥ **Coral Stone Club.** *Vacation Condos.* This exclusive enclave shines in the shadow of the Ritz-Carlton by offering understated barefoot luxury and huge three-bedroom condos. Elegant touches include beveled glass doors, granite-clad kitchens and bathrooms (with stylish raised basins), deco-inspired art, and arched Palladian windows. Top-floor units have the finest views. Many have four-poster beds and oversize jetted tubs, but all have Wi-Fi, a washer/dryer, screened-in sunbathing patio, and flat-screen TV/DVD. Every guest receives a welcome gift (from beach robes to a handcrafted glass platter), the annual attention to detail is exemplary (whether expanding the TV channel selection or converting the pool to gentle saltwater), and management can arrange everything from babysitter to chef. **Pros:** largest ratio of beach and pool space to guests; walking distance to several restaurants and shops; stellar service; excellent off-season deals. **Cons:** expensive in high season; Ritz-Carlton guests sometimes wander over from their packed section of sand trying to poach beach space. ⊠ *West Bay Rd., Box 30105, Seven Mile Beach* ☎ *345/945–5820 or 888/927–2322* ⊕ *www.coralstoneclub.com* ⟲ *35 3-bedroom condos* ⚷ *In-room: kitchen, Wi-Fi. In-hotel: tennis court, pool, gym, beachfront, Wi-Fi hotspot, parking (free)* ⊟ *AE, MC, V* ⏦ *EP.*

$$$$ ▥ **Discovery Point Club.** *Vacation Condos.* This older but ☾ upgraded complex of all oceanfront suites sits at the north end of Seven Mile Beach, 6 mi (9½ km) from George Town, with fabulous snorkeling in the protected waters of nearby Cemetery Reef. Tennis courts, a large pool with hot tub, and sizable screened-in private porches add to the high appeal here; kids six and under also stay free, making it popular with families. Studios—which are really hotel rooms "locked out" from a larger condo—do not have full kitchens or ocean views and represent the worst value (pay the $50 per night premium for a true one-bedroom unit). The open layout enhances the spaciousness, though guest bedrooms are generally cramped, and second bathrooms shower-only; all units (except studios) have a washer/dryer.

As with most of the island's other condo resorts, decor varies according to the owner's taste and whims; unit 23 is particularly smart, with wonderful island photos and granite accents. Units 32 through 40 are also top-of-the-line. **Pros:** sensational snorkeling; caring staff; family-friendly. **Cons:** car necessary to dine out and explore; beach entry is rocky in spots; studios are nothing but overpriced glorified hotel rooms; no elevator. ⊠ *West Bay Rd., Box 439, Seven Mile Beach* ☎ *345/945–4724* ⊕ *www.discoverypointclub.com* ➴ *16 studios, 19 1-bedroom condos, 12 2-room condos* ⚲ *In-room: safe, kitchen (some), DVD, Wi-Fi, Internet. In-hotel: tennis courts, pool, beachfront, laundry facilities* ⊟ *AE, D, MC, V* ⱺ *EP.*

$$$$ ⚟ **Grand Cayman Beach Suites.** *Resort.* The former Hyatt all-suites section, now locally run, offers a terrific beachfront location and trendy eateries. The resort lacks landscaping, so the lackluster setting is one of concrete and elevators. Nevertheless, the ocean-view suites are vividly hued and plush if a tad worn; management is gradually replacing in-room furnishings. The higher the room, the smaller the balcony, but your view becomes increasingly stunning. The configuration is oddly angular and the marble-clad decor a bit formal and fussy, with columns and pilasters, but you'll find the latest gadgetry (Wi-Fi, iPod docking station, 37-inch flat-screen TV/DVD). Nice touches include jetted tubs and canopied beach chairs; the facilities impress, led by a Red Sail Sports outpost, stylish Hemingway's restaurant, and ultra-hip Bamboo lounge. Unfortunately, the parking lot is too small. **Pros:** fine beach; superior dining and water-sports facilities; free use of gym (unusual on Grand Cayman); supermarkets and restaurants within walking distance. **Cons:** most entrances face the street, making it noisy weekends; several units need refurbishment; music often blaring around the pool. ⊠ *West Bay Rd., Box 1588, Seven Mile Beach* ☎ *345/949–1234* ⊕ *www.grand-cayman-beach-suites.com* ➴ *53 suites* ⚲ *In-room: safe, kitchen, DVD, Wi-Fi. In-hotel: 4 restaurants, room service, bars, golf course, pools, gym, spa, beachfront, diving, water sports, children's programs (ages 3–12), Wi-Fi hotspot, parking (free)* ⊟ *AE, D, DC, MC, V* ⱺ *EP.*

$$$$ ⚟ **Grand Cayman Marriott Beach Resort.** *Resort.* The soaring, stylish, if impersonal marble lobby (with exquisite art glass, spectacular blown-up underwater photos, and fun elements like red British-style telephone boxes) sets the tone for this bustling beachfront property. Large adjoining rooms are ideal for families; all have tiny balconies, hardwood furni-

Seven Mile Beach

ture, handsome abstract artworks, and smallish bathrooms. The beach, pool, beach bar, and Red Sail dive center with water toys fill every nautical need. Add a serene spa, lovely lush tropical courtyard and turtle lagoon, clever man-made reef, and solid restaurants, and you never need leave the property (despite the on-site car rental agency). When you do, it's a short walk to more restaurants and stores. **Pros:** lively bars and restaurants; good snorkeling and water sports; convenient to both George Town and Seven Mile Beach. **Cons:** often overrun by tour groups and convention-eers; narrowest section of Seven Mile Beach; pool and bar often noisy late. ⊠ *389 West Bay Rd., Box 30371, Seven Mile Beach* ☎ *345/949–0088 or 800/223–6388* ⊕ *www. marriott.com* ⌖ *273 rooms, 22 suites* ⌂ *In-room: safe, refrigerator, Wi-Fi. In-hotel: 2 restaurants, room service, bars, pool, gym, spa, beachfront, diving, water sports, laun-dry facilities, laundry service, children's programs (3–12), Internet terminal, Wi-Fi hotspot, parking (free)* ⊟ *AE, D, DC, MC, V* ⧆ *EP.*

$$$$ ⊞ **The Grandview.** *Vacation Condos.* This older but well-⟳ groomed property lives up to its ostentatious billing: All 69 two- and three-bedroom units (though sadly only 15 are generally in the rental pool) look smack onto the Caribbean and the beach past splendidly maintained gardens (families play soccer on the expansive lawn). Little painted sandals climbing the office door set the laidback tone. Decor varies wildly but favors soft pastels and marine motifs. First-rate

amenities include huge kitchens and washer/dryers; larger families will also appreciate the sofa beds and the children-under-12-stay-free policy. Snorkeling is excellent, the beach long (a bonus with most older enclaves) if narrow, and the location ideal for walking into George Town or the most bustling part of Seven Mile Beach. Guests receive a discount at nearby King's Gym. **Pros:** terrific snorkeling; restaurants and shops within walking distance; free Wi-Fi (when it's available); screened-in patios keep mosquitoes out. **Cons:** the long beach can be rocky; some units a tad worn though meticulously maintained; not all units have access to the free Wi-Fi signal. ⊠ *95 Snooze La., Seven Mile Beach* ☎ *345/945–4511 or 866/977–6766* ⊕ *www. grandviewcondos.com* ⇆ *69 2- and 3-bedroom condos* ⌂ *In-room: kitchen, DVD, Internet (some), Wi-Fi (some). In-hotel: pool, beachfront, laundry facilities, Wi-Fi hotspot, parking (free)* ⊟ *AE, D, DC, MC, V* ⊺⊙⫼ *EP.*

$–$$ ▦ **Harbour View Apartments.** *Vacation Condos.* This little enclave delivers on the name's promise, with smashing views of the leviathan cruise ships hulking off George Town. The apartments redefine basic, the decor resembling a garage sale; the appliances, though old, are functional; families will appreciate the sofa beds, and the property is well maintained. Cordial owners Rose and Dudley Parsons happily dispense advice and even pre-stock your fridge with a few necessities without even charging. Supermarkets are a couple of minutes away, and you can walk to the action in Seven Mile Beach and George Town. Palm trees and a thatched cabana provide shade on the small beach, and snorkeling is superb right off the pier. **Pros:** sweet, helpful owners; great value; walkable to shops and restaurants. **Cons:** no pool; rocky small beach (but great snorkeling); dilapidated furnishings. ⊠ *West Bay Rd., Box 176, Seven Mile Beach* ☎ *345/949–5681* ⊕ *www.harbourviewapart-ments.com* ⇆ *12 studio and 1-bedroom apartments* ⌂ *In-room: kitchen, Wi-Fi. In-hotel: laundry facilities, beachfront* ⊟ *AE, MC, V* ⊺⊙⫼ *EP.*

$$$$ ▦ **Lacovia Condominiums.** *Vacation Condos.* The carefully manicured courtyard of this handsome arcaded Mediterranean Revival property could easily be mistaken for a peaceful park. Large shade trees somehow escaped hurricane damage in 2004 and 2008, and thick, lush gardens overflowing with flowers bloom everywhere; you can feed the iguanas who stake out the frangipani and hibiscus amid the topiary. What's blissfully missing is the usual pressure of traffic, construction, and concrete walls so common in

Covered chaise longues at the Ritz-Carlton Grand Cayman

this area of Seven Mile Beach. The condos themselves are nicely kept, their contemporary decor accented by classy tapestries and rugs; all units have a washer/dryer. The beach here is wide and soft, with more wonderful shade trees and thatched gazebos. A shopping center, grocery store, restaurants, dive shops, and nightlife are a short walk away. **Pros:** central location; exquisite gardens; extensive beach. **Cons:** rear courtyard rooms can be noisy from traffic and partying from West Bay Road; pool fairly small (though most people prefer the beach). ✉ *697 West Bay Rd., Box 32309, Seven Mile Beach* ☎ *345/949–7599* ⊕ *www.lacovia.com* ↪ *35 1-, 2-, and 3-bedroom condos* ⚏ *In-room: kitchen, Internet. In-hotel: tennis court, pool, gym, beachfront, laundry facilities* ▭ *AE, D, MC, V* ⚏ *EP.*

$$$$ ⌂ **The Meridian.** *Vacation Condos.* The lavish landscaping and neo-Edwardian architecture with gables, Palladian windows, and grillwork balconies sets the understated opulent tone. Everything within is equally posh and plush: Curved enclosed patios larger than many apartments, traditional decor favoring hardwood furnishings, four-poster beds, carved-wood chandeliers, and antique maps. Master bedrooms overlook the beach; their bathrooms have sunken tubs and separate showers. End units offer the most spectacular views (though there's not a bad patio seat in the house). Welcome extras include a fax machine and washer/dryer in each unit. **Pros:** restaurants and supermarket right across the street; meticulously maintained; gorgeous beachfront.

Cons: some find it a little too popular with families; unde-niably elegant but extremely pricey. ⊠ *West Bay Rd., Box 30476, Seven Mile Beach* ☎ *345/945–4002* ⊕ *www.merid-ian.ky* ⌕ *32 2- and 3-room condos* ⌂ *In-room: kitchen, DVD, Wi-Fi. In-hotel: pool, gym, beachfront, concierge* ⊟ *AE, D, DC, MC, V* ⍓ *EP.*

★ **Fodor's**Choice ⌸ **Ritz-Carlton Grand Cayman.** *Resort.* Posh and
$$$$ pampering without pretension, the Ritz-Carlton offers
⟳ unparalleled luxury and service infused with a welcome sense of place including works by top local artists and craftspeople. The 144-acre resort, as exquisitely manicured as its clientele, is anchored by a seven-story behemoth that faces Seven Mile Beach on the west and the North Sound on the east. Top toque Eric Ripert of New York's Le Bernardin, among the world's finest restaurants, created one of the eateries. Greg Norman designed the golf course; tennis is run by Nick Bollettieri (coach of greats like Andre Agassi); La Prairie operates the sybaritic spa; and the Ambassa-dors of the Environment children's program was created by none other than Jean-Michel Cousteau. The staff is professional yet discreet, knowing its business, not yours. Despite its glam romantic trappings, the resort is family-friendly, offering movie screenings nightly at the poolside Periwinkle restaurant, stargazing with astronomers, and incorporating Caymanian culture into the estimable kids' club activities. Rooms are spacious, hedonistic, and outfit-ted with high-tech conveniences. **Pros:** exemplary service; exceptional facilities with many complimentary extras; marvelous local artworks including a corridor-length gal-lery with rotating exhibits. **Cons:** luxury comes with a high price tag; somewhat sprawling with a confusing layout; long walk to beach (over an interior bridge) from most rooms. ⊠ *West Bay Rd., Seven Mile Beach* ⌑ *Box 34328, SMB, KY1-1209, Grand Cayman* ☎ *345/943–9000* ⊕ *www.ritz-carlton.com* ⌕ *329 rooms, 12 suites, 24 condos* ⌂ *In-room: safe, kitchen (some), refrigerator, DVD, Internet, Wi-Fi. In-hotel: 5 restaurants, room service, bar, pools, golf course, gym, spa, diving, children's programs (ages 4–18), laundry facilities, Wi-Fi hotspot* ⊟ *AE, D, MC, V* ⍓ *BP.*

$$ ⌸ **Sunshine Suites Resort.** *Hotel.* This friendly, all-suites hotel is an impeccably clean money saver. The slightly musty rooms were refurbished in early 2009; they lack balconies, patios, and even views, and both windows and bathrooms are tiny, but each has a complete kitchen, flat-screen TV, and free Wi-Fi (laptops can be rented). You can enjoy the great cheap food and gossip at the poolside restaurant, a local fave. It's a five-minute walk to Seven Mile Beach, where the resort provides beach chairs and towels near the Westin Casuarina. Breakfast is served poolside. Guests get free access to the nearby World Gym; the resort provides lockers for dive gear; and a beauty salon and business center were added in April 2009. **Pros:** good value and deals; cheerful staff; rocking little restaurant; thoughtful free extras. **Cons:** poor views; no beach; slightly musty. ⊠ *1465 Esterley Tibbetts Hwy., off West Bay Rd., Box 30095, Seven Mile Beach* ☎ *345/949–3000 or 877/786–1110* ⊕ *www.sunshinesuites. com* ⤳ *130 suites* ⅋ *In-room: kitchen, Internet, Wi-Fi. In-hotel: restaurant, bar, pool, laundry facilities, Wi-Fi hotspot* ⊟ *AE, D, MC, V* ⍉|*CP.*

$$$$ ☷ **Villas of the Galleon.** *Vacation Condos.* People often
☾ overlook this gem due to the lack of pool and its ersatz Greek-isle look (white stucco with turquoise roofs). But its beachfront location, snuggled between the Ritz-Carlton and Westin, is unrivaled, and groceries, restaurants, nightlife, and water-sports concessions are steps away. The buildings are staggered to ensure optimal sea views. All units have full kitchens with a dishwasher and microwave, not to mention free DSL and local calls; two- and three-bedroom units include a washer/dryer. Cribs are provided at no extra cost; families love using the charcoal grills. The on-site manager encourages guests to call any time they need something; energetic and personable, she loves dispensing advice and fresh fruit (often plucked from the sea grape, lime, papaya, and banana trees on the property). Iguanas, including unofficial house pets Papaya, King Tut, and Cleopatra, dart about the pretty grounds. You can feed the iguanas by hand or watch them cavort in a trough designed especially for them. **Pros:** affable management; central location; glorious beach. **Cons:** no pool; slightly boxy room configuration. ⊠ *West Bay Rd., Box 1797, Seven Mile Beach* ☎ *345/945–4433 or 866/665–4696* ⊕ *www.villasofthegalleon.com* ⤳ *74 1-, 2-, and 3-bedroom condos* ⅋ *In-room: kitchen, DVD, Internet. In-hotel: gym, laundry facilities (some)* ⊟ *AE, MC, V* ⍉|*EP.*

$$$– ☷ **Westin Casuarina Resort and Spa.** *Resort.* The Westin has
$$$$ something to offer everyone, from conventioneers to hon-
☾ eymooners to families, not to mention an excellent location. You can walk a perfect beach, enjoy the sumptuous spa, sweat in the Reebok-powered fitness club, get wet with a Red Sail Sports branch, dine at the marvelous Casa Havana (particularly at the lavish Sunday brunch or a winemaker dinner), lounge in the pool with an ocean view, or loll in the

suave lounge after dark. Personalized "pre-concierge" service will place a treadmill in your room or ensure your spa treatment is booked. The sophisticated room decor includes rich hardwood furnishings and marble-clad bathrooms with pampering showers. Many of the ocean-view rooms have better-than-advertised vistas. The Westin-brand signatures have been subtly tailored to the tropics: Locally made rum cakes are offered as turndown treats, a "run concierge" leads jogs at cooler times of day; crafts demonstrations from glass-blowing to thatch-weaving are offered; and the kids' club includes trips to the Butterfly Farm (and piratical skits to scavenger hunts teaching Caymanian history). **Pros:** terrific children's programs; superb beach (the largest resort stretch, at 800 feet); sterling dining. **Con:** occasionally bustling and impersonal when large groups book. ⊠ *West Bay Rd., Box 30620, Seven Mile Beach* ☎ *345/945–3800* ⊕ *www.westincasuarina.net* ⮑ *339 rooms, 8 suites* ♿ *In-room: safe, Internet. In-hotel: 3 restaurants, room service, bars, pool, gym, spa, beachfront, diving, water sports, children's programs (ages 4–12), Internet terminal, Wi-Fi hotspot, parking (free)* ⊟ *AE, MC, V* ⍟ *EP.*

WEST BAY

$$$ ☲ **Cobalt Coast Resort and Suites.** *Resort.* This small eco-friendly hotel is perfect for divers who want a sparkling, spacious room or suite right on the ironshore, far, far from the madding crowds, and who don't want to pay high prices. Units have picture windows overlooking the Caribbean, imported Dutch fixtures, IKEA-style cabinetry, and Constructivist-inspired Marimekko fabrics from Finland. The cutting-edge dive operation DiveTech runs smoothly, catering to a wide array of needs, and Duppies restaurant is surprisingly good. As the gracious, gregarious Dutch-born owner, Arie Barendrecht, says, "The whole idea is to complement the dive experience." The area also lures anglers, so "we'll cook what you bring in." Add great shore diving (especially in the calmer summer season), with a four- or five-minute swim to a 60-foot drop, and this is a no-brainer. **Pros:** superb dive outfit; friendly service and clientele; free Wi-Fi. **Cons:** poky golden sand beach; unattractive concrete pool area; remote location, so a car (included in some packages) is necessary. ⊠ *18-A Sea Fan Dr., West Bay* ☎ *345/946–5656 or 888/946–5656* ⊕ *www. cobaltcoast.com* ⮑ *7 rooms, 11 suites* ♿ *In-room: safe, kitchen (some), refrigerator, Wi-Fi. In-hotel: restaurant,*

Where to Stay in West Bay

0 _____ 2 mi

0 _____ 2 km

Conch Point

Conch Point Rd.

Palmetto Point Rd.

[2]

Capt. Reg Parson's Rd.

[3]

BIRCH TREE HILL

MOUNT PLEASANT

BARKERS

Boatswain's Beach

Hell ○

NW Point

Town Hall Rd.

[4] BATABANO

Head of Barkers

CORAL GABLES

North West Point Rd.

[1]

West Bay

Orange Canyon ◥

Old Homestead ◆

West Bay Public Beach

Little Salt Creek

Trinity Caves ◥

Boat Launch ◆

UPPERLAND

Salt Creek

Cemetery Reef ◥

West Bay Rd.

Grand Cayman Yacht Club ◆

Governors Creek

Seven Mile Beach

A1

GOVERNORS HARBOUR

Welch Point

Cobalt Coast Resort & Suites, 2

Cotton Tree, 3

Lighthouse Point, 1

Shangri-La B&B, 4

bar, pool, diving, laundry facilities, Wi-Fi hotspot ⊟*AE, D, MC, V* ⊠*BP.*

$$$$ 🖼 **Cotton Tree.** *Vacation Villas.* The motto of this exclusive villa enclave in tranquil West Bay could easily be IF LUXE COULD KILL. Peripatetic Cayman-born owner Heather Lockington has created an authentic haven where guests can embrace Caymanian heritage and reconnect with nature without sacrificing comfort. Four enormous, pastel, plantation-style two-bedroom boutique-chic cottages nestle amid lush tropical gardens, steps from the Caribbean (only Almond Cottage lacks sea views). Though individually designed, all feature cathedral ceilings, vibrant local paintings, stunning stone-and-wood statuary, South American teak furnishings, French doors, black-and-white old Cayman photos, 600-thread Egyptian cotton sheets, cutting-edge appliances, high-end utensils, and, in the baths, Elemis products, a spa or rainforest shower, and hot tub. The three 42-inch plasma TVs, an iPod docking station, a Nintendo Wii, free Wi-Fi, a laser printer, and a full media library will please techies. The refrigerator is pre-stocked with morning necessities (complimentary); Continental breakfast can be delivered. Staffing can be arranged. Heather will arrange

Lighthouse Point

hand-picked activities, including biking in Barker's National Park, bird-watching, and art and culinary classes. **Pros:** peaceful and quiet setting; beautifully designed and outfitted accommodations; complimentary airport transfers. **Cons:** luxury comes with a price tag; remote location means a car is required; beach is narrow and tangled with sea-grape trees. ⊠ *375 Conch Point Rd., West Bay* ☎ *345/943–0700* ⊕ *www.caymancottontree.com* ⇆ *4 2-bedroom cottages* ⑂ *In-room: kitchen, DVD, Wi-Fi. In-hotel: pool, gym, spa, beachfront, bicycles, laundry facilities, laundry service, Internet terminal, Wi-Fi hotspot.* ⊟ *MC, V* ⑩ *EP.*

★ **Fodor's Choice** ⌧ **Lighthouse Point.** *Condo Resort.* For travelers
$$$$ who want to "live lightly on the planet," leading scuba operator Divetech's stunning new development takes the lead, from sustainable wood interiors and recycled concrete to an ecosensitive gray water system, energy-saving appliances and lights, and Cayman's first wind turbine generator. But you needn't be an ardent diver or environmentalist to appreciate the nine striking units overlooking the eponymous dive site. Those glossy "granite" and "marble" surfaces might just be recycled beer or vodka bottles, while the mostly reclaimed, artfully distressed hardwood furnishings bespeak elegance. Each unit features an energy-efficient dishwasher and washer/dryer, solar panels, glass block features maximizing natural light, walk-in closets, cathedral recessed ceilings, jetted tubs, flat-screen TV/DVDs, teak furnishings, and enormous patios with sensational sea

views. Distinctive details include public bathrooms with bathysphere-like doors; salvaged antique anchors, buoys, and cannon as found art; Salt Bistro's emphasis on fresh local organic produce; and a half-acre landscaped park on the dramatic ironshore. Best of all, these upscale green lodgings won't cost too much green. **Pros:** eco-friendly; fantastic shore diving (and state-of-the-art dive shop); creative and often recycled upscale look. **Cons:** no real beach; car necessary; bit difficult for physically challenged to navigate. ✉ *571 N.W. Point Rd., West Bay* ☎ *345/949–1700* ⊕ *www. lighthouse-point-cayman.com* ⌁ *9 2-bedroom apartments* ♿ *In-room: safe (some), kitchen, DVD, Internet, Wi-Fi. In-hotel: restaurant, room service (not 24-hour), bar, diving, water sports, bicycles, laundry facilities, Wi-Fi hotspot.* ⊟ *AE, D, DC, MC, V* ⧖⃝ *EP.*

$–$$ 🔲 **Shangri-La B&B.** *B&B.* Accomplished pianist George Davidson and wife Eileen built this lavish lakeside retreat and truly make guests feel at home, along with dogs Roxie and Stella. Understated good taste informs every aspect of the house, from the waterfall pool and hot tub to a screened-in patio overlooking the bird-filled lagoon to the carved hardwood furnishings, tatted linens, and ornately embroidered pillows—not to mention Eileen's scrumptious, sumptuous breakfasts (to-die-for bread-and-butter pudding and French toast). Some rooms have romantic touches like four-poster or canopy beds and jetted tubs. Even the sole room sans balcony, Poinciana, has windows overlooking the water. There's an honor bar, and guests have kitchen privileges (with their own shelf in the refrigerator) as well. Families will appreciate the self-sufficient two-bedroom apartment that sleeps six (with an extra futon) and features jaw-dropping vistas from the rooftop terrace, accessed via a charming spiral staircase. **Pros:** use of kitchen; elegant decor. **Cons:** rental car necessary; not on the beach. ✉ *1 Sticky Toffee La., West Bay* ☎ *345/526–1170* ⊕ *www.shangrilabandb.com* ⌁ *6 rooms, 1 apartment* ♿ *In-room: safe (some), refrigerator, DVD, Wi-Fi. In-hotel: pool, bicycles, laundry facilities, Wi-Fi hotspot* ⊟ *AE, MC, V* ⧖⃝ *BP.*

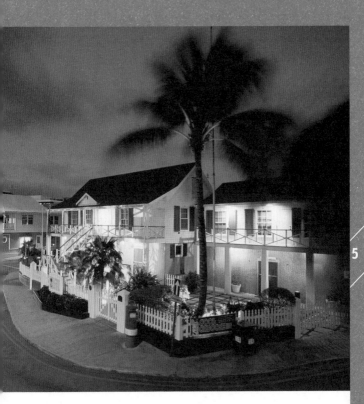

Grand Cayman Nightlife and the Arts

WORD OF MOUTH

"[I]f you plan on hitting the Ritz on Friday night . . . take something hip and stylish. A sexy sequin top, nice pants, and hot shoes, with an evening bag would be fine for women. Hip collared shirt, linen or black pants, nice shoes for men."

—lukesaunt

By Jordan
Simon

DESPITE GRAND CAYMAN'S CONSERVATISM AND SMALL SIZE, the nightlife scene looms surprisingly large, especially on weekends. Choices include boisterous beach-and-brew hangouts, swanky wine bars, pool halls, sports bars, jammed and jamming dance clubs, live entertainment, and cultural events. A smoking ban was instituted in 2010 for nightspots and restaurants (one preexisting cigar bar and a hookah lounge received special dispensation).

Most major resorts, clubs, and bars offer some kind of performance, including lavish rum-and-reggae limbo/fire-eating/stilt-walking extravaganzas. Local bands with a fan(atic) following include soft-rock duo Hi-Tide; the Pandemonium Steelband; reggae-influenced trio Swanky; hard rockers Ratskyn (who've opened for REO Speedwagon, Mötley Crüe, and Bon Jovi); blues/funk purveyors Madamspeaker; and neo-punk rockers the Blow Holes. Other names to look for are Musical Crew, Sucker Box, Ka, Noel's Band, Wild Knights, Island Vibes, Exit, 45 C.I., Lammie, Heat, Gone Country, and Coco Red.

Consult the "Get Out" section in the Friday edition of the *Caymanian Compass* for listings of live music, movies, theater, and other entertainment. Local magazines such as *Key to Cayman, What's Hot,* and *Destination Cayman* can be picked up free of charge around the island, sometimes providing coupons for discounts and/or freebies. Bars remain open until 1 AM, and clubs are generally open from 10 PM until 3 AM, but they can't serve liquor after midnight on Saturday or permit dancing on Sundays. While shorts and sarongs are usually acceptable attire at beachside bars, smart casual defines the dress code for clubbing.

TIPSY TIPS. Don't drive and drink! Local police set sobriety checkpoints in heavily trafficked areas. The law is strict, the punishment (fine and/or prison) harsh. Revel away: The watering holes will happily pour you into a taxi. Or stick to the walkable cluster of bars in George Town and along Seven Mile Beach. Staggering isn't illegal, just embarrassing.

BARS AND MUSIC CLUBS

★ **Aqua Beach Bar** (✉ *426 West Bay Rd., Seven Mile Beach* ☎ *345/949–8498* ⊕ *www.aquabeach.ky*) feels like a country bar gone (coco)nuts: Palm trees burst through thatching; art naïf portraits of musicians explodes in neon reds, yellows,

BEST BETS

■ **A Smokin' Time.** Even if you're not into stogies, Grand Cayman's cigar and wine bars are civilized hangouts where you might see stars or over-hear insider trading tips.

■ **Local Rhythms.** Cayman's musicians have fanatic follow-ings; it's worth a trip to The Reef for the hilarious Barefoot Man. Lammie, Coco Red, Karen Edie, Gary Ebanks & Intransit, and Hi-Tide are other memo-rable musicians.

■ **Fish Feedings.** It's touristy, but watching tarpons pirouet-

ting for bait at sunset reels even locals into waterfront watering holes.

■ **Culture Vultures.** If you want a real feel for Cayman life, take in an original play, particularly such annual special performances and festivals as Rundown and Gimistory.

■ **Full Moon Parties.** Various beach bars host celebrations with almost pagan abandon, and these parties are over-flowing with cocktails and camaraderie.

blues, and greens; private tiki huts provide intimacy; and neon beer ads illuminate the wood paneling. Fairly good Tex-Mex fare is dished out late. There's a variety of live bands, open-mike nights, and theme nights, such as Thurs-day acoustic jams. Also, there are plenty of daily drink-and-eat specials such as Sunday's NASCAR Bud buckets and CI$18 all-you-can-eat-and-drink barbecue.

★ **The Attic** (⊠ *Queen's Court, 2nd fl., West Bay Rd., Seven Mile Beach* ☎ *345/949–7665* ⊕ *www.attic.ky*) is a chic sports bar with three billiard tables, classic arcade games (Space Invaders, Donkey Kong), air hockey, and large-screen TVs (you can nab a private booth with its own flat-panel job). Events encompass daily happy hours, trivia nights, and the Caribbean's reputedly largest Bloody Mary bar on Sundays. Along with downstairs sister hotspot "O" Bar, it's ground zero for the Wednesday Night Drinking Club. For a $25 initiation fee (you get a T-shirt and personalized leather wristband, toga optional) and $10 weekly activity fee, you'll be shuttled by bus to several different bars, with free shots and drink specials all night.

★ **Calico Jack's** (⊠ *West Bay Rd., Seven Mile Beach* ☎ *345/945–7850*), a friendly outdoor beach bar at the north end of the public beach, has a DJ on Monday and open-mike night on Tuesday, bands every Friday night, and riotous parties during the full moon, when even Ritz-Carlton guests let their hair and inhibitions down. It's also a good place for a casual drink.

You can sit at the bar or swing under a century-old poinciana tree at **Coconut Joe's** (✉ *Across from Comfort Suites, West Bay Rd., Seven Mile Beach* ☎ *345/943–5637*) and watch the traffic go by. There are murals of apes everywhere, from gorillas doing shots to a baboon in basketball uniform (in keeping with management's facetious suggestion that you attract your server's attention by pounding your chest while screeching and scratching yourself). It's particularly popular with the younger tourism and hospitality industry crowds (ply them with beer for some hair- and eyebrow-raising backstage stories). Friday really swings with DJs and free happy-hour munchies.

Deckers (✉ *West Bay Rd., Seven Mile Beach* ☎ *345/945–6600* ⊕ *www.deckers.ky*), always bustling and bubbly, takes its name from the red English double-decker bus that forms the focal point of the main outdoor bar. You can luxuriate indoors on cushy sofas over a chess game and signature blood-orange mojito; hack your way through the 18-hole safari miniature golf course; find a secluded nook in the garden terrace framed by towering palms, old-fashioned ornate street lamps, and colonial columns; or groove to the easy-listening potpourri of pop, reggae, blues, and country courtesy of the Hi-Tide duo. Worthy Carib-Mediterranean fusion cuisine is a bonus (try the grilled jerk duck breast in raspberry coulis or coconut shrimp in sweet-and-sour orange marmalade with green papaya salad).

Driftwood Sports Bar (✉ *Rum Point Dr., North Side* ☎ *345/ 927–9015 or 345/927–9596*), right on the beach, is one of the few signs of life along the north shore between Rum Point and the Reef Resort. True to its name, the bar offers live sporting events blasting from three big-screen TVs (expat Americans tackle every seat Sundays in football season; Brits storm the "arsenal" of beer for their Friday football games with a side of free chicken wingdings). Ask when Lammie, a reggae master, is playing, and don't miss the rollicking Sunday afternoon/evening barbecue, where CI$12 buys enough food to last the week.

Fidel Murphy's Irish Pub (✉ *Queen's Court, West Bay Rd., Seven Mile Beach* ☎ *345/949–5189*) has an unusual logo, a stogie-smoking Castro surrounded by shamrocks. Indeed, the congenial Irish wit and whimsy are so thick that you half expect to find Fidel and Gerry Adams harping on U.S.

and U.K. policy over a Harp. The pub's Edwardian decor of etched glass, hardwood, and brass may be prefabricated (it was constructed in Ireland, disassembled, and shipped), but everything else is genuine, from the warm welcome to the ales and cider on tap to the proper Irish stew (though the kitchen also turns out conch fritters and chicken tandoori wraps). Sunday and Monday host all-you-can-eat extravaganzas (fish-and-chips, carvery) at rock-bottom prices. Weekends welcome live televised Gaelic soccer, rugby, and hurling, followed by karaoke and *craic* (if you go, you'll learn the definition soon enough).

Hammerheads Brew Pub and Grill (⊠ *N. Church St., George Town* ☎ *345/949–3080*) offers a classic Cayman sight: Fishers anchor their boats right offshore and display their catch right outside (condo/villa renters, head here if you're in the market for fresh fish!). Needless to say, this is also a prime pyrotechnic sunset-watching spot, where locals laze in locally carved chairs, slowly getting hammered from the house microbrews, on the vast thatch-shaded deck.

The **Hard Rock Cafe** (⊠ *43 S. Church St., George Town* ☎ *345/945–2020*) perfectly replicates its 137-odd brethren around the world, only with more specialty drinks (try the Orangelicious margarita with Monin pomegranate and blood-orange juices) to complement its extensive burger selection (the Big Blue—crumbled blue cheese and horseradish sauce—is surprisingly tasty). The usual T-shirts, plasma-screen TVs streaming videos, and rotating memorabilia (including gold records and autographed photos from the likes of Elton John, the Clash, U2, and *NSYNC before Justin broke out and Lance came out) are the decor. In truth, it only rocks hard on weekends, when the bar can be a prime Grade-A meet market.

Legendz (⊠ *Falls Centre, West Bay Rd., Seven Mile Beach* ☎ *No phone* ⊕ *www.legendz.ky*) is a sports bar with a clubby, retro feel (Marilyn Monroe and Frank Sinatra photos channel the glamour days). Still, it's the usual testosterone test drive with plentiful scoring of both types. Good luck wrestling a spot at the bar for Pay-Per-View and major live sporting events (though 10 TVs, including two 6- by 8-foot-high resolution screens broadcast to every corner). It doubles as an entertainment venue, booking local bands, stand-up comics, and leading island DJs.

Lone Star Bar and Grill (⊠ *West Bay Rd., Seven Mile Beach* ☎ *345/945–5175* ⊕ *www.caymanlonestar.com*) proudly

Calico Jack's Bar and Grill

calls itself Cayman's top dive (and indeed, locals from dive masters to dentists get down and occasionally dirty over kick-ass margaritas). The noisy bar glorifies sports, Texas, T&A, and the boob tube, from murals of Cowboy cheerleaders to an amazing sports memorabilia collection (including items signed by both Bushes), and 10 big-screen TVs tuned to different events.

★ **Macabuca Oceanside Tiki Bar** (✉ *Northwest Point Rd., West Bay* ☎ *345/945–5217* ⊕ *www.crackedconch.com.ky*) is a classic hip-hopping happening beach bar, with a huge deck over the water, thatched roof, wild painted "coral reef" columns, amazing Asian-inspired mosaic murals of waves, spectacular sunsets (and sunset-colored libations), and tiki torches illuminating the reef fish come evening. Macabuca means "What does it matter?" in the indigenous Antillean Taíno language, perfectly encapsulating the mellow vibe. Four big-screen TVs, live bands on weekends, excellent pub grub, and daily specials (Monday all-night happy hour, DJ, and CI$15 all-you-can-eat barbecue) lure everyone from well-heeled loafers to barefoot bodysurfers animatedly discussing current events and dive currents in a Babel of tongues.

Margaritaville (✉ *Island Village, Cardinal Ave., George Town* ☎ *345/949–6274*) is a vast upstairs space that usually bustles with life; the Friday-evening happy hour is especially popular, with an overgrown frat-party ambience,

CLOSE UP

Calling All Corsairs

For 11 days in November, Grand Cayman is transformed into a nonstop, fun-filled festivity every bit as flamboyant as Johnny Depp's Jack Sparrow performances. The annual **Pirates Week Festival** (⊕ *www. piratesweekfestival.com*) is the country's largest celebration, encompassing more than 30 different events, including street dances, five heritage days (where various districts showcase their unique craft and culinary traditions), a float parade, landing pageant, fireworks, song contests, costume competitions, cardboard-boat regattas, golf tournaments, swim meets, autocross, races, kids' fun day, teen music nights, underwater treasure hunt, and more.

Everyone gets involved in the high-spirited high jinks (for example, dive boats stage mock battles and play practical jokes like filling the decks of "rivals" with cornflakes or jam, while swashbucklers "capture" hotel employees and guests). The opening night is an explosion

of sights and sounds, from fireworks to rocking, rollicking bands that keep thousands shaking booty in the George Town streets into the wee hours of the morning. The second day's highlight is the mock pirate invasion of Hog Sty Bay and the spirited defense of the capital, culminating in the buccaneers' trial and extravagantly costumed street parades with ornate floats.

Most of the major events are free. The music sizzles, and the evening functions feature heaping helpings of yummy, affordable local fare (turtle stew, conch, jerk chicken). Given the enormous popularity of the festival, travelers should make reservations for hotel rooms and rental cars well in advance. Even taxis are in short supply for those wanting to attend the farther-flung heritage days. Hotels, shops, and the festival's administrative office do a brisk biz in corsair couture (though you can bring your own stuffed parrot and patch; just leave the sword at home).

5

and though drinks may be a bit pricier than at other waterfront locations, the jollity definitely compensates.

★ **My Bar** (✉ *Sunset House, S. Church St., George Town* ☎ *345/949–7111* ⊕ *www.sunsethouse.com*) is optimally perched on the water's edge, looking almost due west with a perfect vantage point for watching the sunset. The leviathan open-sided cabana is drenched in vivid Rasta colors and crowned by an intricate South Seas–style thatched roof (containing approximately 36,000 palm fronds). Christmas lights and the occasional customer dangle from the rafters year-round. Great grub and a mischievous mix of locals, expats, and tourists from all walks of life prove that eco-centric Cayman offers wild life alongside the wildlife.

The Office (✉ *Shedden Bay Rd., by Cable & Wireless, George Town* ☎ *345/945–5212*) is indeed a preferred hangout for the diverse after-work crowd, which packs the cozy space, absorbing the high-octane cocktails and nightly musical mix (from country to salsa, karaoke to live bands). It's invariably lively, a favorite spot for birthday, office, and bachelor/ette parties, and a prime place to eavesdrop on local gossip.

Rackam's Pub and Restaurant (✉ *N. Church St., George Town* ☎ *345/945–3860* ⊕ *www.rackamswaterfront.ky*) is a hap-penin' bar built on a jetty jutting into the harbor (boat-ers, even snorkelers cruise right up the ladder for drinks while anglers leave their catch on ice) that has complimen-tary snacks on Friday and serves pub fare at fair prices until midnight. A Cayman mosaic of fishers to Who's-the-Hugo-Boss financiers savors sensational sunsets followed by exuberantly pirouetting tarpon feeding at the open-air, marine-theme bar area.

Royal Palms (✉ *West Bay Rd., George Town* ☎ *345/945–6358*) is where notable local bands like Coco Red and Footloose gig weekend nights; it's an outdoor beach bar with plenty of room for dancing under the stars and a great Sunday-afternoon hangout to socialize, sit in the sun, and listen to music.

Rusty Pelican (✉ *Reef Resort, Colliers, East End* ☎ *345/947–3100* ⊕ *www.thereef.com.ky*) draws an eclectic group of dive masters, expats, honeymooners, and mingling singles. The knockout colorful cocktails pack quite a punch, making the sunset last for hours. The bar dialogue is entertainment enough, but Andrew Bacon's occasionally ribald musical games enhance the vivacity. Don't miss local legend, coun-try-calypsonian Barefoot Man, when he plays "upstairs" at Pelican's Reef: He's to Cayman what Jimmy Buffett is to Key West.

★ **South Coast Bar and Grill** (✉ *Breakers, East End* ☎ *345/947–2517*) is a delightful seaside slice of old Cayman (grizzled regulars slamming down dominoes, fabulous views, Fri-day-night dances to local legend Lammie's beats, local Elvis impersonator Errol Dunbar, and reasonably priced

CLOSE UP

Barefoot Man

H. George Nowak, aka "Barefoot Man," is hardly your ordinary Calypsonian. The blond-haired German-born, self-described "Nashville musical reject" moved from Munich to North Carolina after his mother remarried an Air Force officer. But "the inveterate map lover" dreamed of island life.

He started his island-hopping career in the U.S. Virgin Islands, then Hawaii, then the Bahamas ("the smaller, less populated, the better"), finally settling in the Cayman Islands in 1971. "'But there's nothing there,' people said. I replied, 'That's the point!'" Needless to say, Barefoot prefers the casual lifestyle.

He quickly realized that the audience "didn't want 'Folsom Prison Blues,' they wanted 'Banana Boat Song.'" He was dubbed Barefoot Boy ("since the nicest pair of footwear I owned were my Voit diving flippers") in 1971. While he'll still throw in a country or blues tune, Barefoot came to love the calypso tradition, especially its double entendres and political commentary. His witty ditties say it all: "Thong Gone Wrong," "Ship Faced," "The Gay Cruise Ship Song," and "Save the Lap Dance for Me."

One of the most passionate, outspoken, articulate expats on the subject of sustainable tourism, he wittily rants in song and print (including his own self-published *Fun News*, the über-glossy coffee-table *Grand Cayman* magazine, and hilarious tomes like *Which Way to the Islands?*). "I've seen the island go from 3 taxi drivers to, I think 380 in the taxi association...saw how the first high-rise, the former Holiday Inn, changed Cayman irrevocably in the '70s.... I compare tourism to aspirin—a couple are okay, but take the whole bottle you die," he jokes (mostly).

He'll regale you between sets or over beers with colorful (expletive deleted) anecdotes of island life, recounting adventures from a bogus murder charge in the Bahamas to the necessity of scheduling spliff breaks when recording in Jamaica to being mistaken for a DEA agent.

Barefoot sums up his philosophy simply and eloquently in one of his most popular lyrics (add gentle reggae-ish lilt), "I wish I were a captain, Sailin' on the sea. I'd sail out to an island, Take you there with me. I'd throw away the compass, Oh what a dirty scheme...Someday I might wake up, realize where I am, dreamin' like some ten-year-old, out in Disneyland, There is no tomorrow when you're living in a dream."

5

local eats like barbecued ribs and fried crabs). It's also a big politico hangout ("that big shark mural ain't just about nature," one bartender cackled), attested to by the fascinating photos, some historical, of local scenes and personalities. The juke jives, from Creedence Clearwater Revival to Mighty Sparrow.

Stingers Resort and Pool Bar (⊠ *Comfort Suites, West Bay Rd., Seven Mile Beach* ☎ *345/945–3000*) offers tasty food in an appealing setting (check out the stupendous "stinger" mosaic), with cover-free live music and dancing Thursday and Friday. Wednesday and Saturday nights there's a very affordable all-you-can-eat Caribbean luau. The band Heat, a local institution, sizzles with energetic, emotionally delivered calypso, reggae, soca, salsa, and oldies; then the limbo dancers and fire-eaters keep the temperature rising. If you recoil from audience participation, stay far away. More exhibitionistic "spring break" sorts might find their photo adorning the "Wall of Shame," but the worst blackmail is persuading you to buy another blue-green Stingers punch.

You can dance near the water to mellow music at the **Wharf** (⊠ *West Bay Rd., George Town* ☎ *345/949–2231*) on Saturday evening; when there's a wedding reception in the pavilion, the crashing surf and candles twinkling as if competing with the stars bathe the proceedings in an almost Gatsby-esque glow. For something less sedate, you can take part in the free sizzling salsa dancing and lessons on Tuesday, while Fridays morph into a wild 1970s disco night. The stunning seaside setting on tiered decks compensates for often undistinguished food and service. The Ports of Call bar is a splendid place for sunset fanciers, and tarpon feeding off the deck is a nightly 9 PM spectacle.

CIGAR AND WINE LOUNGES

★ **Bamboo Lounge** (⊠ *Grand Cayman Beach Suites, West Bay Rd., Seven Mile Beach* ☎ *345/947–8744* ⊕ *www.grand-cayman-beach-suites.com*) is a quiet, refined, but theatrically designed bar with sublime sushi (and other Asian standbys) and luscious libations (with suggestive names like Foreplay and Love Potion #69) abetted by an extensive wine and sake list. You can roll what you eat during Master Sushi Chef O. G.'s cooking demonstrations at 5:30 most weeknights. The musical menu runs from jazz (luring couples conducting affairs both personal and professional) to Wednesday's

Caymans Captivating Carnival

Held annually during the first week of May (or the week after Easter), the four-day **Batabano Cayman Carnival** (⊕ *www.caymancarnival.com*) is the island's boisterous answer to Mardi Gras, not to mention Carnival in Rio and Trinidad. Though not as hedonistic, the pyrotechnic pageantry, electricity, and enthralled throngs are unrivaled (except for during Pirates Week). Events include a carnival ball, soca and calypso song competitions, massive Mas (masquerade) parade with ornate floats, street dance, and a beach fete. The festivities are enhanced by tasty concession stands offering Caymanian and other Caribbean cuisine and delicacies.

The word *batabano* refers to the tracks that turtles leave as they heave onto beaches to nest. Locating those tracks was reason to celebrate in the olden times, when turtling was a major part of the economy, so it seemed an appropriate tribute to the islands' heritage, alongside the traditional Caribbean celebration of the region's African roots. Indeed, many of the increasingly elaborate costumes are inspired by Cayman's majestic marine life and maritime history from parrots to pirates, though some offer provocative social commentary. Thousands of revelers line the streets each year cheering their favorite masqueraders and boogying to the Mas steel pan and soca bands. The organizers also hold a stand-alone street parade for Cayman's youth called Junior Carnival Batabano the weekend before the adult parade. Equally exciting, it stresses the importance of teaching students the art of costume-making and Mas, ensuring Carnival won't become another dying Caymanian custom.

"Bamboozled" nights, when younger soigné singles sweat elegantly on the minuscule dance floor.

★ **Havana Club Restaurant and Cigar Lounge** (✉ *Regency Court, 672 West Bay Rd., Seven Mile Beach* ☎ *345/945–5391* ⊕ *www.havanaclub-cigars.com*) is the latest venture of Cubano-phile Raglan Roper, who sailed his boat from Florida to Grand Cayman 20 years ago, stopping off along the way. The restaurant serves authentic Cuban cuisine (scrumptious steak in garlic sauce and near-definitive black-bean soup). Ironically, it's smoke-free, though you can purchase not just Cuban cigars but cigarettes (there's a small adjacent hut for fuming). The back lounge is intimate, with back-to-the-future touches like curved bars and chartreuse walls amid the handsome mahogany furnishings. Live jazz

A wall mural at the Havana Club Restaurant and Cigar Lounge

and blues animate the evenings from Thursday through Saturday. A state-of-the-art ventilation system ensures the air remains clean. Best of all is meeting and admiring the dexterity of septuagenarian Jesus Lara Perez, the in-house *torcedor,* or cigar roller, who started working in Cuban factories when he was 14 and has since traveled from the Bahamas to Belgium demonstrating his craft.

Macumba Lounge (✉ *Falls Centre, West Bay Rd., Seven Mile Beach* ☎ *345/946–6161 or 345/928–5565* ⊕ *www.macumbalounge.com*) lives up to its name, from an African word meaning "party," with events every evening, from Monday karaoke to Friday bingo to Sunday comedy acts. A DJ plays mixes from R&B to Bollywood-esque Bhangra nightly, and there's live salsa on Wednesday and jazz on Saturday. The handsome, dimly lit space features billowing curtains, plush leather couches, and big video screens.

Don't let the location of **Nectar** (✉ *Seven Mile Shops, Seven Mile Beach* ☎ *345/946–3496*), which is in the back of a plain strip mall, fool you. This is a chic New York–style martini lounge and sushi-tapas bar with more than 30 different drinks—including many 'tinis with 'tude. Choose from bar, tall tables, or sofas in the sleek, slick, mostly red-and-black space with chrome accents and blue lighting. There's new art on the walls every month, DJs spinning Thursday and Friday, and special shisha (hookah) evenings.

★ **Silver Palm Lounge** (⊠ *Ritz-Carlton, West Bay Rd., Seven Mile Beach* ☎ *345/943–9000*) drips with cash and cachet. One section faithfully replicates a classic English country library (perfect for civilized proper afternoon tea or a pre- or post-dinner champagne or single malt). Then there's the sexy, über-hip, black-clad Taikun lounge, with hardwood wainscoting, carved bamboo, marble floors, lacquer tables, and model (in both senses) waitstaff. Also on tap: fab cocktails including specialty martinis (the Sundancer is a winner—Belvedere Cytrus, Pomarancza, Moët champagne, mango juice, and orange juice); pages of wines by the glass; an impressive list of cigars, Cognacs, and aged rums; and marvelous sushi and creative tapas. Everyone's chic-by-jowl after 10 pm, especially on funked-out DJ Fridays, when Arab sheiks mingle with American CEOs, while tonsorially challenged agent-types wear trophy wives (and mistresses) on their arms like Rolexes: It puts the sin in scintillating.

DANCE CLUBS

For a rowdy time, zoom into **Jet** (⊠ *West Bay Rd., opposite Marriott, Seven Mile Beach* ☎ *345/946–6398*), a new late-night, yup-scaled, slim-hipper-than-thou version of previous tenant, Next Level that delivers a dancing high, spinning everything from retro remixes to hip-hop for Jessica Alba wannabes poured into spandex and Gap poster-boy slackers (potential hell for anyone over 30 years old or 20% body fat).

★ **"O" Bar** (⊠ *Queen's Court, West Bay Rd., Seven Mile Beach* ☎ *345/943–6227 ⊕ www.obar.ky*) is a trendy black-and-crimson, industrial-style dance club with mixed music and juggling, flame-throwing flair bartenders—practically local celebs—flipping cocktails with cojones. It's as close to a stand-and-pose milieu as you'll find on Cayman, with the occasional fashion fascist parading in Prada. An upper-level private loft is available by reservation.

THE ARTS

Grand Cayman mounts special events throughout the year, including November's respected Cayman Jazz Fest (which has hosted such headliners as Natalie Cole, BeBe Winans, and Jeffrey Osborne). The Cayman National Orchestra performs in disparate venues from the Cracked Conch

Preserving Caymans Cultural Heritage

CLOSE UP

Several worthy organizations are dedicated to keeping Caymanian traditions alive, including the National Trust of the Cayman Islands, which restores historic buildings and offers craft demonstrations and talks. The Cayman National Cultural Foundation mounts story-telling, musical, dance, and theatrical presentations, as well as readings and art exhibits that respect the "old ways" while seeking new forms of expression. The National Gallery also seeks to ensure vibrant vital world-class artistic development.

Respected local artist Chris Christian and his wife, Trina (who curate the Ritz-Carlton Gallery exhibits), founded **Cayman Traditional Arts** (*CTA* ⊠ *60 W. Church St., West Bay* ☎ *345/946-0117* ⊕ *www. getaway.ky*), which offers interactive classes for children and adults interested in learning authentic Caymanian arts, crafts, and recipes: Thatch weaving, kite-making, gig-making and spinning, rope-making, and an old-style cookout on the wood-burning oven called a caboose are just some of the topics. The network of freelance artisans has practiced these traditional crafts and customs their entire lives, often handed down over several generations, and represent the best in their disciplines. You can get a taste, literally, if you visit the "ambassadors" Trina organizes on Cayman Street at Boatswain's Beach, but you really get hands-on in Chris and Trina's "living museum" headquarters, a 1917 mauve-and-mint wattle-and-daub cottage with iron-wood posts that also doubles as a studio for Chris and Carly Jackson. It's a unique interactive immersion in local culture.

restaurant to First Baptist Church. There's a burgeoning theater scene. Many new works use religious themes as a launching pad for meditations on issues relevant to current events, such as the Cayman Drama Society (⊕ *www. caymandrama.org.ky*), which put on a provocative offering, *The Judith Code*, updating the biblical heroine's story to a present-day London of TV talk-show hosts and terrorist coalitions; the company also produces stimulating children's fare (*Mort*, based on Terry Pratchett's *Discworld* novels about a young boy apprenticed to Death), as well as escapist crowd-pleasing revivals like *Annie Get Your Gun* and *You're a Good Man, Charlie Brown*.

TELLING TALES. The Cayman National Cultural Foundation started "Gimistory" as a means of preserving the rich but vanishing oral-culture tradition once passed from generation to generation. Held annually the last week of November, it features storytellers, often in elaborate garb, from Cayman and the Caribbean "spinnin' yarn" about old-time legends (duppies, spirits who return as bogeymen; or Pierrot Grande, the clown dressed in a colorful patchwork quilt of rags) as well as their travels and experiences. Free admission includes Caymanian delicacies like conch fritters and swanky (lemonade).

VENUES

Harquail Theatre (✉ *17 Harquail Dr., George Town* ☎ *345/949–5477*) is a state-of-the-art facility seating 330 for theatrical performances, concerts, dance recitals, fashion shows, beauty pageants, art exhibits, and poetry readings sponsored by the Cayman National Cultural Foundation.

Lions Centre (✉ *Harquail Dr., Red Bay* ☎ *345/945–4667 or 345/949–7211*) hosts events throughout the year: "Battle of the Bands" competitions, concerts by top names on the Caribbean and international music scene such as Maxi Priest, stage productions, pageants, and sporting events.

Prospect Playhouse (✉ *223B Shamrock Rd., Prospect* ☎ *345/947–1998 or 345/949–5054*) is a thrust proscenium stage where the Cayman Drama Society and its partner arts organizations mount comedies, musicals, and dramas (original and revival) year-round.

Performances at **Vivendi Cabaret** (✉ *The Strand, West Bay Rd., Seven Mile Beach* ☎ *345/943–2060 or 345/943–7469*), a relatively new dinner theater (tickets without food cost CI$34), combine elements of opera, Broadway-style choreography, acrobatics, skating, juggling, and Caribbean culture. More than 25 international artists in various disciplines compose the troupe; shows include 200 costume changes and props from flowing curtains to hoops. Some might dub the performances Cirque du So-lame, but many elements are world-class. An à la carte tapestry of tapas complements the prix-fixe dinner, and dance lessons from meringue to mambo are also offered.

The Lowdown on Rundown

Rundown is a steamy Caymanian fish stew combining a potpourri of ingredients. A rundown is also a quick summary, and this enduringly popular show performed annually in October since 1991 puns on both definitions. The format is a series of skits, music, stand-up comedy, monologues, cabaret, dance, and impersonations—written from scratch each year by playwright-actor Dave Martins: a light-hearted, topical, satirical lampoon of daily Caymanian life, current events, politics, personalities, and nationalities. Caymanians call it their answer to *The Daily Show* and *Colbert Report.*

Martins started Rundown because he'd "seen topical shows in other Caribbean countries... and felt something similar would work here, but Cayman is very conservative and people said that would get me in hot water." After seeing caricatures of prominent people hanging in their offices, "I concluded that Caymanians were ready to laugh at themselves and wrote the first show. Some of the cast were very apprehensive in rehearsals, but it was a hit from day one." Every year provides fodder and inspiration aplenty,

but the show is more gently mocking than controversial, and the targets of its barbs usually laugh along with everyone else.

The audience's nonstop guffawing may bemuse tourists. Martins explains, "A lot of the stuff I write... is very contextual and almost always local, so the lyrics generally make little sense to someone outside that frame." Recent skits spoofed the red tape involved in putting up a little backyard shed to play dominoes; interplay among a crowd of people lining up to get Caymanian Immigration Status (the rollover policy); a Jamaican trying to teach a Londoner to speak the J dialect; and a lost tourist trying to get directions from a group that includes a Cuban, a Barbadian, a Pakistani, a Jamaican, a Chinaman, and, of course, a Caymanian... "all of whom are incomprehensible to the visitor.... To understand it fully, you'd need to have lived here 10, 15 years." He doesn't Americanize or clean up the dialect, but that augments the honest authenticity. And much of the material, from frustrating daily interactions to bureaucratic blundering, transcends any cultural divide.

Grand Cayman Sports and Outdoor Activities

WITH BEACHES

WORD OF MOUTH

"I definitely recommend buying snorkel gear before you go and bringing it with you. We kept it in our rental car and were able to just pull over and snorkel anywhere we found a great beach."

—MMN

WATER, WATER, AND STILL MORE WATER rippling from turquoise to tourmaline; and underneath lies nature's even more kaleidoscopically colorful answer to Disney World for scuba divers and snorkelers. The Cayman Islands' early aggressive efforts on behalf of marine conservation paid off by protecting some of the most spectacular reefs in the western hemisphere. There are innumerable ways to experience their pyrotechnics without getting your feet or hair wet, from submarines to remote-controlled robots, not to mention a bevy of other water sports from windsurfing to wrangling big-game fish, parasailing to paddling kayaks through mangrove swamps.

While most activities on Grand Cayman are aquatic in nature, landlubbers can do more than just loll on the lovely beaches. There are nature hikes, bird-watching treks, and horseback rides through the island's wilder, more remote areas. The golf scene is well above par for so small an island, with courses designed by Jack "The Golden Bear" Nicklaus and, fittingly, "The White Shark" Greg Norman. Even the most seasoned sea salts might enjoy terra firma, at least for half a day.

BEACHES

Grand Cayman is blessed with many fine beaches, ranging from cramped, untrammeled coves to long stretches basking like a cat in the sun, lined with bustling bars and water-sports concessions. All beaches are public, though access can be restricted by resorts. Remember that the Cayman Islands are a conservative place: Nudity is strictly forbidden and punishable by a hefty fine and/or prison time.

★ **Barkers**. A series of secluded, spectacular beaches are accessed via a dirt road just past Papagallo restaurant. There are no facilities (that's the point!), but some palms offer shade. Unfortunately, the shallow water and rocky bottom discourage swimming, and it can be cluttered at times with seaweed and debris. ⊠ *Conch Point Rd., Barkers, West Bay.*

East End Beaches. Just drive along and look for any sandy beach, park your car, and enjoy a stroll. The vanilla-hue stretch at Colliers Bay, by the Reef and Morritt's resorts, is a good, clean one with superior snorkeling. ⊠ *Queen's Hwy., East End.*

BEST BETS

■ **A Ray-diant Experience.** Feeding and stroking the silky denizens of Stingray City and Stingray Sandbar are highlights of any Cayman trip.

■ **Snorkeling or Diving from Shore.** Whether you make it to Stingray City or even scuba dive, you're all wet if you don't check out the pyrotechnic reef life glittering just offshore.

■ **Hiking the Mastic Trail.** The ecocentric should hike (and sometimes hack their way) through this mix of ecosystems, including ancient dry forest that embraces 716 plant species as well as (harmless) wildlife.

■ **ROV-ing the Ocean's Depths.** Deep See Cayman's ROV robot explores 2,000 feet under the sea while you watch in comfort on a yacht; the kids can steer if they're handy with joysticks.

■ **Putting on the Nightlights.** Kayak when the moon is waning to a bioluminescent bay; millions of microorganisms glow like fireflies when disturbed.

6

Old Man Bay. The North Side features plenty of hidden coves and pristine stretches of perfect sand, where you'll be disturbed only by seabirds dive-bombing for lunch and the occasional lone fishers casting nets for sprats, then dumping them into buckets. This area is easily accessed off Frank Sound Road. Off the Edge restaurant is less than 1 mi (1½ km) west. Otherwise, it's fairly undeveloped for miles, save for the occasional private home. Snorkeling is spectacular when waters are calm. ⊠ *Queen's Hwy., just off Frank Sound Rd., North Side.*

★ **Rum Point.** This North Sound beach has hammocks slung in towering casuarina trees, picnic tables, the thatched Wreck Bar and Grill, a "fancier" dining option, well-stocked shop for seaworthy sundries, and Red Sail Sports, which offers various water sports and boats to explore Stingray City. The barrier reef ensures safe snorkeling and soft sand. The bottom remains shallow for a long way from shore, but it's littered with small coral heads, so kids shouldn't wrestle in the water here. The Wreck is ablaze with color—yellow with navy blue trim and lime and mango picnic tables— as if trying to upstage the snorkeling just offshore; an ultra-casual hangout turns out outstanding pub grub from fish-and-chips to wings, as well as lethal mudslide cocktails. Showers are available. Just around the bend, another

quintessential beach hangout, Kaibo, rocks during the day. ⊠ *Rum Point, North Side.*

★ Fodor's Choice **Seven Mile Beach.** Grand Cayman's west coast is dominated by the famous Seven Mile Beach—actually a 6½-mi-long (10-km-long) expanse of powdery white sand overseeing lapis water stippled with a rainbow of parasails and kayaks. The width of the beach varies with the season; toward the south end it narrows and disappears altogether south of the Marriott, leaving only rock and ironshore. It starts to broaden into its normal silky softness anywhere between Tarquyn Manor and the Reef Grill at Royal Palms. Free of litter and pesky peddlers, it's an unspoiled (though often crowded) environment. Most of the island's resorts, restaurants, and shopping centers sit along this strip. At the public beach toward the north end you can find chairs for rent ($10 for the day, including a beverage), a playground, water toys aplenty, two beach bars, restrooms, and showers. The best snorkeling is at either end, by the Marriott and Treasure Island or off the northern section called Cemetery Reef Beach. ⊠ *West Bay Rd., Seven Mile Beach.*

★ **Smith's Cove.** South of the Grand Old House, this tiny but popular protected swimming and snorkeling spot makes a wonderful beach wedding location. The bottom drops off quickly enough to allow you to swim and play close to shore. Although slightly rocky (its pitted limestone boulders resemble Moore sculptures), there's little debris and few coral heads, plenty of shade, picnic tables, restrooms, and parking. Surfers will find some decent swells just to the south. Note the curious obelisk cenotaph IN MEMORY OF JAMES SAMUEL WEBSTER AND HIS WIFE ARABELLA ANTOINETTE (NÉE EDEN), with assorted quotes from Confucius to John Donne. Local scuttlebutt calls it a place for dalliances during work hours; it's also a romantic sunset spot. ⊠ *Off S. Church St., George Town.*

South Sound Cemetery Beach. A narrow, sandy driveway takes you past the small cemetery to a perfect beach. The dock here is primarily used by dive boats during winter storms. You can walk in either direction; the sand is talcum-soft and clean, the water calm and clear (though local surfers take advantage of occasional small reef breaks; if wading, wear reef shoes, since the bottom is somewhat rocky and dotted with sea urchins). You'll definitely find fewer crowds. ⊠ *S. Sound Rd., Prospect.*

Spotts Beach. Families often barbecue weekends at this idyllic spot caught between ironshore cliffs and a barrier reef. A jungle gym and swing set keep the kids occupied when they're not chowing down at the picnic tables and cabanas. During the week it's usually deserted. Follow South Church Street through South Sound past Red Bay; you'll see yet another little cemetery with a turnoff to the beach. ⊠ *Queen's Hwy., Spotts Newlands, East End.*

Water Cay. If you want an isolated, unspoiled beach, bear left at Rum Point on the North Side and follow the road to the end. When you pass a porte cochere for an abandoned condo development and see a soft, sandy beach, stop your car. Wade out knee deep and look for the large, flame-hued starfish. (Don't touch—just look.) Locals also call it Starfish or Ivory Point. ⊠ *North Side.*

SPORTS AND ACTIVITIES

BIRD-WATCHING

6

The Cayman Islands are an ornithologist's dream, providing perches for a wide range of resident and migratory birds—219 species at last count, many of them endangered, such as the Cayman parrot. The National Trust organizes regular bird-watching field trips conducted by local ornithologists through the Governor Michael Gore Bird Sanctuary, Queen Elizabeth II Botanic Park, Mastic Reserve, Salina Reserve, Central Mangrove Wetland, Meagre Bay Pond Reserve in Pease Bay, Colliers Pond in East End, and Palmetto Pond at Barkers in West Bay. Prime time for bird-watching is either early in the morning or late in the afternoon; take strong binoculars and a field guide to identify the birds.

Silver Thatch Tours (☏ *345/925–7401* ⊕ *www.earthfoot.org/ places/ky001.htm*) is run by Geddes Hislop, who knows his birds and his island (though he's Trinidadian by birth). He specializes in customizable five-hour natural and historic heritage tours that generally culminate at the Queen Elizabeth II Botanic Park's nature trail and lake. The cost is $45 per hour for one to four people. Serious birders leave at the crack of dawn, but you can choose the time and leave at the crack of noon instead. The cost includes guide service, pickup and return transport, and refreshments such as local drinks (a great excuse for discourse on herbal medicinal folklore).

One of the world's leading dive destinations, Grand Cayman has dramatic underwater topography that features plunging walls, soaring skyscraper pinnacles, grottoes, arches, swim-throughs adorned with vibrant sponges, coral-encrusted caverns, and canyons patrolled by lilliputian grunts to gargantuan groupers, darting jacks to jewfish, moray eels to eagle rays. Gorgonians and sea fans wave like come-hither courtesans. Pyrotechnic reefs provide homes for all manner of marine life, ecosystems encased within each other like an intricate series of Chinese boxes.

REEF WATCH. This progressive program, a partnership between the Department of the Environment and Cayman Islands Tourism Association, debuted in 1997 during Earth Day activities. The DOE designed a field survey to involve diving and snorkeling tourists in counting and cataloging marine life. To date, more than 1,000 surveys have been completed, helping estimate species' populations and travel patterns based on sightings and their distance from buoys and other markers, as well as gauging how often equipment touches the fragile reefs. Though not scientifically sound, it does enhance awareness through interaction.

DIVE SITES
There are more than 200 pristine dive sites, many less than a half-mile from the island and easily accessible, including wreck, wall, and shore options. Add exceptional visibility from 80 to 150 feet (no rivers deposit silt) and calm, current-free water at a constant bath-like 80°F. Cayman is serious about conservation, with stringently enforced laws to protect the fragile, endangered marine environment (fines up to $500,000 and a year in prison for damaging living coral, which can take years to regrow), protected by the creation of Marine Park, Replenishment, and Environmental Park Zones. Local water-sports operators enthusiastically cooperate: Most boats use biodegradable cleansers and environmentally friendly drinking cups. Moorings at all popular dive sites prevent coral and sponge damage due to continual anchoring; in addition, diving with gloves is prohibited to reduce the temptation to touch.

Pristine water, breathtaking coral formations, and plentiful marine life including hammerheads and hawksbill turtles

CLOSE UP

Learn to Dive

Diving is an exciting experience that does not have to be strenuous or stressful. Almost anyone can enjoy scuba, and it's easy to test the waters via a three-hour resort course costing $100–$120. After a quick rundown of dos and don'ts, you stand in the shallow end of a pool, learning how to use the mask and fins and breathe underwater with a regulator. The instructor then explains some basic safety skills, and before you know it you're in the drink. The instructor hovers as you float above the reef, watching fish react to you. Don't worry—there are no dangerous fish in Cayman, and they don't bite (as long as you're not "chumming," or handling fish food). You can see corals and sponges, maybe even a turtle or ray. It's an amazing world that you can enter with very little effort.

The resort course only permits shallow, instructor-guided dives in Cayman's calm, clear waters. The next step is full Open Water certification (generally three to four days, including several dives, for around $450, less as part of a hotel package). This earns you a C-card, your passport to the underwater world anywhere you travel. From there, addicts will discover dozens of specialty courses. The leading teaching organizations, both with their adherents, are PADI (Professional Association of Dive Instructors) and NAUI (National Association of Underwater Instructors), affectionately nicknamed "Not Another Underwater Idiot" and "Pay and Dive Immediately" (those are the polite versions in scuba's colorful slang). Worry not: Cayman's instructors are among the world's best. And the water conditions just might spoil you.

mark the **North Wall**—a world-renowned dive area along the North Side of Grand Cayman.

Trinity Caves, in West Bay, is a deep dive with numerous canyons starting at about 60 feet and sloping to the wall at 130 feet. The South Side is the deepest, with the top of its wall starting 80 feet deep before plummeting, though its shallows offer a lovely labyrinth of caverns and tunnels in such sites as **Japanese Gardens** and **Della's Delight.**

The less-visited, virgin East End is less varied geographically beyond the magnificent **Ironshore Caves** and **Babylon Hanging Gardens** (trees of black coral plunging 100 feet), but it teems with "Swiss-cheese" swim-throughs and exotic life in such renowned gathering spots as **The Maze** (a hangout

Dive Tips

Here are a few helpful hints to maximize your enjoyment:

■ If you're not strong, ask someone to carry your tank and don't go in rough water from shore.

■ Always orient yourself on the sandy bottom near the boat: Check gauges and camera/video equipment, fine-tune your buoyancy, and ensure that your buddy is also secure.

■ Use a flashlight to explore crevices and illuminate the true dazzling colors of soft corals, sponges, and tunicates.

■ Check overhangs and outcroppings where grouper, tarpon, minnows, and other fish hang out in the shade.

■ Never touch black coral, usu-ally found near 100-foot depths under outcroppings or inside tunnels. It's quite fragile, growing a mere inch every two to three years.

■ Fire coral is prevalent in the tropics and assumes many forms. Skin contact is painful (explaining the name). Vinegar or isopropyl alcohol helps alleviate pain; hydrocortisone cream or gel ameliorates the itch.

■ When shore diving off George Town, always use a surface float marker to indicate your position to the snorkeler/boater traffic.

■ If you become fatigued, float on your back; the seawater buoys you.

for reef, burse, and occasional hammerhead sharks), **Snapper Hole,** and **Grouper Grotto.**

The Cayman Islands government acquired the 251-foot, decommissioned **USS Kittiwake.** Once sunk, it will become an exciting new dive attraction, as well as necessary relief for some of the most frequently visited dive sites.

The new **Cayman Dive 365** (⊕ *www.divecayman.ky/dive365*) initiative is part of a commitment to protect reefs from environmental overuse. New dive sites will be introduced while certain existing sites will be "retired" to be rested and refreshed. Visitors are encouraged to sponsor and name a new dive site from the list of selected coordinates.

★ **Fodor's Choice** Most dive operators offer scuba trips to **Stingray City** in the North Sound. Widely considered the best 12-foot dive in the world, it's a must-see for adventurous souls. Here dozens of stingrays congregate—tame enough to suction squid from your outstretched palm. You can stand in 3 feet of water at **Stingray Sandbar** as the gentle

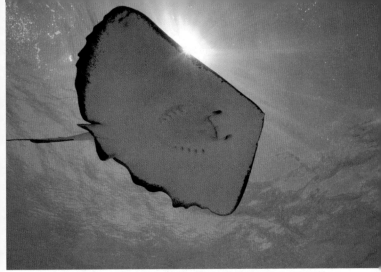
A stingray at Stingray City, widely considered the best 12-foot dive in the world

stingrays glide around your legs looking for a handout. Don't worry—these stingrays are so acclimated to tourist encounters that they pose no danger; the experience is often a highlight of a Grand Cayman trip.

SHORE DIVING

Shore diving around the island provides easy access to kaleidoscopic reefs, fanciful rock formations, and enthralling shipwrecks. The areas are well marked by buoys to facilitate navigation. If the water looks rough where you are, there's usually a side of the island that's wonderfully calm.

★ If someone tells you that the silverside minnows are in at **Eden Rock,** drop everything and dive here (on South Church Street in George Town across from Harbour Place Mall by Paradise Restaurant). The schools swarm around you as you glide through the grottoes, forming quivering curtains of liquid silver as shafts of sunlight pierce the sandy bottom. The grottoes themselves are safe—not complex caves—and the entries and exits are clearly visible at all times. Snorkelers can enjoy the outside of the grottoes as the reef rises and falls from 10 to 30 feet deep. Avoid carrying fish food unless you know how not to get bitten by eager yellowtail snappers.

★ Its neighbor, **Devil's Grotto,** resembles an abstract painting of anemones, tangs, parrotfish, and bright purple Pederson cleaner shrimp (nicknamed the dentists of the reef, as they gorge on whatever they scrape off fish teeth and gills). Extensive coral heads and fingers teem with blue wrasse, horse-eyed jacks, butterfly fish, Indigo hamlets, and more. The cathedral-like caves are phenomenal, but tunnel entries here aren't clearly marked, so you're best off with a dive master.

Turtle Reef, at the Cracked Conch restaurant in West Bay, begins 20 feet out and gradually descends to a 60-foot mini-wall pulsing with sea life and corals of every variety. From there it's just another 15 feet to the dramatic main wall. Ladders provide easy entrance to a shallow cover perfect for pre-dive checks, and since the area isn't buoyed for boats, it's quite pristine.

DIVE OPERATORS

As one of the Caribbean's top diving destinations, Grand Cayman is blessed with many top-notch dive operations offering diving, instruction, and equipment for sale and rent. A single-tank boat dive averages $70, a two-tank dive about $100. Snorkel-equipment rental is about $15 a day. Divers are required to be certified and possess a "C" card. If you're getting certified, to save time during your limited holiday you can start the book and pool work at home and finish the open-water portion in warm, clear Cayman waters. Certifying agencies offer this referral service all around the world.

When choosing a dive operator, here are a few things to ask: Do they require that you stay with the group? Do they include towels? camera rinse water? protection from inclement weather? tank-change service? beach or resort pick-up? snacks between dives? Ask what dive options they have during a winter storm (called a nor'wester here). What kind of boat do they have? (Don't assume that a small, less crowded boat is better. Some large boats are more comfortable, even when full, than a tiny, uncovered boat without a marine toilet. Small boats, however, offer more personal service and less-crowded dives.)

Strict marine protection laws prohibit you from taking any marine life from many areas around the island. Always check with the **Department of Environment** (☎345/949–8469) before diving, snorkeling, and fishing. To report violations, call **Marine Enforcement** (☎345/948–6002).

Ambassador Divers (✉ *Comfort Suites, West Bay Rd., Seven Mile Beach* ☎345/743–5513 ⊕ *www.ambassadordivers.*

com) is an on-call guided scuba-diving operation offering dive trips to parties of two to eight persons. Co-owner Jason Washington's favorite spots include the excellent dive sites on the West Side and South and North Wall. Ambassador offers two boats, a 28-foot custom Parker (maximum six divers), another 28-foot completely custom overhauled boat, and a 26-footer primarily for snorkeling. They are available around the clock, and interested divers can be picked up from their hotels or condos. The price for a two-tank boat dive is $105 ($90 for two or more days).

Cayman Aggressor IV (☎ *985/385–2628, 345/949–5551, or 800/348–2628 ⊕ www.aggressor.com*), a 110-foot live-aboard dive boat refitted in 2007, offers one-week cruises for divers who want to get serious bottom time, as many as five dives daily. Nine staterooms with en suite bathrooms sleep 18. The fresh food is basic but bountiful (three meals, two in-between snacks), and the crew offers a great mix of diving, especially when weather allows the crossing to Little Cayman. Digital photography and video courses are also offered (there's an E-6 film processing lab aboard) as well as Nitrox certification. The price is $2,395–$2,895 double-occupancy for the week.

🕙 **Deep Blue Divers** (✉ *Cayman Islands Yacht Club, C27, Governors Harbour* ☎ *345/947–0116 or 345/916–1293 ⊕ www. deepbluediverscayman.com*) has two custom-designed 27-foot outward driven Dusky boats, which ensure a smooth, speedy ride and can access sites that much larger boats can't. They accept a maximum of eight guests, under the watchful eyes of Patrick Weir and Nick Buckley, who joke that diving is "relaxing under pressure." Personalized valet attention and flexibility have ensured a high repeat clientele; Nick's particularly good with kids and has taught three generations of families. He's often asked by happy customers to join them on dive trips around the world. He and his crew delight in telling stories about Cayman culture and history, including pirate tales and often hilarious anecdotes about life in the Cayman Islands. He offers underwater photo/video services and a range of PADI- and NAUI-certified courses; beach pickup is included.

★ **Fodor's**Choice **Divetech** (✉ *Cobalt Coast Resort & Suites, 18-A*
🕙 *Sea Fan Dr., West Bay* ☎ *345/946–5658 or 888/946–5656 ⊕ www.divetech.com* ✉ *Lighthouse Point, near Boatswain's Beach, 571 N.W. Point Rd., West Bay* ☎ *345/949–1700*) has opportunities for shore diving at its two north-coast

locations, which provide loads of interesting creatures, a mini-wall, and, of course, the North Wall. With quick access to West Bay, the boats are quite comfortable. Technical training (a specialty of owner Nancy Easterbrook) is unparalleled, and the company offers good, personable service as well as the latest gadgetry such as underwater CCR scooters. They even mix their own gases, and there are multiple dive instructors for different specialties, with everything from extended cross-training Ranger packages to Dive and Art workshop weeks, popular photography/video seminars with Courtney Platt to deep diving, less disruptive free diving, search and recovery, stingray interaction, reef awareness, and underwater naturalist. Snorkel and diving programs are available year-round for children ages eight and up, SASY for five and up. Excellent multi-day discounts are a bonus.

Don Foster's Dive Cayman Islands (✉ *218 S. Church St., George Town* ☎ *345/949–5679 or 345/945–5132* ⊕ *www.donfosters.com*) has a pool with a shower and also snorkeling along the ironshore at Casuarina Point, easily accessed starting at 20 feet, extending to depths of 55 feet. There's an underwater photo center, night dives, and Stingray City trips with divers and snorkelers in the same boat (perfect for families). Specialties include Nitrox courses and Underwater Naturalist guided dives. Rates are competitive, and there's free shuttle pickup/drop-off along Seven Mile Beach. If you go out with Don, he might recount stories of his wild times as a drummer in the islands, but all the crews are personable and efficient. The drawback is larger boats and groups.

Eden Rock Diving Center (✉ *124 S. Church St., George Town* ☎ *345/949–7243* ⊕ *www.edenrockdive.com*), south of George Town, provides easy access to Eden Rock and Devil's Grotto. It features full equipment rental, lockers, shower facilities, and a full range of PADI courses from a helpful, cheerful staff. Costs for guided shore dives and two-tank dives on its Pro 42 jet boat are cheaper than those of most other outfits, without sacrificing quality or comfort.

★ **Indigo Divers** (✉ *Box 30445, Seven Mile Beach* ☎ *345/946–7279 or 345/525–3932* ⊕ *www.indigodivers.com*) is a full-service PADI teaching facility specializing in exclusive guided dives from its 28-foot Sea Ray Bow Rider or 32-foor Donzi Express Cruiser. Comfort and safety are paramount, the attention to detail superior. Luxury

Divers exploring one of Grand Cayman's famous reefs

transfers in a Chevy Avalanche are included, and the boat is stocked with goodies like fresh fruit and homemade cookies. Captain Chris Alpers has impeccable credentials: a licensed U.S. Coast Guard captain, PADI Master Scuba Diver Trainer, and Cayman Islands Marine Park officer. Katie Alpers specializes in wreck, DPV, dry suit, boat, and deep diving, but her primary role is resident videographer, and she edits superlative DVDs of your adventures, complete with music and titles. They guarantee a maximum of six divers. The individual attention is a bit pricier, but the larger your group, the more you save.

Neptune's Divers (⊠ *West Bay Rd., Seven Mile Beach* ☎ *345/ 945–3990* ⊕ *www.neptunesdivers.com*) offers competitive package rates, in addition to free shuttle service along Seven Mile Beach. It's also one of the best companies for physically challenged divers. Captain Keith Keller and his staff try to customize trips as best they can, taking no more than eight divers out on their 30-foot custom Island Hopper and 36-foot Poseidon Crusader. A wide range of PADI courses are available; the instructors are patient and knowledgeable about reef life. The operation is computer-friendly to permit longer bottom time.

★ **Fodor's Choice Ocean Frontiers** (*Compass Point,* ⊠ *346 Austin Connelly Dr., East End* ☎ *345/947–7500 or 800/348–6096* ⊕ *www.oceanfrontiers.com*) is an excellent ecocentric operation, offering friendly small-group diving and a technical training facility, exploring the less trammeled, trafficked East End. Some trips also depart from the Kaibo Yacht Club in Cayman Kai to explore the North Wall; you may even go as far as 12-Mile Bank, where an old 250-foot fuel barge wreck sits in 115-feet depth with strong currents—not for recreational divers, but an astonishing site exploding with color from rare yellow jackfish to strawberry sponges, with visibility up to 200 feet. The company provides valet service, personalized attention, a complimentary courtesy shuttle, and an emphasis on green initiatives and specialized diving, including unguided computer, Technical, Nitrox, and cave diving for advanced participants. But even beginners and rusty divers (there's a wonderful Skills Review and Tune-Up course) won't feel over their heads. Special touches include hot chocolate and homemade muffins on night dives; owner Steve is an ordained minister and will conduct weddings in full face masks.

☪ **Red Sail Sports** (☎ *345/949–5965 or 877/733–7245* ⊕ *www. redsailcayman.com*) offers daily trips from most of the major hotels. Dives are often run as guided tours, a perfect option for beginners. If you're experienced and your air lasts a long time, consult the boat captain to see if he requires that you come up with the group as determined by the first person who runs low on air. There is a full range of kids' dive options for ages 5 to 15. The company also operates Stingray City tours, dinner and sunset sails, and just about every major water sport from wave-runners to windsurfing.

Sundivers (✉ *The Cracked Conch, N.W. Point Rd., West Bay* ☎ *345/916–1064 or 345/949–6606* ⊕ *www.sundivers.ky*), owned by Ollen Miller, one of Cayman's first dive masters, has the newly renovated on-site dive shop at the Cracked Conch restaurant next to Boatswain's Beach, offering competitive rates for air, lessons, and rentals; shore access to Turtle Reef' and such amenities as showers, rinse tanks, and storage.

Sunset Divers (✉ *Sunset House, 390 S. Church St., George Town* ☎ *345/949–7111 or 800/854–4767* ⊕ *www.sunset-house.com*), a full-service PADI teaching facility located at George Town hostelry and catering to the scuba set, has great shore diving and five dive boats to hit all sides of the island. Divers can be independent on their boats as long as they abide by the maximum time and depth standards. Instruction and packages are comparatively

Learning In-Depth

A common kitschy T-shirt reads DIVERS DO IT DEEPER AND LONGER, but that's certainly the goal of any scuba enthusiast. That's where new specialized equipment and courses come in. Technical diving refers to advanced dives conducted beyond the 130-foot depth limit, requiring a decompression stop, or into an overhead environment. DiveTech's Nancy Easterbrook compares it to "skiing a really steep mogul-ly double black diamond, or scaling a sheer cliff face. It takes practice and determination." The courses and equipment are also much more expensive.

Terms you'll soon hear are Nitrox, Advanced Nitrox, Normoxic, Trimix, and Advanced Trimix. These all enable divers to explore deeper depths safely at greater length. Nitrox, for example, is highly oxygenated nitrogen (32% as opposed to "normal" air, with 21%), which enables you to dive for a longer time before reaching decompression limits. And just like the oxygen-bar craze of the last decade, Nitrox invigorates you, reducing fatigue after dives.

Rebreather diving (Closed Circuit Rebreathers, or CCR) is another popular way to extend dive time, up to three hours 100 feet down. You breathe warmer, moister air (reducing the chance of chills at lower depths). As a bonus, denizens of the deep are less wary, as there are no bubbles.

inexpensive. Though the company is not directly affiliated with acclaimed underwater shutterbug Cathy Church (whose shop is also at the hotel), she'll often work with the instructors on special courses.

FISHING

The Cayman Islands are widely hailed as a prime action-packed destination for all types of sportfishing, from casting in the flats for the wily, surprisingly strong "gray ghost" bonefish to trolling for giant, equally combative blue marlin. Conditions are ideal for big game fish: The water temperature varies only 8 to 10 degrees annually, so the bait and their pelagic predators hang out all year. The big lure for anglers is the big game-fish run near the coast, as close as a quarter-mile offshore.

Experienced, knowledgeable local captains charter boats with top-of-the-line equipment, bait, ice, and often lunch included in the price (usually $500–$750 per half-day, $800–$1,500 for a full day). Options include deep-sea, reef, bone, tarpon, light-tackle, and fly-fishing. June and July are particularly good all-around months for reeling in blue marlin, yellow- and blackfin tuna, dolphinfish (dorado), and bonefish. Bonefish have a second season in the winter months, along with wahoo and skipjack tuna. Marine Park laws prohibit fishing or taking any type of marine life in protected areas. Local captains promote conservation and sportsmanship through catch-and-release of both reef and pelagic fish not intended for eating and all billfish, unless they are local records or potential tournament winners.

★ Longtime fisherman Captain Eugene Ebanks established **Bayside Watersports** (☎ 345/949–3200 ⊕ www.baysidewater-sports.com) in 1974. The family-run West Bay–based company operates two first-class fishing boats, the "Hooker" fleet, ranging from 31 feet (*Lil Hooker*) to 53 feet (the *Happy Hooker,* which sleeps six for overnight charters farther afield). The tradition began with the original *Hooker,* named after the Moldcraft Hooker lure, whose team led by son Al Ebanks caught a 189.4-pound yellowfin tuna in 1989 that still stands as the island record. They do reef-, tarpon-, and bonefishing trips as well, but their real specialty is deep-water fishing, such as at 12-Mile Bank, a 3-mi (5-km) strip just 90 minutes west of Grand Cayman, where leviathan fighters congregate around the submerged peak of an underwater mountain.

Black Princess Charters (☎ 345/916–6319 *or* 345/949–0400 ⊕ www.fishgrandcayman.com), owned by Captain Chuckie Ebanks, who offers deep-sea and reef fishing as well as snorkel trips on his fully equipped and supplied eponymous 40-foot Sea Ray. His rates are comparatively reasonable, and he can arrange clean, inexpensive local accommodations.

Captain Asley's Watersports (☎ 345/949–3054 ✎ cayfish@candw.ky) prides itself on personable, flexible, and customized charter services for deep-sea, light-tackle, and bonefishing. The cost for a privately chartered fishing vessel can run from $400 (small boat, half-day) to $1,500 (big boat, full day). The owner of this family-run operation, Captain Asley has plied these waters since the 1960s; now his affable, patient kids and extended family (usually Darrin, Dwight, and Kevin) captain the five boats. They're all expert coaches, coaxing a confident approach even from first-timers, though they'll take experts to troll all the lesser-known depths; ESPN's Bass Pros selected them as a "preferred outfitter guide." Like many other operators, they also run snorkeling, diving, and sunset and dinner cruises.

The excellent, environmentally conscious dive outfit **Ocean Frontiers** (⊠ *Compass Point, Austin Connelly Dr., East End* ☎ *345/947–7500 or 800/348–6096* ⊕ *www.oceanfrontiers. com*) also offers fishing on a 26-foot, diesel-powered Mer-Panga with depth sounder, GPS, six lines, and all safety gear including life jackets and emergency radio beacons. Captain Joey Welcome plies his secret spots along the East End, where marlin, wahoo, and tuna congregate within a mile offshore, and at Coxain Bank, which teems with snapper. The inner reef is ideal for shore and night fishing, providing a sheltered site for tarpon, snapper, and barracuda.

Oh Boy Charters (☎ *345/949–6341 or 345/926–0898* ⊕ *www. ohboycharters.com*) charters a 60-foot yacht with complete amenities for day (and overnight) trips, as well as sunset and dinner cruises, plus a 34-foot Crusader. Alvin Ebanks—son of Caymanian marine royalty, the indomitable Captain Marvin Ebanks (still going strong in his 90s)—jokingly claims he's been playing in and plying the waters for a century and tells tales (tall and otherwise) of his father reeling him in for fishing expeditions. No more than eight passengers on the deep-sea boats ensures the personal touch (snorkeling on the 60-footer accommodates more people). Guests always receive a good selection of their catch; if you prefer others to do the cooking, go night fishing, which includes dinner. All trips include a free Seven Mile Beach shuttle.

★ Captain Ronald Ebanks of **R&M Fly Shop and Charters** (☎ *345/947–3146 or 345/946–0214* ⊕ *www.flyfishgrand-cayman.com*) is arguably the island's most knowledgeable fly-fishing guide, with more than 10 years' experience in Cayman and Scotland. He also runs light-tackle trips on a 24-foot Robalo. Everyone from beginners—even children—to experienced casters will enjoy and learn from the trip; free transfers are included.

★ **Sea Star Charters** (☎ *345/949–1016; 345/916–5234 after 8* AM), aka Clinton's Watersports, is run by Clinton Ebanks, a fine and very friendly Caymanian who will do whatever it takes to make sure that you have a wonderful time on his two 25- and 31-foot cabin cruisers, enjoying light-tackle, bone-, and bottom-fishing. He's a good choice for beginners and offers a nice cultural experience, as well as sailing charters and snorkeling with complimentary transportation and equipment. Only cash and traveler's checks are accepted.

White Rose Charters (☎ *345/949–1012, 345/325–1472 cell*), owned by Captain Alphonso Ebanks, has one of the highest catches in bone-, tarpon-, reef, and drift fishing. He has two boats, the 24-foot *White Rose #1* and 39-foot *White Rose #2,* both fully equipped for fishing and comfort, and he knows every crevice and cranny along the shore.

GOLF

The 9-hole, 3,515-yard, par-36 **Blue Tip** (⊠ *Ritz-Carlton Grand Cayman, West Bay Rd., Seven Mile Beach* ☎ *345/943–9000 or 345/815–6500* ⊕ *www.ritzcarlton. com*) was designed by Greg Norman and built on previously sacrosanct mangroves. Five of the holes are par-4s, and two are par-5s, including a 600-yarder. The course is open only to guests of the Ritz-Carlton and to owners of the Residences (luxury condominiums). No jeans are allowed, and you must wear a collared golf shirt. Club rentals are available at the pro shop. Greens fees are $125 for 9 holes, $200 for 18 holes.

The **Britannia** (⊠ *West Bay Rd., Seven Mile Beach* ☎ *345/745–4653 or 345/949–3406* ⊕ *www.britannia-golf.com*) golf course, next to the Grand Cayman Beach Suites, was designed by Jack Nicklaus. The course is really three in one—a 9-hole, par-70 regulation course; an 18-hole, par-57 executive course; and a Cayman course played with a Cayman ball that travels about half the distance of a regulation ball. Signature tough holes include 3 and 10; beware tricky winds on 7 through 11. Greens fees are $100 for 9 holes, $150 for 18 ($75/$100 during the off-season). Amenities include a full pro shop and the Britannia Golf Grille (particularly good breakfasts and local fare).

Formerly the Links at Safehaven, the par-71, 6,605-yard, 18-hole **North Sound Club** (⊠ *Off West Bay Rd., Seven Mile Beach* ☎ *345/947–4653* ⊕ *www.northsoundclub.com*) is infamous among duffers for its strong gusts, giving the ball unexpected loft or backspin. Roy Case factored the wind into his design, which incorporates lots of looming water and sand traps; the handsome setting features many mature mahogany and silver thatch trees. Wear shorts at least 14 inches long (15 inches for women); no T-shirts are allowed, only collared shirts. Greens fees change seasonally; in winter it's $175 ($105 for 9 holes), including cart. There's a twilight discount, fine pro shop, and open-air bar with large-screen TVs.

GUIDED TOURS

Taxi drivers will give you a personalized tour of Grand Cayman for about $25 per hour for up to three people. Or you can choose a fascinating helicopter ride, a horseback or mountain-bike journey, a 4x4 safari expedition, or a full-day bus excursion. Ask your hotel to help you make arrangements.

Costs and itineraries for island tours are about the same regardless of the tour operator. Half-day tours average $40–$50 a person and generally include a visit to Hell and the Turtle Farm at Boatswain's Beach aquatic park in West Bay, as well as shopping downtown. Full-day tours ($60–$80 per person) add lunch, a visit to Bodden Town (the first settlement), and the East End, where you stop at the Queen Elizabeth II Botanic Park, blowholes (if the waves are high) on the ironshore, and the site of the wreck of the *Ten Sails* (not the wreck itself—just the site). The pirate graves in Bodden Town were destroyed during Hurricane Ivan in 2008, and the blowholes were partially filled. As you can tell, land tours here are low-key. Children under 12 often receive discounts.

A. A. Transportation Services (✉ *Grand Cayman* ☎ *345/949–6598 or 345/926–8294*) offers taxis and tour buses—ask for Burton Ebanks.

Cayman Safari (✉ *Grand Cayman* ☎ *345/925–3001 or 866/389–8559* ⊕ *www.caymansafari.com*) hits the usual sights but emphasizes interaction with locals, so you learn about craft traditions, folklore, and herbal medicines.

Majestic Tours (✉ *Grand Cayman* ☎ *345/949–7773* ⊕ *www. majestic-tours.com*) caters mostly to cruise-ship and incentive groups but also offers similar options to individuals and can customize tours; it's particularly good for West Bay, including Boatswain's Beach and Hell.

McCurley Tours (✉ *Grand Cayman* ☎ *345/949–7222*) is owned by B.A. McCurley, a free-spirited freewheeling Midwesterner who's lived in Cayman for 24 years and knows everything and everyone on the East End. Not only is she encyclopedic and flexible, she also offers car rentals and

CLOSE UP

Turtles and Cats

Blessed with arguably the world's largest turtle nesting grounds, Cayman developed into the center of the Caribbean turtle industry for nearly two centuries. English settlers on Jamaica became particularly proficient turtlers. Once they hunted the population into near-extinction by the early 1800s, Caymanians went to sea for months, trapping and supplying turtles from Cuba and Nicaragua well into the 20th century. Even today roughly 20 locals are licensed to catch four turtles annually, and the Cayman Turtle Farm (an environmentally sensitive "working" part of the Boatswain's Beach marine theme park) supplies the local market with farm-raised meat.

Turtling led indirectly to one of the proud Caymanian contributions to shipbuilding, the catboat. The design of this basic sailboat (not a catamaran) is usually credited to Cayman Brac's Daniel Jervis circa 1904, though Cape Cod and Chesapeake Bay boaters debate the origin. He decided to bring the stern to a sharp point, similar to New England/Canadian whalers and peapods, placing the mast in the bow. Supposedly, the shape permitted quicker course reversal and less drag, while the lack of keel depth facilitated beaching the boat. Ballast provided stability, and only a yoke was used to steer the rudder. Turtlers would place their necks in a groove that helped focus the quest, then was used to haul in catch.

The Cayman Catboat Club holds several annual regattas as well as free rides during special events, including Pirates Week.

transfers for travelers staying on the East End; don't be surprised if she tells you what to order at lunch, especially if it's off the menu.

Tropicana Tours (⊠ *Grand Cayman* ☎ *345/949–0944* ⊕ *www. tropicana-tours.com*) offers several excellent Cayman highlights itineraries on its larger buses, including Stingray City stops, as well as reef-runner adventures across the North Sound through the mangrove swamps.

HIKING

★ The National Trust's internationally significant **Mastic Trail** (⊠ *Frank Sound Rd., entrance by fire station at botanic park, Breakers, East End* ☎ *345/749–1121 for guide reservations* ⊕ *www.nationaltrust.org.ky*), used in the 1800s as the only direct path to and from the North Side, is a rugged 2-mi (3-km) slash through 776 dense acres of woodlands, black mangrove swamps, savannah, agricultural remnants, and ancient rock formations. It embraces more than 700 species, including Cayman's largest remaining contiguous ancient forest (one of the heavily deforested Caribbean's last examples). A comfortable walk depends on weather—winter is better because it's drier, though flowering plants like the banana orchid set the trail ablaze in summer. Call the National Trust to determine suitability and to book a guide for $25; tours are run daily from 9 to 5 by appointment only, regularly on Wednesday at 9 AM. Or walk on the wild side with a $5 guidebook that provides information on the ecosystems you traverse, the endemic wildlife you might encounter, seasonal changes, poisonous plants to avoid, and folkloric uses of various flora. The trip takes about three hours.

HORSEBACK RIDING

Coral Stone Stables (☎ 345/916–4799 ⊕ www.csstables.com) offers 90-minute leisurely horseback rides along the white-sand beaches at Bodden Town and inland trails at Savannah; complimentary photos are included. Your guide is Nolan Stewart, whose ranch contains 20 horses, chickens, and "randy" roosters. Nolan offers a nonstop narrative on flora, fauna, and history. He's an entertaining, endless font of local information, some of it unprintable. Rides are $80; swim rides cost $120.

Horseback in Paradise (☎ 345/945–5839 or 345/916–3530 ⊕ www.caymanhorseriding.com) is the domain of gregarious Nicki Eldemire, who loves telling stories about horse training and life on Cayman. She leads guided tours through Barkers National Park on the West End: a pristine peninsular area filled with enthralling plant and animal life along the beaches and wetlands. The steep price of $100 includes transportation, but it's a private, exclusive experience with no more than four riders per group.

Mary's Stables & Equestrian Center (☎ 345/949–7360 or 345/516–1751), the top-notch training facility for the Cayman national equestrian team, offers classic English riding lessons (dressage is also an option) and allows you to help groom the exotic horses.

Pampered Ponies (☎ 345/945–2262 or 345/916–2540 ⊕ www.ponies.ky) offers what is called "the ultimate tanning

Horseback riding in Barkers National Park

machine": horses walking, trotting, and cantering along the beaches. You can do either private tours or a variety of guided trips, including sunset, moonlight, and swim rides along the uninhabited beach from Conch Point to Morgan's Harbour on the north tip beyond West Bay.

KAYAKING

🕙 **Cayman Kayaks** (☎ *345/746–3249 or 345/926–4467* ⊕ *www.*
★ *caymankayaks.com*) explores Grand Cayman's protected mangrove wetlands, providing an absorbing discussion of the indigenous animals (including a mesmerizing stop at a gently pulsing, non-stinging Cassiopeia jellyfish pond) and plants, the effects of hurricanes, and conservation efforts. Even beginners will find the tours easy (the guides dub it low-impact aerobics), and the sit-on-top kayaks are quite stable and comfortable. The Bio Bay tour involves more-strenuous paddling, but the underwater light show is magical as millions of bioluminescent microorganisms called dinoflagellates glow like fireflies when disturbed. It runs only on moonless nights for full effect and books well in advance. All tours depart from Kaibo Beach Bar in Cayman Kai; costs run from $39 to $55 (some tours offer kids' discounts).

SAILING

Though Cayman has a large sailing community, it isn't a big charter-yacht destination. Still, you can skipper your own craft (albeit sometimes under the watchful eye of the boat's captain). The protected waters of the North Sound are especially delightful, but chartering a sailboat is also a wonderful way to discover lesser-known snorkeling, diving, and fishing spots around the island.

Cayman Island Sailing Club (✉ *Selkirk Dr., Red Bay* ☎ *345/947–7913* ⊕ *www.sailing.ky*) is a private club that sometimes offers lessons to non-members but always has boats, including J-22s, for hourly or half- and full-day rental (CI$30–CI$300). The club's a great hangout, and chatting up the friendly members provides invaluable insights into all subjects Caymanian.

Mike High and Neil Galway, both experienced RYA Yacht Masters, run **Sail Cayman** (☎ *345/945–4474 or 345/916–4333* ⊕ *www.sailcayman.com*), offering 33-foot Nautica rib ecotours and a plush 44-foot Nautigal Gibsea for full-day or half-day private sailing or snorkeling. Though not bareboating, it is hands-on: You can crew and even captain if you enjoy sailing. Mike and Neil personalize the cruise to suit any family or group, accommodating a maximum of 12–15 passengers. A half-day runs $600–$700, full day $1,000–$1,200: if you have a large group, it's little more than the total price for crowded excursions with twice as many strangers.

SEA EXCURSIONS

The most impressive sights in the Cayman Islands are on and under water, and several submarines, semi-submersibles, glass-bottom boats, and Jules Verne–like contraptions allow you to see these underwater wonders without getting your feet wet. Sunset sails, dinner cruises, and other theme (dance, booze, pirate) cruises are available from $30–$60 per person.

☪ **Atlantis Submarines** (☎ *345/949–7700 or 800/887–8571*
★ ⊕ *www.atlantisadventures.com*) takes 48 passengers safely and comfortably along the Cayman Wall down to 100 feet. You peep through panoramic portholes as good-natured guides keep up a humorous but informative patter. A guide dons scuba gear to feed fish, who form a whirling frenzy of color rivaling anything by Picasso. At night, the 10,000-

Getting SASY

A few years ago, Wayne Hasson, a Cayman resident and owner of the live-aboard dive boat *Cayman Aggressor*, faced a dilemma. He and his wife, Anne, were both ardent, accomplished scuba divers and marine environmentalists. His children, then 5 and 7, understandably longed to share the diving experience, but their mother insisted that they simply snorkel atop the surface until they reached the age minimum of 12. They hated breathing in water and sputtering. So Hasson developed an ingenious compromise device that has already profoundly impacted the scuba industry and ocean education.

Hasson rigged a life vest with a pony bottle and regulator and let his kids try breathing from an air tank while positively buoyant at the surface. They remained face down without inhaling water, mimicking the feel of actual diving. The family worked on R&D for nearly a year with Custom Buoyancy, inventing and refining SASY (Supplied Air Snorkeling for Youth). The units resemble the real thing with life vest, small scuba tank (13 cubic feet as opposed to 19) in an adjustable holder,

and regulator (all integrating crucial safety features like child-proof attachments and stabilizing straps); any kid 5 or older could now enjoy "diving" with Mom and Dad safely and comfortably. Recognizing adults might also feel awkward with snorkeling gear, Hasson created SASA (Supplied Air Snorkeling for Adults), which differs in the tank size (19 to 30 cubic feet). Although "snuba" allows you to go underwater, the hose can prove cumbersome and restrict the scope of your movement; kids as young as 4 can enjoy the feel of dive equipment with SASY, but the snuba minimum age is 8.

The device promotes interest in diving from a younger age, but equally important, the patent, trademarks, and income from sales and licensing agreements belong to Oceans for Youth, a nonprofit organization the Hassons subsequently founded to educate youth about the marine environment and the vital connection between sea and land life. As Hasson states, "...the health of the world's oceans will soon become the responsibility of today's children."

watt lights show the kaleidoscopic underwater colors and nocturnal stealth predators more brilliantly than during the day. Try to sit toward the front so you can watch the pilot's nimble maneuverings and the depth gauge. If that literally in-depth tour seems daunting, get up-close and personal on the *Seaworld Observatory* semi-submersible (glorified glass-bottom boat), which just cruises the harbor (including glimpses of the *Cali* and *Balboa* shipwrecks). Cost for the submarine is $99, $49 for the semisubmersible. Children get discounts.

★ **Fodor's Choice** Scientists often call our oceans just as mysteri-
☺ ous as deep space, and **Deep See Cayman** (☎ 345/926–3343 ⊕ *www.deepcayman.com*) provides spellbinding proof. Its personable owner was pilot for Paul Allen's *Octopus,* one of the world's largest yachts; helped film David Attenborough's compelling *The Blue Planet;* and currently works with Scripps on underwater research with his little toy, an ROV underwater robot that plumbs the Cayman Trench's depths down to 2,400 feet while you comfortably watch the real-time high-definition images it transmits aboard a luxury yacht, the *Deep Seeker.* Some wrecks have gradually sunk to those depths, but the real prize is otherworldly oddly-shaped creatures straight out of sci-fi. The two-hour excursions depart from the West Bay dock several times daily (including a night tour), with an 8-person maximum, costing a reasonable $74 ($5 discount for advance online booking). Gary will even let kids particularly adept with joysticks from video game mastery navigate the Little Tyche (an appropriate name, given the eager would-be pilots).

☺ The **Jolly Roger** (☎ 345/945–7245 ⊕ *www.jollyrogercayman. com*) is a two-thirds-size replica of Christopher Columbus's 17th-century Spanish galleon *Nina;* the company also owns the *Valhalla,* a wooden Norwegian brig built in 1934 that holds more than 100 passengers. On the afternoon snorkel cruise, play Captain Jack Sparrow while experiencing swashbuckling pirate antics including a trial, sword fight, and walking of the plank; the kids can fire the cannon, help hoist the main sail, and scrub the decks (it's guaranteed that they will love it even if they loathe doing chores at home). The evening options (sunset and dinner sails) are more-standard booze cruises, less appropriate for the kids. Food is more appropriate to the brig, and it's more yo-ho-hokum than remotely authentic, but fun. Prices range from $40 to $60.

On the semisubmersible **Nautilus** (☎ 345/945–1355 ⊕ *www. nautilus.ky*) you can sit above deck or venture below, where you can view the reefs and marine life through a sturdy glass hull. A one-hour undersea tour is $50. Watch divers feed the fish, or take the Captain Nemo's Tour, which includes snorkeling; there's also a catamaran cruise to Stingray City and land-sea tours. As on the Atlantis semisubmersible, you get a close-up look at the Cheeseburger Reef and two of Cayman's mysterious shipwrecks (*Cali* and *Balboa*), with a bit of entertaining educational narrative.

☺ **Sea Trek** (☎ *345/949–0008* ⊕ *www.seatrekcayman.com*) offers helmet diving, permitting you to walk and breathe 26 feet underwater—without getting your hair wet—for an hour. No training or even swimming ability is required, and you can wear glasses. Guides give a thorough safety briefing, and a sophisticated system of compressors and cylinders provides triple the amount of air necessary for normal breathing, while a safety diver program ensures four distinct levels of backup. The result at near-zero gravity resembles an exhilarating moonwalk. The minimum age is eight. The cost is $89 per person ($79 per person for groups of four or more).

SKATING AND SKATEBOARDING

★ **Fodor'sChoice Black Pearl Skate and Surf Park** (⊠ *Red Bay Rd.,*
☺ *Grand Harbour* ☎ *345/947–4161 or 345/925–8576* ⊕ *www. blackpearl.ky*), a great skating park (skateboards, in-line skates), is the size of a football field (at 62,000 square feet the world's second-largest such facility), with stairs, half-pipe, rails, 20-foot vert ramp, and flow course offering innumerable lies. International professional skaters like Tony Hawk, Ryan Sheckler, and Mark Appleyard have practiced their kickflips, tailslides, wheelies, and grinds here. The park also has one of only three Waveloch standing wave-surf machines in the world, which generates adjustable 11-foot swells. You can arrange lessons or rent anything you need at the adjacent skate/surf shop. The outdoor patio of the surprisingly elegant Brick House restaurant (terrific pizzas and playground) is the perfect vantage point for the rad performances that local daredevils mount Friday and Saturday nights.

SNORKELING

The proximity of healthy, Technicolor reef to the Grand Cayman shore means endless possibilities for snorkelers. Some sites require you to simply wade or swim into the surf; others are only accessible via boat. Nearly every snorkeling outfit follows the same route, beginning with the scintillating Stingray City and Sandbar. They usually continue to the adjacent Coral Gardens and often farther out along the Barrier Reef. Equipment is included, sometimes drinks, snacks, and lunch. Half-day tours run $35–$40, full-day $60–$70, and there are often extras such as kids' discounts and a complimentary shuttle to and from Seven Mile Beach resorts. Other popular trips combine Eden Rock, Cheeseburger Reef, and the wreck of the *Cali* off George Town. Most decent-size boats offer cover, but bring sunscreen and a hat.

SNORKELING SITES

A **Barrier Reef** separates the North Sound and Cayman's celebrated wall drop-off (part of a 6,000-foot underwater mountain). You can snorkel along the shallow side, which is crawling with critters of all shapes, sizes, and colors.

★ **Cemetery Reef** sits 50 yards out from the north end of Seven Mile Beach, within walking distance of several condo resorts. Fish here are also accustomed to being fed, so blue tangs to blue-headed wrasse and bat jacks to black durgeon could swarm around you.

Cheeseburger Reef earned its unusual moniker thanks to its location straight out from the downtown Burger King. It's also known as Soto's Reef after legendary diver Bob Soto, one of the islands' original dive operators. The eye-popping, 12,000-year-old coral formations begin 20 yards offshore, with larger heads a mere 10 feet down, though it reaches depths of 40 feet. You can swim through numerous tunnels where turtles and tarpon hang out; people have long fed fish in the area, and they're not shy, wanting it their way, but beware of snapping snappers if you bring food.

Coral Gardens, which is very near Stingray Sandbar, attracts nurse sharks, moray eels, queen conch, lobster, and not just schools but universities of jacks, tangs, sergeant majors, parrotfish, yellowtails, and others playing hide-and-seek with riotously colored soft and hard corals. It really is like swimming in an aquarium.

Eden Rock, in George Town next to Paradise Bar & Grill, is even more spectacular for divers, who can explore its caves and tunnels, then proceed to Devil's Grotto. Still, from the surface you can see schools of sergeant majors, yellowtail snappers, parrotfish, tarpon, Bermuda chubs, even the occasional stingray and turtle.

Stingray City

Hundreds of gray and khaki Atlantic Southern stingrays, resembling inquisitive alien life forms, enact an acrobatic aqua-ballet as they circle this North Sound site seeking handouts from divers and snorkelers. The area actually encompasses two separate locations: Stingray City, called by many the world's great 12-foot dive, and the nearby sandbar, where people can wade in waist-deep water.

Steve Irwin's tragic demise rekindled humankind's age-old fear of these beautiful, mysterious "devil" creatures with their barbed tails. The Atlantic southern stingrays are a different, smaller species than the stingray that killed Irwin and as close to tame as possible. Shy and unaggressive by nature, they use their tails only in defense; nonetheless, don't pick rays up unless you follow your guide's careful instructions.

Stingray City's origins can be traced to local fishermen who would moor inside the fringe reef, then clean their catch, tossing the scraps overboard. Captain Marvin Ebanks, who still runs trips in his nineties, recalls feeding them as a child. The rays, who hunt via keen smell (and sensitive electro-receptors stippling their underside, near the mouth), realized they'd discovered their own restaurant and began hanging around. They slowly became inured to human interaction, rarely displaying the species' typical timidity. They glide like graceful giants (up to 4 feet in diameter), practically nuzzling you with their silken bellies, begging pet-like for food. Indeed, crews recognize them (and vice versa), fondly giving the rays nicknames (Hoo-Ray, X-Ray, Gamma Ray), insisting they have distinct personalities.

Instead of teeth, their mouths contain vise-like sucking grips. Keep your palms face-up and as flat as possible so they don't unintentionally "swallow" your fingers (their eyes are located atop their bodies, so they hover over and practically hoover your hand in excitement).

More formal visitation guidelines have now been established because 5 to 20 boats visit twice daily, and the population is growing at an alarming rate. Feeding is restricted to appointed tour operators; only natural bait fish like ballyhoo and squid are permitted; the food amount is limited; and any remains and litter must be removed. Many Caymanians and divers oppose altered feeding because it changes the ecosystem's natural food chain. But they concede the good outweighs the bad: The interaction is magical, not to mention fostering greater appreciation and environmental awareness.

★ Fodor'sChoice **Stingray City and Sandbar** is the stellar attraction on Grand Cayman and simply not to be missed; dozens of boats head there several times daily. The area is always less crowded if you can go on a day when there are fewer cruise ships in port.

The **Wreck of the** *Cali* sits offshore in George Town harbor roughly 50 yards out from Rackam's and Hammerheads pubs. You can still identify parts such as engines and winches of this old sailing freighter, which settled about 20 feet down. The sponges are particularly vivid, and tropical fish, shrimp, and lobster abound. Many operators based in George Town and Seven Mile Beach come here, as well as Eden Rock.

SNORKELING OPERATORS

Bayside Watersports (☎ *345/949–3200* ⊕ *www.baysidewatersports.com*) offers half-day snorkeling trips, North Sound beach lunch excursions, Stingray City and dinner cruises, and full-day deep-sea fishing. The company operates several popular boats out of West Bay's Morgan's Harbour. Full-day trips include lunch and conch diving in season (November–April).

☼ **Captain Crosby's Watersports** (☎ *345/945–4049 or 345/916–1725* ⊕ *www.captaincrosbyswatersports.com*) offers favorably priced snorkeling (and dive) excursions on a well-equipped 47-foot trimaran; $30 includes lunch. Captain Crosby is one of the more colorful captains among a group of genuine characters (he maintains a friendly rivalry with his fellow sailors regarding who really jump-started Stingray City tours). He's actively involved in preserving Cayman's maritime heritage as a founder of the Catboat Association. As a bonus, the trips are usually a little longer in duration; expect a sing-along with the captain on his guitar at some point. You can also arrange deep-sea fishing charters.

Captain Marvin's (☎ *345/949–4590, 345/945–6975, or 345/945–7306; 866/978–0022* ⊕ *www.captainmarvins.com*) offers multi-stop North Sound snorkel trips, as well as fishing charters and land tours. The indomitable, irrepressible Captain Marvin, one of the first regular Stingray City operators (in business since 1951), is still going strong in his early 90s. Full-day trips include lunch and conch dives in season (November–April), when the crew prepares marinated conch as the appetizer. The half-day (three hours) is a better deal than the quickie trips; the only drawback is

the relatively large groups. Reservations can be made only from 10 am to 3 pm on weekdays.

🌤 **Ebanks Watersports** (☎ *345/925–5273* ⊕ *www.ebanks-watersports.com*) is run by a large family long known for its aquatic activities. Shawn Ebanks offers a range of watersports activities, including various snorkeling tours, private charters, fishing, and his popular Yamaha wave-runner snorkel tours (the last are costlier, $125 for single riders, $150 for two). The crew is both friendly and experienced; they're particularly adept at holding the stingrays for the ultimate photo op; they'll even teach you how to pick one up yourself. His two custom-fitted boats (a 45-foot Garcia and 21-foot Sea Ray) include GPS navigation, VHS radio, freshwater shower, and other necessities.

🌤 Captain Dexter Ebanks runs **Fantasea Tours** (☎ *345/945–2182 or 345/916–0754* ⊕ *www.caymanislandsstingray-tours.com or www.dexters-fantaseatours.com*) on his 38-foot trimaran, *Don't Even Ask*. He doesn't pack you in like sardines (20 people max) and is particularly helpful with first-timers. Like many of the captains, he has his own pet names for the rays (ask him to find Lucy, whom he "adopted") and rattles off fascinating factoids during an entertaining, non-stop narration. It's a laid-back trip, with Bob Marley and Norah Jones on the sound system, and fresh fruit and rum punch on tap. He even has a money-back guarantee—if you don't enjoy, you don't pay.

Kirk Sea Tours (☎ *345/949–7278 or 345/949–6986* ⊕ *www.kirkseatours.com*) caters to cruise-ship passengers on 60- to 65-foot boats, as well as the 28-passenger glass-bottom *Reef Roamer,* snorkeling along the West Wall including Cheeseburger Reef. Sometimes it seems the snorkelers outnumber the fish, but the price is right and it's less frenzied obviously when fewer cruise ships are in port. Kirk also rents kayaks for $20 (and can arrange guided tours), Jet Skis ($65 single, $90 double per half-hour), paddle boats ($20), and snuba gear (with instruction).

🌤 **Red Sail Sports** (☎ *345/949–5965 or 877/733–7245* ⊕ *www.redsailcayman.com*) offers Stingray City, sunset, and evening sails (including dinner in winter) on their luxurious 65-foot catamarans, the *Spirits of Cayman, Poseidon,* Calypso, and *Ppalu*. They often carry large groups; although the service may not be personal, it will be efficient. In addition to the large cats, a glass-bottom boat takes passengers to Stingray City/Sandbar and nearby coral reefs. The cost ranges from $40 to $88.

SQUASH AND TENNIS

Most resorts and condominium complexes have their own courts, often lit for night play, but guests have top priority. When empty, you can book a court, which normally costs around $25 per hour.

The Courts (⊠ *West Bay Rd., Seven Mile Beach* ☎ *345/943–9000*) is a collaboration between Ritz-Carlton Grand Cayman and tennis coach Nick Bollettieri (former mentor of Andre Agassi, Monica Seles, Jim Courier, and the Williams sisters at his legendary Florida academy). The club offers three French-style clay courts and a Wimbledon-worthy grass court. Bollettieri personally trained the director, who gives private lessons ($125); Bollettieri himself occasionally drops by for tournaments and clinics. Court rental is $40 per hour.

South Sound Squash Club (⊠ *S. Sound Rd., George Town* ☎ *345/949–9469*) has seven international courts, changing room, bar and lounge, and coaches. It's a private club, but temporary memberships can be arranged.

WINDSURFING AND KITEBOARDING

The East End's reef-protected shallows extend for miles, offering ideal blustery conditions (15 to 35 mph in winter, 6- to 10-knot southerlies in summer) for windsurfing and kiteboarding. Boarders claim only rank amateurs will "tea-bag" (kite-speak for skidding in and out of the water) in those "nuking" winds. They also rarely "Hindenburg" (stall due to lack of breeze) off West Bay's Palmetto Point and Conch Point.

Cayman Windsurfing with Red Sail Sports at Morritt's (⊠ *Morritt's Tortuga Resort, Colliers, East End* ☎ *345/947–2097* ⊕ *www.tortugadivers.com*) offers a full range of top-flight equipment as well as lessons. Rentals start at $40 per hour; lessons are $65 per hour.

Cayman Windsurfing with Red Sail Sports at the Westin (⊠ *Westin Casuarina, West Bay Rd., Seven Mile Beach* ☎ *345/945–5965* ⊕ *www.redsailsports.com*) currently only offers lessons.

Kitesurf Cayman (⊠ *Barkers, near Papagallo's Restaurant, West Bay* ☎ *345/916–7742* ⊕ *www.kitesurfcayman.com*)

takes full advantage of the gusty conditions at Barkers beach. Head instructor Jhon Mora is a member of the Columbian National Kitesurfing Team; lessons, including tricks like loops and rolls, are geared toward experienced boarders.

Ocean Frontiers (✉ *Compass Point, Austin Connelly Dr., East End* ☎ *345/947–7500 or 800/348–6096* ⊕ *www.ocean-frontiers.com*) offers kiteboarding rentals and instruction, working with the respected Kitehouse team, with locations from Costa Rica to Key West. Private two-hour lessons are $250; half-day rental is $75. They'll help you achieve 60 feet of big air to practice your triple loops.

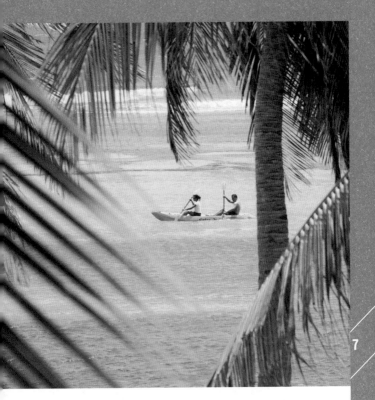

Cayman Brac

WORD OF MOUTH

"Cayman Brac is VERY laid-back. Hardly anyone there. Most tourists are divers. The diving at Brac was the best dive vacation we have done."

—Kima

By Jordan
Simon

**CAYMAN BRAC IS NAMED FOR ITS MOST DISTINCTIVE
FEATURE,** a moody, craggy limestone bluff (*brac* in the
Gaelic of the Scottish highlands fishermen who settled the
islands in the 18th century) that runs up the spine of the
12-mi (19-km) island, culminating in a sheer 140-foot cliff
at its eastern end, the country's highest and easternmost
point. The Bluff holds the angry Atlantic at bay, gradually
tapering like a coil losing its spring in the west. Nature's
artistry—and awesome power—is also evident in the many
caves and sinkholes that stipple the crag, long rumored
to hold pirates' gold. The island-scape is by far the most
dramatic in the Cayman Islands, though divers the world
over come for the spectacular underwater topography and
sponge-encrusted wrecks.

The Brac, as it's commonly called, sits just 90 mi (143 km)
northeast of Grand Cayman, accessible only via Cayman
Airways (and private boat), but it's nothing like the cosmopolitan and Americanized Grand Cayman. With only
1,800 residents—they call themselves Brackers—the island
has the feel and easy pace of a small town. Brackers are
known for their friendly attitude toward visitors, so it's
easy to strike up a conversation. You're never treated like a
stranger; locals wave at passing and might invite you home
for a traditional rundown (a thick, sultry fish stew) and
storytelling, usually about the sea, the turtle schooners, and
the great hurricane of 1932 (when the caves offered shelter
to islanders). Brackers are as calm and peaceful as their
island is rugged, having been violently sculpted by sea and
wind, most recently by Hurricane Paloma, which leveled the
island in November 2008 (locals quip that all 18 churches
sustained significant damage—but no bars).

Columbus first discovered the island by mistake during
his final voyage in 1503; explorers and privateers made
infrequent pit stops over the next three centuries, the Bluff
serving as a vital navigational landmark. Though the Brac
wasn't permanently settled until the 1830s, its short history
seethes with dramatic incident, from marauding pirates to
ravaging hurricanes. Today, despite its small size (roughly
12 mi by 1½ mi, or 14 square mi), the Brac is reinventing
itself as an ecocentric, adventure destination. Aside from
diving, bonefish in the shallows and game fish in the deeper
offshore waters lure anglers. The island hosts numerous
ecosystems from arid semi-desert stubbled with cacti to
ancient dry woodlands thick with exotic, fragrant flowers
and trees. More than 200 bird species, both indigenous

and migratory—including the endangered Cayman Brac parrot—flutter about. Nature trails filigree the interior, and several caves can be easily accessed. No surprise that the island is also considered one of the world's most exotic rock-climbing destinations, famous for its sheer vertical cliffs.

Hamlets with names like Watering Place, Cotton Tree Bay, Creek (Rock), and Spot Bay hold charming restored homes typical of seafaring architecture embroidered with carefully tended yards bursting with tropical blooms. Dozens of tiny churches line the road, bordered by sand graveyards. Despite the expats gradually boosting the year-round population, development remains as blissfully slow as the pace, though one longtime escapee from the stateside rat race grumbles about fancier cars and faster driving. There's still no stoplight, and traffic is defined by two locals stopping in the middle of the road to chat. It's as idyllic as a semi-developed island can be. Indeed, the Brac is the affectionate butt of jokes from other Caymanians: "Two 60-year-old Brackers were so bored they decided to put in a bomb threat," starts one; the punch line, depending on the teller, is that they fall asleep first—or that nothing results. Another, referring to the three or four families dominating the phone book, runs: "The most confusing day of the year on the Brac is Father's Day."

But Brackers take it all in stride, knowing their tranquil existence and abundant natural splendors give them the last laugh in the tourism sweepstakes.

ORIENTATION AND PLANNING

ORIENTATION

The island is quite easy to navigate for the most part. One main road hugs the north coast, another the south, while a paved rollercoaster bypass (Ashton Reid Drive) across the bluff roughly bisects the island, linking the two sides. Numerous gravel and dirt roads crisscross the island, but these are best avoided. The main hotel development and nicest beaches lie near the airport in the West End (the island's lowest point, at sea level). The southern road climbs the Bluff, passing spectacular caves and cliffs, ending at the Parrot Reserve and Lighthouse, with their splendid panoramic trails. The north road accesses the tiny towns of Stake Bay and Spot Bay, where several historic attractions are located.

TOP EXPERIENCES

■ **Diving.** This is unquestionably one of the world's great scuba destinations, from walls and wrecks exploding with kaleidoscopic marine life to wondrous manmade creations like the "Lost City of Atlantis" underwater installation.

■ **Lighthouse Walk.** In addition to thrilling Caribbean vistas and an eerie, almost lonely lunar look, you experience Nature's fierce elemental savagery, the crescendo of crashing surf and whipping wind.

■ **Local Crafts.** Several "old-timer" artisans keep traditions alive. Visiting their shops (often in their homes) is a marvelous immersion in Bracker culture.

■ **Caving.** Several caves are accessible—most easily, some via a mildly strenuous hike; in addition to striking natural formations, they played a vital role in sheltering islanders during storms.

■ **Museum-hop.** The Cayman Brac Museum pays tribute to this remote island's maritime tradition; though small, it's jam-packed with odd, often poignant little artifacts.

PLANNING

WHEN TO GO

The Brac is sleepy year-round, and there's slightly less difference price-wise between low and high season than on other islands, since diving, climbing, and fishing excel throughout the year, as does bird-watching (though winter attracts the migrant fowl). Still, summer represents savings, though some properties might close for maintenance in September during hurricane season.

GETTING HERE AND AROUND

BY AIR

Cayman Airways Express provides Twin Otter service several times daily from Grand Cayman to Cayman Brac. Depending on the flight route, you may land on Little Cayman first. The flight is approximately 40 minutes nonstop. Cayman Brac has its own small airport, Gerrard Smith International Airport (CYB).

BY CAR

You need a car to really explore Cayman Brac, though hotels often provide complimentary bikes. Your own valid driver's license is necessary to obtain a temporary local driving permit ($7.50), which can be used on any of the

Cayman Islands. Figure $40 to $45 per day, with compacts and mid-size generally at the low end, Jeeps and full-size median, and SUVs high-end.

Driving is on the left, British-style. Gasoline is quite expensive; there are only two stations (one at each end of the island), whose hours can be erratic. The main road circumnavigating the island and the bypass over the Bluff connecting the north and south coasts are well maintained. Yellow lines on roads indicate no parking zones. Most locals park on the side of the road.

Brac Rent-A-Car Ltd. offers mid-size cars, minivans, and Suzuki 4x4s. Rates are competitive and include unlimited mileage; the car will be delivered to the airport at no extra cost if you've reserved in advance (highly recommended). Four D's, which carries mostly Nissans, tends to have cheaper rates, though rarely offers discounts; pick-up and drop-off are included. B&S Motor Ventures offers compacts, mid-size vehicles, Jeeps, SUVs, and vans. The only on-site airport agency, CB Rent-A-Car, has Hondas, Toyotas, and Mitsubishis from compact to SUV.

Contacts B&S Motor Ventures (✉ West End ☎ 345/948–1646 or 345/948–2517 ⊕ www.bandsmv.com). **Brac Rent-A-Car Ltd.** (✉ Stake Bay ☎ 345/948–1515 or 345/948–0277 ⊕ www.bracrentals.com). **CB Rent-A-Car** (✉ Airport Dr., Gerrard Smith Airport, West End ☎ 345/948–2424 or 345/948–2847 ⊕ www.cbrentacar.com). **Four D's Car Rental** (✉ KIDCO Building, South Side, Spot Bay ✍ 4_d@candw.ky ☎ 345/948–1599 or 345/948–0459).

BY TAXI

Brackers often wear several hats, so your tour guide might also take you out fishing or serve you drinks; all of them are fonts of local lore and legend. An island day tour generally costs $24 per person, with a minimum of two people. Occasionally, you may have to wait to be picked up. Your hotel can arrange airport transfers. Rates are generally fixed: $8 to the closest hotels like Brac Reef Beach Resort, $15 to Cayman Breakers near the southeastern tip, $20 to the Bight and Spot Bay on the north side. Drivers will generally load up passengers from several properties, including individual villas.

The tourist office and the hotels have a list of preferred providers, including D&M Taxi and Tours, run by David Hurlston, who has a minivan as well as a 24-passenger bus for larger groups. He and his daughter Monica are courteous, knowledgeable guides, as is his father, O'Neil, who sometimes spells him and can regale you with soft-spoken stories of scaling the Bluff to collect water or herd cattle at 4 AM, as well as his adventures running bananas from Ecuador to Virginia.

Contacts **D&M Taxi and Tours** (☎ 345/939–0583 or 345/916–7226).

VISITOR INFORMATION

From 8:30 to 5 weekdays, the affable staff at the Sister Islands office of the Cayman Islands Department of Tourism can supply brochures on accommodations, dive outfits, activities, and nature and heritage trails. This office also services Little Cayman.

Contacts **Cayman Islands Department of Tourism** (⊠ 209 West End Community Park, West End ☎ 345/948–1649 ⊕ www.cayman-islands.ky).

RESTAURANTS

Most resorts offer optional meal plans, but there are several independent restaurants on the island, some of which provide free transport from your hotel. Local restaurants serve island fare (local seafood, chicken, and curries, as well as addictive beef patties). On Friday and Saturday nights the spicy scent of jerk chicken fills the air; several roadside stands sell take-out dinners. Look for the local specialty, a sweetish pillow-soft round bread.

WHAT IT COSTS IN U.S. DOLLARS					
	¢	$	$$	$$$	$$$$
Restaurants	under $8	$8–$12	$12–$20	$20–$30	over $30
Hotels*	under $80	$80–$150	$150–$250	$250–$350	over $350
Hotels**	under $125	$125–$250	$250–$350	$350–$450	over $450

*EP, BP, CP **AI, FAP, MAP; restaurant prices are for a main course, excluding the customary 10% service charge. Hotel prices are for two people in a double room in high season, excluding the 7½% VAT, customary 10% service charge, and meal plans (except at all-inclusive hotels).

HOTELS

Lodgings are small and intimate, and guests are often treated like family, congregating in the lobby or bar to swap stories, tall or otherwise, of their exploits. There are only a few full-service resorts, two of them condo complexes. There are also a couple of cozy guesthouses and several private villas (usually second homes for snowbirds) for rent throughout the island. In November 2008, Hurricane Paloma wiped out most of the island's larger properties. All have been rebuilt, in some cases from the ground up; two had only partially reopened as of this writing.

EXPLORING CAYMAN BRAC

The Brac abounds in both natural and historic attractions. Many of the former include botanic gardens and preserves set aside to protect threatened indigenous species. The latter revolve around the maritime heritage and hardscrabble lives of the earliest settlers and their descendants up until the island developed better communication with the outside world in the 1970s. *For more specific listings of caves and nature trails of particular significance, see ⇨ Sports & the Outdoors, below.*

If you're exploring on your own, be sure to pick up the *Cayman Brac Heritage Sites & Trails* brochure, available at the tourist office and most hotels; it lists all the major points of interest.

The **Sister Islands District Administration** (☎ *345/948–2222 Ext. 4420, ask for organizer Chevala Burke ⊕ www.nature-cayman.com*) offers free government-sponsored guided nature and cultural tours with trained local guides Cantrell Scott and Keino Daley. Options include the Parrot Reserve, nature trails, wetlands, Lighthouse/Bluff View, caving, birding, and heritage sites. You just supply the wheels and spirit of adventure.

WHAT TO SEE

★ **Cayman Brac Museum**. Here you'll find a diverse, well-displayed collection of historic Bracker implements from scary dental pliers to pistols to pottery. A meticulously crafted scale model of the Caymanian catboat *Alsons* has pride of place. The front room faithfully reconstructs the customs, treasury, bank, and post office as they would have looked decades ago. Permanent exhibits focus on the 1932 hur-

Cayman Brac

Restaurants
Alexander Hotel
Restaurant, **3**
Aunt Sha's Kitchen, **1**
Captain's Table, **2**
Coral Isle Club, **4**
La Esperanza, **5**

Hotels
Alexander Hotel, **4**
Brac Caribbean and
Carib Sands, **2**
Brac Reef
Beach Resort, **1**
Captain's Cove, **7**
Cayman Breakers, **9**
Cayman Cottage, **3**
Featherstone, **11**
Island Time, **12**
La Esperanza, **10**
Pirate's Dream, **8**
Sea Feather, **5**
Sunset Cottage, **14**
3 Palms Beach House, **6**
Walton's Mango
Manor, **13**

KEY
- Beaches
- Dive Sites
- **1** Restaurants
- (1) Hotels

0 1 mi
0 1 km

Caribbean Sea

CAYMAN BRAC

West End Pt.
Gerrard-Smith Airport
M.V. Capt. Keith Tibbets
Buccaneer's Beach
Frenchman's Fort
West End
Rebecca's Cave
Brac Reef Beach
Tiara Beach
Deadman's Pt.
Stake Bay Pt.
Cayman Brac Museum
Lost City of Atlantis
The Bight
Christopher Columbus Gardens
Bat Cave
Cedar Pt.
Public Beach
Sea Feather Bay
Tibbetts Turn
Parrot Reserve
Tom Jennett's Bay
Cat Head Bay
North East Bay
Heritage House
Booby Pt.
Spot Bay
Peter's Cave
Spellman McLaughlin Home
Pollard Bay
North East Pt.
Great Cave
East End Lighthouse

ricane, turtling, shipbuilding, and typical old-time home life, including a re-creation of a child's bedroom; the back room hosts rotating exhibits such as herbal folk medicine. ⊠ *Old Government Administration Bldg., Stake Bay* ☎ *345/948–2622 or 345/244–4446* ⊴ *Free* ☉ *Weekdays 9–noon and 1–4, Sat. 9–noon.*

Heritage House. The acre of beautifully landscaped grounds dotted with thatched gazebos and fountains includes an old-fashioned well and tannery, as well as Cola Cave (used to shelter the former estate owners during hurricanes), with informational panels. The main building, though new, replicates a traditional house; the interior has a few displays and videos depicting Brac history, but the treat is watching local artists at work. It's a great resource for books on natural history and Caymanian crafts, when daily slide shows, various cultural events, and talks by visiting naturalists are often scheduled. Call ahead before visiting to make sure that the house is open. ⊠ *Northeast Bay Rd., Spot Bay* ☎ *345/948–0563* ⊴ *Free* ☉ *Weekdays 9:30–1 and 2–5, Sat. 10–3.*

★ **Parrot Reserve.** The likeliest place to spot the endangered Cayman Brac parrot—and other indigenous and migratory birds—is along this National Trust hiking trail off Major Donald Drive, aka Lighthouse Road. Prime time is early morning or late afternoon; most of the day they're camouflaged by trees, earning them the moniker "stealth parrot." The loop trail incorporates part of a track used by Brackers in olden days to cross the Bluff to reach their provision grounds on the south shore or to gather coconuts, once a major export crop. It passes through several types of terrain: old farmland under grass and native trees from mango to mahogany unusually mixed with orchids and cacti. Wear sturdy shoes, as the terrain is rocky, uneven, and occasionally rough. The 6-mi (10-km) gravel road continues to the lighthouse at the bluff's eastern end, where there's an astonishing view from atop the cliff to the open ocean—the best place to watch the sunrise. ⊠ *Lighthouse Rd., Tibbetts Turn, ½ mi (1 km) south of town* ☎ *345/948–0319* ⊴ *Free* ☉ *Daily sunrise–sunset.*

★ **Spellman McLaughlin Home.** This green-trimmed, whitewashed clapboard house, built by Captain Spellman McLaughlin between 1926 and 1930, is one of the last surviving examples of classic Bracker architecture (most were blown away by the great 1932 hurricane). McLaughlin constructed

the house from pine timber he ferried on his own schooner from Mobile and Pensacola. Eschewing the expedient custom of using precut lengths for prefabricated designs, he instead cut the planks to specification on-site. It's supported on 60 full-section log posts sunk into the ground. Wooden pegs (rather than rust-able nails) join many sections. Three individually pitched gable ends tower above the veranda roof (fashioned from salvaged curved boat boards), forming the optical illusion of a second story. The eight exterior rooms surround the dining room, the focal point of Bracker life; each features a window and door to the wraparound veranda, ensuring that the house captures the light and the breezes. His youngest daughter, Mrs. Brunzil Rivers, still lives in her childhood home and proudly shows people around, almost apologizing for the modern modifications (the kitchen once occupied a separate building to minimize fire risk and reduce heat, and closets have replaced the wardrobes standard at the time). Especially exceptional are the dining room's diagonal wall patterning and the front north parlor's domed beaded ceiling. ⊠ *Northeast Bay Rd., Creek* ☎ *345/949–0121* ⊡ *Free* ⊙ *Weekdays 9:30–1 and 2–5, Sat. 10–3.*

THE GREAT HURRICANE OF '32. Brackers were ill-prepared for hurricanes, especially the deadly storm with 200 MPH winds that blustered its way over the island in 1932, destroying virtually everything in its path. Most Brackers took shelter in the caves sculpted from the Bluff. Others flooded into the McLaughlin home, which miraculously stood fast, saving 130 people. A "tear of sea" (archaic argot for a tidal wave) crashed onto shore, sending a boulder hurtling through the front door. Other than some damage from flooding, the house withstood the brunt of the storm quite well, and even the windows remained unbroken. Even younger Brackers still discuss the storm with awe.

WHERE TO EAT

$$–$$$ ✕ **Alexander Hotel Restaurant.** *Continental.* This potentially fine eatery is all over the place, from cuisine to decor. The kitchen's one-from-column-A approach tries to accommodate all tastes, running from conch fritters in fruit chutney to Parmesan-crusted chicken in chardonnay sauce to steak Diane. The space likewise lacks identity, resembling a sterile conference room gussied up with burgundy chairs,

wainscoting, and genre watercolors. Service is smiling, however, and the chef promises to infuse more individual (and local) flair into the menu. ☒ *West End* ☎ *345/948–8222* ⊕ *www.alexanderbrac.com* ⌂ *Reservations essential* ☰ *AE, D, DC, MC, V.*

$–$$ ✕ **Aunt Sha's Kitchen.** *Caribbean.* Sharon Connolly is the eponymous owner of this unassuming spot, which is usually packed with locals, from ladies in hair nets to fishers with buckets of catch flirting or gossiping (the island's best eavesdropping). Sea-green and sky-blue walls, ceramic fish, nature photos, and fringe lamps lend some decorative flair, but you come here for stellar Caymanian cuisine, from brown stew tuna to conch fritters, Cayman-style lobster (the most expensive item by far, also prepared curried or broiled in mushroom sauce), or even fried chicken, all served with heaping helpings of sides such as dumplings. You can add heat with homemade hot sauce (pickled peppers, cabbage, onions, and tomato) that will knock your socks (and shoes) off. Everyone swears by Aunt Sha's velvety Key lime pie. ☒ *West End* ☎ *345/948–1581* ☰ *D, MC, V* ⊗ *No dinner Sun.*

$$–$$$ ✕ **Captain's Table.** *Continental.* This weathered, powder-blue wooden building wouldn't be out of place on some remote New England shore, except perhaps for the garish pirate at the entrance. The nautical yo-ho-hokum continues inside (painted oars, model sailboats, faux portholes, droll touches like a skeleton with a chef's toque), but fortunately the kitchen isn't lost at sea, despite voyaging from India to Italy. Teriyaki chicken and lobster rigatoni with roasted bell peppers are worthy house specialties. Lunch is cheaper, from standbys (wraps, burgers, nachos) to more creative options like jerk chicken pizza and blackened shrimp quesadilla. The outdoor poolside bar is a popular hangout for dive masters. ☒ *Brac Caribbean, West End* ☎ *345/948–1418* ⌂ *Reservations essential.* ☰ *AE, MC, V.*

$–$$ ✕ **Coral Isle Club.** *Caribbean.* This seaside eatery daubed in a virtual rainbow of blues from turquoise to teal serves up fine local food, emphasizing fresh seafood and, on weekends, mouth- and eye-watering barbecue. The lusciously painted outdoor bar offers equally colorful sunsets, cocktails, and characters (one regular swears, "If I were any better, I'd be dangerous," before buying another round). At night, spotlights illuminate the reef sharks and lobsters lurking in the turtle grass below the patio. The congenial owner, Carlton Ebanks, plans on offering regular entertainment from fashion shows to domino tournaments. ⊠ *Off South Side Rd., West End* ☎ *345/925–4848* ═ *D, MC, V.*

$–$$ ✕ **La Esperanza.** *Caribbean.* Known island-wide as Bussy's— after the larger-than-life owner—this combination grocery store, restaurant, and club encompasses a wildly colored lounge, alfresco bar with elevated gazebo, and covered pier jutting into the Caribbean. Drink in the sunset views, and then dine on fresh-caught seafood (conch is particularly yummy, whether as fritters or prepared "Cayman-style" in lemon-butter sauce with onions and bell peppers). Burgers, fish-and-chips, and chicken chop suey are evergreen favorites. The place really jumps Friday and Saturday nights, when Bussy cranks up his grills and "jerks" chicken (he'll give you impromptu "jerking" lessons). Wife Velma makes a luscious Key lime pie that would give Aunt Sha's a run for the top prize if the Brac had county-fair-style bake-offs. ⊠ *The Creek, Stake Bay* ☎ *345/948–0531* ═ *AE, D, MC, V* ⊗ *No dinner Sun.*

WHERE TO STAY

Cayman Brac has a handful of hotels and resorts, as well as a decent B&B and several apartments. Several private villas on Cayman Brac can also be rented, most of them basic but well maintained, ranging from one to four bedrooms. The rental fees are quite reasonable, and normally the price for extra couples in the larger units is only $200 per week (singles $100–$135, children often free), representing substantial savings for families or couples traveling together, while the kitchen helps reduce the price of dining out. In addition, government tax and often a service fee are sometimes included in the quoted rate (be sure to verify this), and most villa owners arrange a 10% discount with car-rental agencies. As a general rule of thumb, properties are thoroughly cleaned before your arrival; you must pay extra if you want daily maid service, and a one-time cleaning fee of $50 to $75 is usually assessed for end-of-rental cleaning. Owners can sometimes arrange to prestock the fridge. Each villa has a manager who must meet you at the airport (or car rental agency), then escort you to your home; you'll be provided with his or her contact information during the reservation process. Rates are sometimes discounted in the off-season.

Most villa owners mandate a three- to seven-night minimum stay in high season (assume at least one week's booking during the Christmas holiday unless otherwise noted), though this is often negotiable. Some owners will leave a kayak or snorkeling gear out for guests' use. If such amenities are included, they're mentioned. Unless otherwise noted, properties have landline phones; local calls are usually free, but phones are generally locked for international calls. If your GSM provider works in the Cayman Islands, activate the international capability, but note that service is poor or nonexistent at some villas on the south side beneath the Bluff.

$$ ☂ **Alexander Hotel.** *Hotel.* This chic boutique business hotel
★ elevates Brac lodging to a new level, though with no on-site activities to offer vacationers who make up the larger proportion of Brac travelers, its ultimate target audience is unclear. The hotel is extremely handsome inside and out, seamlessly merging classic (modified cupolas to colonnades) with contemporary (striking blown-up nature photos and giant Constructivist-style squares in lime and melon dominate the lobby). Stylishly appointed rooms feature an earthy color scheme from champagne to chocolate with chrome and black accents, flat-screen TV, kitchenette, pillow-top mattress, and Wi-Fi, but the lighting is not good; bathrooms have only a shower. Though the hotel is set back from the water, rooms 210–214 offer the best views. The bar is a fun hangout, overlooking the sea and a saltwater pond bustling with whistling ducks; the sound level can be fairly high on karaoke nights. **Pros:** high-tech amenities; stylish yet affordable; next door to small shopping mall for sundries and food; delightful alfresco bar. **Cons:** two-minute walk to a pebbly beach; small pool; inadequate bedside and bathroom lighting; no on-site activities. ✉ *Box 132, West End, Cayman Brac* ☎ *345/948–8222* ⊕ *www.alexanderbrac.com* ⇋ *29 rooms, 2 2-bedroom suites* ☖ *In-room: safe, refrigerator, DVD (some), Wi-Fi. In-hotel: restaurant, bar, pool, laundry service, Internet terminal, Wi-Fi hotspot.* ⊟ *AE, D, DC, MC, V.* ⦿|*EP.*

$$ ☂ **Brac Caribbean and Carib Sands.** *Resort.* These neighboring beachfront sister complexes, almost completely rebuilt (and expanded) after Paloma, offer condos with one to four bedrooms, all individually owned and decorated beyond a "starter" design. The Brac Caribbean balconies overlook the sea; those at Carib Sands overlook the water across the extensive pool area. The nattily nautical Captain's Table restaurant and poolside bar at Brac Caribbean are a popular hangout for locals and visitors alike. The Sands grounds are particularly pretty, with buttonwood and ficus "fences" and fragrant oleander bushes buzzing with butterflies. The units here tend to be more vivid though often weirdly configured. Many have nice touches like hand-painted mirrors and walk-in closets. Numbers 111 and 114 are particularly stylish digs with splendid views. The Brac Caribbean units feature a more-flowing layout but more-generic decor; ground-floor units formerly obscured by foliage have better views while the trimmed plants regrow. **Pros:** lively restaurant-bar; excellent value for families, especially with weekly discounts. **Cons:** pretty but narrow, often unmaintained beach; limited staff. ⌂ *Box 4 SPO, Cayman Brac KY2-2101* ☎ *345/948–2265, 345/948–1121, or 866/843–2722* ⊕ *www.866thebrac.com* ⬦ *65 condos* ⌂ *In-room: kitchen, DVD (some). In-hotel: restaurant, bar, pools, beachfront, bicycles, laundry facilities, Wi-Fi hotspot* ⊟ *AE, MC, V* ⍾*CP.*

$$ ⊺**Brac Reef Beach Resort.** *Resort.* Popular with divers, this
★ well-run resort, entirely rebuilt from the ground up (including a new pool and dining room), features a beautiful sandy beach shaded by sea-grape trees. The dock is illuminated nightly, attracting stingrays, tarpon, and other creatures to entertain you on your after-dinner stroll. The motel-style rooms are simple but spotless, with handsome new hardwood furnishings and granite-clad baths. The second-floor and end units (118–121, 219–221) offer the best views; 10 junior suites include microwave, not to mention more style and amenities (dual shower heads, leather recliners, iPod docks, and flat-screen TV/DVD). There's a library with video and board games for use in bad weather. Even the buffet-style food is surprisingly good: killer peppery conch chowder, silken lobster bisque, scrumptious garlic bread, live carving station, and plentiful choices like mahimahi with mushroom demi-glace. The crowd tends to be older, with a handful of honeymooners thrown in and a few small meetings and vacationing families in summer. **Pros:** lovely beach; great dive outfit; friendly staff and clientele; free Wi-Fi in public areas. **Cons:** noise from planes; view often obscured from ground-floor units. ⌂ *Box 56, West End, Cayman Brac KY2-2001* ☎ *345/948–1323; 727/323–8727 for reservations in Florida, 800/594–0843* ⊕ *www.bracreef.com* ⬦ *40 rooms* ⌂ *In-room: safe (some), refrigerator (some), DVD (some), Internet. In-hotel: 2 restaurants, room service, bar, tennis court, pool, gym, spa, beachfront, diving, water sports, bicycles, laundry service, laundry facilities, Internet terminal, Wi-Fi hotspot* ⊟ *AE, D, MC, V* ⍾*BP.*

7

$$ ⊞ **Captain's Cove.** *Private Villa.* This tasteful, welcoming
★ home was built in vernacular style with a "welcoming"
double staircase, modified mansard-style gray-shingle roof,
fantastic deck with gingerbread trim, and bougainvillea-
draped coral facade set off by indigo shutters and doors.
The setting, caught between the Bluff and beach lined with
sea grapes, coconut palms, and orchids, is stunning. A small
but inviting pool overlooks the sea. The airy, sun-drenched
interior chicly contrasts hand-painted tables, vibrant rugs
and artworks, and lovely ceramic lamps with period-style
armoires and handsome beach-scene photos. Large bed-
rooms feature splashes of parrot-green, lemon, and scarlet;
gorgeous island crafts and quilts; and stained-glass windows
depicting marine life. **Pros:** remote location gives privacy;
great snorkeling; stylish decor; eco-friendly. **Cons:** isolated;
rocky but nice beach; uncertain cell service. ⊠ *South Side
Rd. E, South Side* ☎ *734/854–5228 direct to owner* ⊕ *www.
caymanbraccaptainscove.com* ⇨ *2 bedrooms, 2 baths* ♿
DVD, pool, beachfront, laundry facilities, no smoking
⊟ *No credit cards.*

$$ ⊞ **Cayman Breakers.** *Vacation Condos.* This attractive pink-
★ brick colonnaded condo development sitting between the
bluff and the southeast coastal ironshore caters to climbers, who scale the bluff's sheer face, as well as divers, who
appreciate the good shore diving right off the property.
Spacious, two-bedroom units favor soft seashell colors,
beach photos, and frilly touches (Aubusson-style rugs,
shell-embedded mirrors, painted wooden fish) and have full
open kitchens including a dishwasher, as well as a sleeper
sofa and washer/dryer. A private shore-dive entrance with
a shower and rinse tank is located at the cabana/pool area,
slung with hammocks and offering breathtaking views
of the bluff and beach. **Pros:** spectacular views; thoughtful extras like complimentary bikes, jigsaw puzzles, and
climbing route guides; very attentive managers who live
onsite. **Cons:** nearest grocery is a 15-minute drive; gorgeous beach is rocky and has rough surf; some units slightly
musty and faded. ⊡ *Box 202 SPO, South Side Rd., East
End KY2-2101* ☎ *345/948–1463* ⊕ *www.caybreakers.com*
⇨ *18 2-room condos* ♿ *In-room: kitchen, DVD. In-hotel:
pool, beachfront, bicycles, laundry facilities, Wi-Fi hotspot*
⊟ *AE, MC, V* ⊙ *EP.*

$ ⊞ **Cayman Cottage.** *Private Villa.* Owner Sue Smart escapes
her dry, mountainous, landlocked New Mexico home several times a year to bask on her wonderful stretch of sand;
she and her husband planted every coconut palm and the

rock walls that prevent beach erosion. Her "cove" is lovely indeed, forming a mini-reef-encircled lagoon ideal for safe swimming and snorkeling. The detached quiet guest cottage is within a mile's stroll of dive operations, restaurants ("or you can take a floatie down to the Captain's Table"), bars, the post office, car rentals, and gift shops. Small but comfy at 600 square feet, it's homey, simple, and immaculate in white, cream, and beige tones. **Pros:** alluring beach with great snorkeling; affable owner often on property; easy walk to town. **Cons:** cramped with tiny kitchen; no dishwasher; owner's house has better views. ⊠ *Box 100, WPO, South Side Rd. E, West End, Stake Bay* ☎*345/948–1617* ⊕ *www.caymancottage.com* ➪*1 bedroom, 1 bath* ⚐ *Beachfront, laundry facilities* ⊟ *Cash only* ☞ *3-night minimum high season.*

$ ☷ **Featherstone.** *Private Villa.* Owner Minnie Branch is an interior decorator, and her sense of style and love of nature inform every aspect of this self-contained, new two-story cottage behind her own rebuilt seaside home. The property enjoys 280-degree views of the Bight, with the Bluff visible to the east and Little Cayman to the west on clear days. The screened porch overlooks the lush landscaping, a virtual jungle, gazebo with billowing drapes and a rock-walled cactus garden. The wonderful 1.4-acre sandy beach, anchored by scaevola and palms (with plentiful hammocks and loungers), is situated well off the public roads with no immediate neighbors. Even the power and telephone wires are buried to enhance the isolated feel. The classic look encompasses handsome natural wicker and hardwood furnishings with tropical accents downstairs, and gauzy curtains, organdy dust ruffles, and a cobalt-and-white color scheme in the upstairs bedroom. **Pros:** refined decor; glorious garden; nice extras like use of a kayak and hot tub under a shady almond tree. **Cons:** main house has better views; lovely but very chatty owner. ⊠ *The Bight* ☎*345/948–0488* ⊕ *www.cayman-featherstone.com* ➪*1 bedroom, 1 bath* ⚐ *Beachfront, bicycles, water toys* ⊟*AE, MC, V* ☞ *7-day minimum high season.*

$$ ☷ **Island Time.** *Private Villa.* This airy, attractive villa plays off its beachfront location, with prominently displayed marine photos and soft blue colors inside, dive-gear rinsing/drying station, and outdoor shower. Other nice decorative touches include vividly painted wooden fish, flags, iron sconces, and a four-poster master bed. Despite the cathedral ceiling, the rooms themselves feel slightly cramped, but with additional bunk and sofa beds, large families are

easily accommodated. **Pros:** splendid sea views; good snorkeling; well equipped; good for families; thoughtful extras for divers. **Cons:** no pool; surf occasionally rough; shower only. ⊠ *Off Spot Bay Rd., Stake Bay* ☎ *972/530–8660 direct to owner* ⊕ *www.bractime.com* ⋟ *3 bedrooms, 2 baths* ⚬ *Dishwasher, DVD, Wi-Fi, beachfront, laundry facilities.* ⊟ *MC, V* ⦿ *EP.*

$ 🖼 **La Esperanza.** *Vacation Condos.* This fun, funky seaside cluster of mango and teal buildings with magenta accents is run by industrious, affable owners who also rent cars and offer free use of (and sometimes transportation to) their private beach 6 mi (10 km) away on the gentler south shore. The apartments and houses are surrounded by towering shade trees and across the street from the restaurant and rocky beach (#1 has the best view). Accommodations are attractive if slightly worn, favoring clashing lemon, burnt orange, and fuchsia fabrics with gaudy, often religious artworks and garage-sale furnishings; the houses include washer/dryers. For years this was one of the few spots where folks could mingle and exchange news over drinks (remember, even TVs were few until the mid-1990s), and the restaurant-bar remains an evergreen favorite. Two of the original founders, Bussy and Velma Dilbert, still run the place and ensure personalized attention (they're always handy with advice and local lore). It's a tranquil spot, at least until weekends, when it's usually party central. **Pros:** fun ambience; good snorkeling; party time on weekends; grocery on-site. **Cons:** slightly threadbare; weekend parties get loud. ⊡ *Box 28, SPO, The Creek, Stake Bay,* ☎ *345/948–0531 or 345/948–0591* ⊕ *www.laesperanza. net* ⋟ *4 2-bedroom apartments, 2 3-bedroom houses* ⚬ *In-room: kitchen. In hotel: restaurant, bar, laundry facilities (some)* ⊟ *AE, D, MC, V* ⦿ *EP.*

$$ 🖼 **Pirate's Dream.** *Private Villa.* The old real estate man-
★ tra—location, location, location—applies to this opulent oceanfront home featuring fantastic water views from every room (even the kitchen's cooking island is optimally positioned) and constantly blowing trade winds that graze the hammocks strategically placed under coconut, mango, and papaya trees. French doors throughout saturate the rooms with sunlight. Beamed vaulted ceilings enhance the spaciousness. Cushy furnishings, handsome throw rugs, and white and turquoise fabrics contrast attractively with the terra-cotta tile floors and polished hardwood cabinetry and ceiling. The master bedroom features an oversize shower and private covered patio looking seaward. The main guest

bedroom on the opposite end of the house, offering total privacy for everyone, also has a private covered porch (with super sunset rather than sunrise vistas). Festive quilts and sculpted fish provide just enough color. The deck, larger than most Manhattan studios, at more than 600 square feet, opens to the beach. Many dive-master guests rave about the stupendous reef/wall shore dive here, but it's a fair swim out—at least 300 yards—to the mooring buoy that starts with a 60-foot drop and keeps going. **Pros:** great value; terrific shore diving. **Cons:** no pool; occasional cellphone reception problems. ⊠ *912 South Side Rd., Hawksbill Bay, East End* ☎ *757/481–5090 direct to owner* ⊕ *www.caymanbrac.com/rentals/piratesdream.html* ⌁ *3 bedrooms, 3 baths* ⌂ *Wi-Fi, beachfront, laundry facilities* ⊟ *Cash only* ⌁ *7-day min. high season.*

$$ ⊡ **Sea Feather.** *Private Villa.* This two-bedroom retreat offers location, location, location on one of the Brac's prettier stretches of sand, best appreciated from the long screened patio. Immaculate white walls, floors, and standing lamps play off hardwood and natural wicker, marine photos, shell art, handmade wall-hanging quilts, and fabrics in the full range of Caribbean colors, from aqua to azure. The kitchen is nicely equipped, and the master bedroom opens onto the patio. **Pros:** nice if pebbly beach; good snorkeling; well-stocked library of books and media. **Cons:** no pool; no Wi-Fi; bedrooms lack great views. ⊠ *South Side Rd., Sea Feather Bay* ☎ *860/435–0630 direct to owner* ⊕ *www.caymanseafeather.com* ⌁ *2 bedrooms, 2 baths* ⌂ *Dishwasher, DVD, beachfront, laundry facilities.* ⊟ *MC, V.* ⋈ *EP*

$$ ⊡ **Sunset Cottage.** *Private Villa.* This light-filled little hideaway is small but appealing, with an enclosed patio that delivers on the name. Immaculate in white with aquamarine accents, its standard Caribbean look is animated by dried sea fans, driftwood, and gorgeous photos of sunsets and the lighthouse. The master bedroom has smashing views; both bedrooms feature walk-in closets large enough to sleep a kid comfortably. You can walk to the tourist office and snack shops. **Pros:** fabulous sunsets; excellent snorkeling. **Cons:** rocky beach with rough surf; no Internet; no stereo system. ⊠ *62 Georgianna Dr., West End* ☎ *949/219–0715 direct to owner* ⊕ *www.caymanbraccottage.com* ⌁ *2 bedrooms, 2 baths* ⌂ *DVD, beachfront, laundry facilities* ⊟ *D, MC, V* ⌁ *3-night minimum high season.*

$$ ⊡ **3 Palms Beach House.** *Private Villa.* This spacious, spanking new oceanfront home, completed in spring 2007, is one of the most luxuriously appointed villas on the Brac,

with gleaming tile floors, hardwood and rattan furnishings (including gorgeous armoires and headboards carved in palm-tree shapes), dried sea fans and shells as accents, and French doors and oversize windows that permeate the rooms with light. The trappings are just as upscale, including 350-thread-count linens, top-notch stainless-steel appliances, 32-inch flat-screen TV/DVD (airing more than 100 channels of DirecTV), Wi-Fi, and Xbox setup (with several games and movies). Two bedrooms with a shared bath bracket the living room and kitchen; the front "master" units have delightful ocean views, while the back bedrooms both have twin beds. The home is perfectly priced for families and ideal for divers (there's terrific snorkeling off the 100-foot private beach frontage in numerous small coral reefs, thoughtful touches like an outdoor shower and rack for hanging scuba gear, and a coconut "totem" on the beach to propitiate the diving deities). **Pros:** high-tech by Brac standards; excellent value; great snorkeling. **Cons:** shared bathrooms; immature landscaping; rocky beach. ✉ *552 Southside Rd. E, South Side* ☎ *345/948–8045 or 661/816–3322 direct to owner* ⊕ *www.threepalmsonthebrac.com* 🛏 *4 bedrooms, 2 baths* ⚭ *Dishwasher, DVD, Wi-Fi, laundry facilities* ═ *AE, MC, V.*

$ 🖫 **Walton's Mango Manor.** *B&B.* This beautifully restored
★ traditional West Indian home has five rooms (all with bath), accented with lovely antique furnishings, nautical gadgets, maps, model catboats, and bric-a-brac from the Waltons' world travels. Upper-floor units are desirable: Their tiny balconies oversee the 500-foot sweep of verdant grounds down to the sea. A spacious, private, split-level seaside cottage called Sea Dreams (fully renovated after Paloma) has a full kitchen, washer/dryer, and Internet access. The tranquil ironshore beach is usually unoccupied; its gazebo has hosted many a wedding ceremony. Walk with owner George, a native Bracker, through the extravagant, enchanted landscaping, which includes a tiny exquisite synagogue (that he and his wife constructed themselves from imported Honduras mahogany, Minnesota granite, Ferrara marble, and more), mosaic gazebo, organic garden in a failed swimming pool, and turtle pond with bridge. Breakfasts feature fresh fruit and luscious jellies from the remaining fruit trees (several types of mango, Key limes, coconuts, plum, tamarind), wife Lynne's homemade challah French toast, and local dishes like salt cod and plantain. **Pros:** true Caymanian hospitality; beautiful grounds; excellent snorkeling; free Wi-Fi access. **Cons:** poky beach across the

street; car required. ⌂ *Box 56 SPO, Stake Bay KY2-2101*
☎ *345/948–0518* ⊕ *www.waltonsmangomanor.com* ⌖ *5
rooms, 1 2-bedroom cottage* ⌂ *In-room: kitchen (some),
no TV (some), Internet (some), Wi-Fi. In-hotel: beachfront,
Wi-Fi hotspot* ▭ *D, MC, V* ⍟*BP.*

BEACHES

Much of the Brac's coastline is ironshore, though there
are several pretty sand beaches, mostly along the southwest coast (where swimmers will also find extensive beds
of turtle grass, which creates less than ideal conditions
for snorkeling). In addition to the hotel beaches, where
everyone is welcome, there is a public beach with good
access to the reef; it's well marked on tourist maps. The
north-coast beaches, predominantly rocky ironshore, offer
excellent snorkeling.

Buccaneer's Beach. Just north of the airport, the rocky stretch
is somewhat rough, but the snorkeling is sublime; you'll
recognize the area when you see the 1860 windlass (winch)
of the SS *Kersearge* in the ironshore. ⊠ *Georgiana Dr., just
before North Side Rd. E, West End.*

Pollard Bay. The beach by Cayman Breakers is fairly wide
for this eastern stretch of the island. You can start clam-
bering east underneath the imposing Bluff, past the end
of the paved road, to find strikingly beautiful deserted
stretches accessible only on foot, but the water here starts
churning like a washing machine. It becomes progressively
rockier, littered with driftwood; you might stumble upon
locals searching for whelks here. Flocks of seabirds darken
the sun for seconds at a time, while blowholes spout as if
answering migrant humpback whales. Don't go beyond
the gargantuan rock called First Cay—the sudden swells
can be hazardous—unless you're a serious rock climber.
⊠ *South Side Rd. E, East End.*

Public Beach. Roughly 2 mi (3 km) east of the Brac Reef and
Carib Sands/Brac Caribbean resorts, just past the wetlands
(the unsightly gate is visible from the road; if you hit the
Bat Cave you've passed it), lie a series of strands culminating in this relatively deserted beach (despite its name). The
surf is calm and the crystalline water fairly protected for
swimming. There are picnic tables and showers in uncer-
tain condition. Snorkeling is quite good. ⊠ *South Side Rd.
W, South Side.*

House of Worship

CLOSE UP

The pale blue, circular Temple Beth Shalom nestles incongruously in the Waltons' serene garden, replete with the only consecrated Jewish cemetery in the Cayman Islands. A plaque by the imposing carved mahogany door reads HOUSE OF WELCOME, MAY ALL WHO ENTER HERE FIND PEACE. Brooklyn-born Lynne presides over services, though rabbis and cantors fly in for special occasions and holidays. George erected the synagogue as a gift to his wife but says, "I hope that any person from around the world will talk to God as they understand Him without intervention.... Protestants love the temple; they spend more time here than the Jews, even one of the most hard-core Baptist families we have." Indeed, visitors from Argentina to Austria to Australia have renewed their spirits here.

Swiss architect Fredy Schulteiss designed the building, but George and Lynne practically built it by themselves. It includes stained glass, Italian marble accents from Italy, and polished gray Minnesota granite floors they laid themselves. Lynne carved everything from the marble to the Honduran wood doors and inlaid scrolling fashioned from dead limbs of wild plum, cedar, mahogany, ironwood, and candlewood trees. Her father created a menorah in the shape of a shofar; another was a family heirloom brought by Lynne's grandmother from Odessa. The synagogue is actually one structure encased within another, "one for the Torah, the other to reach toward the heavens, in a small way making a statement to God that we're trying to get there." The 28-foot ceiling fittingly depicts a starry sky, with the 12 lights representing the 12 tribes of Israel. As a bonus, the space has splendid acoustics and a piano. Members of the Cayman National Orchestra, including flutists, pianists, and cellists, occasionally perform memorable classical concerts.

Sea Feather Bay. The central section of the south coast features several lengthy ribbons of soft ecru sand, with little shade aside from the occasional coconut palm, no facilities, and blissful privacy (aside from the occasional villa). ✉ *South Side Rd. just west of Ashton Reid Dr., Sea Feather Bay, South Side.*

SPORTS AND THE OUTDOORS

BIRD-WATCHING

Bird-watching is sensational on the sister islands, with almost 200 species patrolling the island from migratory to endemic, including the endangered Cayman Brac parrot and brown booby. The best place to spy the feathered lovelies is on the north coast and in the protected woodland reserve (*see* ⇨ *Parrot Reserve in Exploring Cayman Brac, above*) on the Bluff. Other species to look out for include the indigenous vitelline warbler and red-legged thrush. The wetlands and ponds in the West End teem with herons and shorebirds, including splendid frigates, kestrels, ospreys, and rare West Indian whistling ducks. Most coastal areas offer sightings, but the best may be just inland at the **Westerly Ponds** (which connect during rainy season; otherwise boardwalks provide excellent viewing areas). A hundred species flap about, particularly around the easternmost pond off Bert Marson Drive by Mr. Billy's house: The old Bracker feeds them late afternoon and occasionally early morning, when the whistling ducks practically coat the entire surface of the water.

DIVING AND SNORKELING

Cayman Brac's waters are celebrated for their rich diversity of sea life, from hammerhead and reef sharks to stingrays to seahorses. Divers and snorkelers alike will find towering coral heads, impressive walls, and fascinating wrecks. The snorkeling and shore diving off the **north coast** are spectacular, particularly at West End, where nearby coral formations attract all kinds of critters. The walls feature remarkable topography with natural gullies, caves, and fissures blanketed with Technicolor sponges, black coral, gorgonians, and sea fans. Some of the famed sites are the West Chute, Cemetery Wall, Airport Wall, and Garden Eel Wall.

The **South Wall** is a wonderland of sheer drop-offs carved with a maze of vertical swim-throughs, tunnels, arches, and grottoes that divers nickname Cayman's Grand Canyon. Notable sites include Anchor Wall, Rock Monster Chimney, and the Wilderness.

Notable diving attractions around the island include the 330-foot MV *Capt. Keith Tibbetts,* a Russian frigate purchased from Cuba and deliberately scuttled in 1996 within

A diver swimming between coral formations

swimming distance of the northwest shore, accessible to divers of all levels. Many fish have colonized the Russian frigate—now broken in two and encrusted with magnificent orange and yellow sponges. Other underwater wrecks include the *Cayman Mariner,* a steel tugboat, and the *Prince Frederick,* a wooden-hulled twin-masted schooner that allegedly sank in the 19th century.

Oceanic Voyagers, a 7-foot-tall bronze statue created by world-renowned marine sculptor Dale Evers, depicts spotted dolphins cavorting with southern stingrays and was sunk off the Brac's coast near Stake Bay in January 2003 as part of the Cayman Islands' year-long quincentennial celebration. An artist named Foots has created an amazing underwater Atlantis off Radar Reef.

Other top snorkeling/shore diving spots include the south coast's **Pillar Coral Reef, Tarpon Reef,** and **Lighthouse Reef;** the north shore counters with **Greenhouse Reef, Snapper Reef,** and **Jan's Reef.**

★ **Indepth Watersports** (✉ *South Side* ☎ *345/948–8037 or 866/476–2195* ⊕ *www.indepthwatersports.com*) has a newly custom-refitted, speedy, state-of-the-art former Navy Seal boat that enables aficionados to dive both the Brac and Little Cayman on the same trip. When not diving, the owners can also take you out fishing.

★ **Reef Divers** (✉ *Brac Reef Beach Resort, West End* ☎ *345/948–1642* ⊕ *www.bracreef.com*) offers five boats and enthusiastic experienced staff. Certified divers can purchase à la carte dive packages even if they aren't guests of the hotel. Most dives are done at mooring balls to protect the reefs.

FISHING

Cayman Brac offers superior bonefishing along the shallows off the southwest coast and even finer light-tackle action. The offshore waters mostly compose a marine park, so fishers go out a few hundred feet from the dive buoys, themselves ranging ¼ to ½ mi (½ to 1 km) from shore. The pristine environment teems with wahoo, marlin, and sushi-grade tuna. Most charter-boat operators also run snorkeling trips; a memorable excursion is to Little Cayman Brac, passing several fanciful rock formations.

When not out diving, Craig Burhart, Katie Wand, and Carl Nash of **Indepth Watersports** (✉ *South Side* ☎ *345/329–6348, 345/948–8037, or 866/476–2195* ⊕ *www.indepthwatersports.com*) are usually on their refitted ex-Seal 34-foot *Karma*. A full day on the well-equipped, comfortable *DeJa Vu* costs $1,000.

Robin Walton (✉ *Stake Bay* ☎ *345/948–2382*) has been fishing the waters commercially for years and knows the best times and secret spots where mahimahi, wahoo, marlin, grouper, and tuna hang out. His 21-foot Bayliner Trophy, *TLC*, is equipped with GPS tracking, he quips, "Because I'm lazy." He takes you to truly wonderful sites since he doesn't like the dive-boat traffic. The maximum is four anglers, though he can fit up to eight comfortably for snorkeling. His rates are also fairly reasonable ($125 per hour) because you subsidize his income with your catch, though he generally allots 50% "or whatever you can manage" to his guests, most of whom cook at their rental condos or villas.

HIKING

Public footpaths and hiking trails filigree the island, with interpretive signs identifying a staggering variety of resident and non-resident bird species that call the Brac home. You'll also find reptile habitats, indigenous flora, and historically and geologically significant sites. Arguably the most scenic route traverses the eastern Bluff to the tip, where the remains of a lighthouse stand sentinel over the roaring Caribbean. This is one of the routes taken by early

CLOSE UP

Sculpting Cayman

A Brac sculptor who is known only as Foots (after his size-16 feet) fantasized of re-creating Plato's lost city of Atlantis. Four decades later, he's fulfilling that dream by creating, then sinking mammoth sculptures 45 feet off the Brac's north shore. The resulting artificial reef is an astounding artistic achievement and engineering feat with more than 100 pieces covering several acres.

An architect-contractor who was fascinated by ruins and mythology, Foots found his niche restoring historic buildings, including churches in Germany, Austria, and Iran. To secure permits, Foots submitted a video of his ideal site and a 140-page environmental impact report to the Department of the Environment, noting the good will and revenue it would generate in the scuba and tourism industries. "I have money, I just need your blessing," Foots wrote.

He's sunk thousands of dollars ("What price making a dream come true?") and years of his life into the project, which launched officially in May 2005, when 150,000 pounds of sculpture were submerged. Specially constructed barges help position the pieces by cranes, lift bags, and drag floats. By Phase 4's completion, the technical marvel will encompass more than 300,000 pounds. The scale is immense, but, as Foots says, "Hopes and dreams make the world livable ... I'm promoting new life and marine growth through art that will last an eternity."

The story starts at the Archway of Atlantis (its two bases weigh 21,000 pounds each). The Elders' Way, lined with 5-foot temple columns, leads to the Inner Circle of Light, centering a 2,600-pound sundial. Two 50,000-pound pyramids tower 20 feet with eight swim-throughs. One ambitious project, the Colossus, a toppled 30-foot statue broken into pieces like 7-foot-long feet and a scepter, will suggest the Lost City's destruction.

Foots is modeling the statues after actual people who have contributed to Cayman. He fashions exact plaster-of-Paris molds of their faces (and sometimes hands), then casts in limestone-based cement. Copper piping and doorknobs ingeniously replicate papyrus scrolls; apothecary bottles complete the Medicine Men.

The vision for the entire project has continually evolved inside Foots's head since childhood, without architectural renderings: "I invent so many phases I'd never live long enough to finish.... Atlantis will only end when I do."

7

Great (Tenson) Scott!

Quite the character, Tenson will regale you with fishing tales, tall and otherwise. Ask him how to catch wahoo without a hook—if he doesn't volunteer this "dynamite, power-packed information" first. Don't blame him if you try it unsuccessfully: He explains, "It's like watching a good love story that turns into Rambo; every fish is different." Another tangent might be a discourse on booby eggs collected from the cliff face for egg punch, "our version of egg nog. . . . Why go? Man eats the eggs for a month, it improves his performance. . . . I'm not Spiderman, just a normal Caymanian, but don't go over the

cliff just to get Nature's Viagra." You might also hear the story of when he went "fishering" at 14, stopping for fresh rainwater by a hulking boulder known as Slaughterhouse on the southeast coast (he states the name derives from the reputed habit of pirates to spill blood as if consecrating spots where they bury their booty—and the wind-sculpted image of a skull). Tenson tried digging for the long-rumored gold but hit what he thought was a rock. A few years later, some Brackers used a metal detector and sure enough found buried treasure. "I'd have spent it all by now anyway," he shrugs.

Brackers scaling the bluff via the steep **Lighthouse Steps** up past Peter's Cave (*see ⇨ Spelunking, below*), then down the 2½-mi (4-km) **Lighthouse Footpath** adjacent to Major Donald Drive (aka Lighthouse Road). This was used to bring cattle to pasture, as well as to access plantations of cassava, peppers, beans, tomatoes, sweet potatoes, mangoes, bananas, and other crops. The panoramas are awe-inspiring, especially once you reach the lighthouse. Even though the path along the edge is fairly even, it's not suitable for the elderly, very young, or infirm due to high winds (don't venture onto the dramatic bleached limestone outcroppings: A sudden gust could send you hurtling into the air with the brown boobies that nest in ledges and caves here). It's a compellingly desolate, eerie area, as if future spacefarers were terra-forming the moon with hardy "maypole" cacti, century plants, aloes, and wind-lashed silver thatch palms bowing almost as if in deference to Nature.

Free printed guides to the Brac's many heritage and nature trails can be obtained from the **Brac Tourism Office** (⊠ *West End Community Park, west of airport, Cayman Brac* ☎ *345/948–1649*); you can also get the guides at the airport or at your hotel. Traditional routes across the bluff have been cleared and marked; trailheads are identified with signs along the road. It's safe to hike on your own, though some trails are fairly hard going (wear light hiking boots) and others could be better maintained.

For those who prefer less-strenuous walking, **Christopher Columbus Gardens** (⊠ *Ashton Reid Dr. [Bluff Rd.], just north of Ashton Rutty Centre*) has easy trails and boardwalks. The park showcases the unique natural flora and features of the bluff, including two cave mouths. This is a peaceful spot dotted with gazebos and wooden bridges that traverses several ecosystems from cacti to mahogany trees.

The **Sister Islands District Administration** (☎ *345/948–2222 Ext. 4420*) arranges free government-sponsored guided nature and cultural tours with trained local guides. Options include the Parrot Reserve, nature trails, wetlands, Lighthouse/Bluff View, caving, birding, and heritage sites. You just supply the wheels and spirit of adventure.

ROCK CLIMBING

Aficionados consider the Brac among the world's leading exotic climbing destinations. If you are experienced and like dangling from ropes 140 feet above a rocky, churning sea, the Brac is the place for you. Unfortunately, if you want to learn the ropes, no organization promotes climbing or rents equipment such as ropes and safety gear—you need to bring your own. Through the years, climbers have attached permanent titanium bolts to the **Bluff** face, creating some 70 routes in seven prime regions around the East End, most notably the Spot Bay Areas, the North Wall, the East Wall, and the South Wall. Access is often via private property, so be respectful (though most Brackers will just invite you in for cold drinks and stimulating conversation). The number is still growing as aficionados create new ascents. Difficulty is high; the "easiest" routes are graded 5.8 by the Yosemite Decimal system; most are rated 5.10 to 5.12, though many experienced climbers argue some approach the dizzying 5.14 range, especially around the sheer, "pumpy" (rock-speak for adrenaline-flowing) Northeast Point. This is steep, gnarly terrain of varying stability, suitable only for experienced climbers. Most of the Bluff's faces are hard vertical to overhanging; many walls vault abruptly, if exhilaratingly, to the savage sea.

Climbing the Brac is rocking, but precautions are vital. Sturdy hiking boots are mandatory, since you'll traverse a wide variety of terrain just accessing routes. Leather gloves are also recommended, as most of the high-quality limestone is smooth but has sharp and jagged areas. Two ropes are necessary for many climbs, the longest of which requires 19 quickdraws. Gear should include ascending devices like prussiks and Tiblocs and shoulder-length slings with carabiners. Don't attempt climbs alone, and you're on your own even in teams should disaster occur. Agree upon rope tug signals, since the wind, waves, and overhangs make hearing difficult. Always analyze surf conditions and prevailing winds (which are variable) before rappelling, and double-check rap setup, anchors, and harnesses. Though titanium glue-ins replaced most of the old stainless steel bolts, many are deteriorating due to stress corrosion cracking; avoid any old bolts.

The Cayman Breakers condo complex has route maps and descriptions (⇨ *see Where to Stay*). Several world-renowned climbers have built (second) homes on the Brac, including Liz Grenard, John Byrnes, and Ian Stewart.

READ ABOUT THE BRAC. Ian Stewart wrote a fine article on Brac climbing for the Web site of the Sister Islands Department of Tourism (⊕ *www.caymanbrac.com/islandattractions/climbing.html*). The TradGirl blog (⊕ *www.wiki.tradgirl.com*), started by Dawn Alguard and co-maintained by John Byrnes, includes a major section on the Brac. The J.W. Harper blog also contains useful links (⊕ *www.jharp.net*). Though some of these articles and trip reports were written a few years ago, they're still pertinent.

SPELUNKING

Residents and geologists are still discovering "new" caves and sinkholes in the Brac's 25- to 30-million-year-old dolomite rock. Most of these caves were formed when the sea receded after the last Ice Age as rainwater dissolved the carbonate rock over millennia through cracks made by plants rooting in the limestone. Mineral deposits fashioned fanciful formations in many caves, as well as more typical pillars, stalagmites, and dagger-like stalactites.

Buccaneers (supposedly including Henry Morgan and Edward "Blackbeard" Teach) of the 17th and 18th centuries stopped like most mariners at the Cayman Islands to restock stores of water, wood, and turtles. Many locals still believe buried treasure lies deep within the recesses of the Bluff. But more vitally, the caves served as shelter during the fearsome storms of the first part of the 20th century.

Most caves are closed to the public—even to experienced spelunkers—but several are easily accessed and considered safe. If you plan to explore Cayman Brac's caves, wear good sneakers or hiking shoes, as some paths are steep and rocky and some entrances reachable only by ladders.

Peter's Cave offers a stunning aerial view of the picturesque northeastern community of Spot Bay. The climb is easier from atop the Bluff; the other access is steep, and purchase isn't always easy even with railings. The chambers feature few formations but some pretty multi-hued striations. **Great Cave,** at the island's southeast end, has numerous chambers and photogenic ocean views. It's the least accessible yet most impressive. You won't fund Bruce Wayne or his Boy Wonder in the **Bat Cave,** but you may see Jamaican fruit bats hanging from the ceiling (try not to disturb them), as well as nesting barn owls. The bats play a crucial role in the ecosystem's food chain because they devour overripe fruits, thereby pollinating plants, disseminating seeds, and reducing insect pests. There are some whimsical formations, and sections cracked and crawling with undergrowth, trees, and epiphytes. **Rebecca's Cave** poignantly houses the grave-side of an 18-month-old child who died during the horrific hurricane of 1932. A plaque commemorates her short life (DAUGHTER OF RAIB AND HELENA 'MISS MISSY' BODDEN), and people still leave flowers. It's actually a ¼-mi (½-mi) hike inland along a well-marked trail called the Saltwater Pond Path, which continues to the north side. Today it's a prime bird-watching walk lined with indigenous flora like red birch, jasmine, silver thatch palms, agave, dildo cactus, balsam, cabbage trees, duppy bushes, and bull hoof plants.

CAYMANITE. Found only in the crevices of the Bluff, this stone is actually an amalgam of several metals and minerals, including magnesium, iron, calcium, sodium, copper, nickel, phosphorus, and more: practically a quarter of the periodic table. Its striations supposedly represent different geologic eras, ranging from rus-set to white; no two pieces are identical. Special tools including diamond-tipped cutting wheels and grinders hone the extremely hard rock to a dazzling marble-like finish.

Thatch Weaving

"Laying rope" is an old-time tradition that originated so that women could support themselves while the men were away at sea, often for months at a time. The Brac was particularly noted for the method of stripping silver thatch palm leaves and drying them in the sun, both creating a labor-intensive twisted hemp-like rope that was exported to Jamaica, usually in barter, and various baskets for carrying sand (for gardens) and provisions from little farms atop the Bluff.

You can visit the home-studio/-shop of the craft's foremost practitioner, **Annelee Ebanks** (✉ *35 White Bay Rd., West End* ☎ *345/948–1326*), whose skill is such that the Ritz-Carlton commissions her to create pieces as gifts, decorative accents, towel hampers, and waste baskets. Miss Annelee began more than half a century ago at 13 watching her father make traditional baskets. She enjoyed it and "decided as the years went on to start new patterns. I dream at night, sketch the idea, then go back to sleep."

The stripped dried thatch "strings" have several gradations in hue from silvery mint to buff; bunches are tied off in places to ensure the sun doesn't bleach out all the color. She also uses darker brown dried stripped coconut leaves to create multicolored pieces: place mats with matching coasters and napkin rings, hats, baskets, purses, sandals, hand fans, even brooms and switches ("for bad boys"), since thatching originally served utilitarian purposes. It takes her three days to create one beach bag: one day to weave, a second to line and stitch, another to decorate (she uses magic marker and spray paint, as well as raffia from Jamaica for binding and decorative curlicues).

Amazingly nimble, she'll gladly demonstrate the process but might recruit you if you prove adept. A bunch (usually two to eight strands) is tied at the bottom; use the thumb and index finger to hold and weave, pleating in and out. "Bend and crease it good at the bottom, then you be the boss of it."

SHOPPING

Shopping is limited on the Brac; there are few small stores, though many local ladies sell their wares from home. You'll also find boutiques at the "big" hotels, Brac Reef Beach Resort and Brac Caribbean/Carib Sands. The prize craft specialties are woven thatch items and Caymanite jewelry.

Kirk Freeport (✉ *Next to the museum, Stake Bay* ☎ *345/948–2612*) is a miniature version of its ritzy Grand Cayman sister outposts, offering a smattering of upscale duty-free items from Waterford to Wedgwood, scents, watches, and jewelry from international to local designers.

★ **NIM Things** (✉ *Northeast Bay Rd., Spot Bay* ☎ *345/948–0582 or 345/939–5306*) stands for Native Island Made. Artist and raconteur Tenson Scott fashions exquisite jewelry from Caymanite (he climbs down from the lighthouse without ropes to chisel the stone), triton shells, sea eggs, and more unusual materials. His wife, Starry, creates delicate works from sea urchins, hardening the shell with epoxy: cute turtles, bud vases, and planters decorated with minuscule shells.

Treasure Chest (✉ *Tibbetts Sq., West End* ☎ *345/948–1333*) carries simple resort wear, T-shirts, bonnets, handbags (usually with the Brac logo), and black coral and Caymanite jewelry, as well as a small selection of books, including pamphlets on local birds and fish.

NIGHTLIFE

Divers are notoriously early risers, but a few bars keep things hopping if not quite happening, especially on weekends, when local bands (or "imports" from Grand Cayman) often perform. Quaintly reminiscent of *Footloose* (without the hellfire and brimstone), watering holes are required to obtain music and dancing permits. Various community events including talent shows, recitals, concerts, and other stage presentations at the Aston Rutty Centre provide the rest of the island's nightlife.

★ **Bucky's** (✉ *West End Rd., West End* ☎ *345/948–2449)* This restaurant is popular for its all-you-can-eat West Indian lunch buffets. But the real allure is free Wi-Fi and the very cushy lounge adjacent to the restaurant, which resembles a small Vegas sports bar with leather armchairs, cool black-and-white photos, and team pennants and jerseys galore.

Edd's Place (✉ *West End Rd., West End* ☎ *345/926–0376)* is a combination restaurant (the specialties are burgers and chop suey) and sports bar, known for its joyous happy hours on weekends. It tends to attract a rowdier, more local crowd, and features a friendly rivalry with Bussy's for "best" jerk on island. You can't miss the colorful mural of revelers splashed across the exterior.

★ **La Esperanza** (✉ *The Creek, Stake Bay* ☎ 345/948–0531), aka Bussy's, overflows with drinks, good cheer, and seemingly half the island on weekends, when Bussy fires up the grill and does a huge beach jerk barbecue. You can shoot pool and the breeze in the indoor lounge or head outside for the sensational sunsets (and drinks in matching colors). The music, heavy on the reggae with the occasional salsa tune thrown in, blares, encouraging everyone to sway along.

Tipsy Turtle Pub (✉ *Brac Reef Beach Resort, West End* ☎ 345/948–1323), the only spot open until midnight or later nightly, overflows with good cheer and strong drinks. The mudslides are particularly potent, and there are usually some good Cubanos. The alfresco bar serves excellent pub grub (jerk chicken pizza, Caesar salad wrap, portobello-and-Swiss cheeseburger, messy marvelous spare ribs, tempura shrimp) for around $10. Popcorn and Ping-Pong are free. It's the kind of casual congenial hangout where almost everyone ends up buying a round at some point ("What are you drinking?" might elicit a response like "Oh, a little bit of everything"). Depending on your tastes, stop by for Wednesday karaoke on the outside patio, which attracts large, enthusiastic crowds.

Little Cayman

WORD OF MOUTH

"The diving in Little Cayman was phenomenal. We dove with Paradise Divers at Paradise Villas. They did a great job of pointing out cool marine life and little things we would have missed on our own (like a tiny seahorse)."

—RatherBeDiving

By Jordan
Simon

**THE SMALLEST AND MOST TRANQUIL OF THE THREE CAY-
MAN ISLANDS,** Little Cayman has a full-time population
of only 170, most of whom work in the tourism industry;
they are easily outnumbered by iguanas and rare birds. This
12-square-mi (31-square-km) island is practically pristine
and has only a sand-sealed airstrip, sharing its "terminal"
building with the fire department and a few other vehicles.
The grass runway was finally paved with blacktop a couple
of years ago, and locals no longer have to line up their cars
at night to guide emergency landings in by headlight. But
some things don't change. The speed limit remains 25 mph,
as no one is in a hurry to go anywhere. In fact, the island's
population of resident iguanas uses roads more regularly
than residents; signs created by local artists read IGUANAS
HAVE THE RIGHT OF WAY.

With little commercial development, the island beckons
ecotourists seeking wildlife encounters, not urban wild life.
It's best known for its spectacular diving in world-renowned
Bloody Bay Marine Park, including Bloody Bay Wall and
adjacent Jackson Wall. The ravishing reefs and plummeting
walls encircling the island teem with more than 500 different species of fish and more than 150 kinds of coral. Fly-,
lake-, and deep-sea fishing are also popular, as well as snorkeling, kayaking, and biking. And the island's certainly for
the birds. The National Trust Booby Pond Nature Reserve
is a designated wetland of international importance, which
protects around 20,000 red-footed boobies, the Western
Hemisphere's largest colony. It's just one of many superlative spots to witness avian aerial acrobatics.

Secluded beaches, unspoiled tropical wilderness and
wetlands, mangrove swamps, lagoons, bejeweled coral
reefs—Little Cayman practically redefines "hideaway"
and "escape." Yet aficionados appreciate that the low-
key lifestyle doesn't mean sacrificing the high-tech amenities, and some of the resorts cater to a quietly wealthy yet
unpretentious crowd.

Which isn't to say Little Cayman lacks for lively moments.
Halloween parties and Mardi Gras festivities bring out
wildly imaginative costumes and floats. It's just one of
those rare places that attract more colorful types who are
in search of privacy, not just the ardently ecocentric. One
of the largest private homes was built and owned by the
late actor Burgess Meredith; island rumors persist to this
day of planefuls of high-school cheerleaders visiting his digs

TOP EXPERIENCES

■ **Wall-to-Wall Fun.** Divers can't miss the hallowed Bloody Bay, lauded by every Cousteau worth his sea salt.

■ **Booby Watching.** Even if you're not a birder, learning about the rare red-footed booby from its fanatics at the National Trust and spying them through telescopes are more fun than you'd think.

■ **Beachcombing.** A jaunt to Owen Island or Point o' Sand rewards you with practically virgin strands, breathtaking views, and scintillating snorkeling.

■ **Pirates Pointing.** A meal with Gladys Howard at her peerless little resort is memorable not only for the food but the company.

■ **Something Fishy.** The deep-sea fishing is superior, but the light-tackle option should lure any angler.

for weeks at a time. Then there's a local who allegedly grew marijuana. The island's two bobbies (who do a four-year stint from Great Britain and learn when to look the other way) caught him with a joint. "But it can't be mine," he protested, "'cuz I woulda smoked it by now." The plants were impounded and placed in a tub in the jail's only cell, while the accused went free.

That doesn't provide a license for misbehavior on this beautiful, idiosyncratic landfall. But this is definitely a place to mellow out; drugs won't be needed. As one regular cackles, "If the island were any more laid-back, it'd be double-jointed."

ORIENTATION AND PLANNING

ORIENTATION

Little Cayman is bracketed by lighthouses at the West and East Ends, whose terrain couldn't be more different. The semi-arid East End has a remote, end-of-the-world feel: Limestone sinkholes called karst stitched with xeric shrub give it a pitted moon-like appearance. The West End is much greener. But beaches, snorkeling, nature trails, and bird-viewing areas embroider the entire island. One main road, mostly paved, essentially circumnavigates the coast. Several packed-dirt side roads crisscross the island, often

8

accessing the more remote beaches. These can become muddy and almost impassable in heavy rain.

PLANNING

WHEN TO GO

Though diving and fishing excel in summer as well, the traditional high-season months of December through April apply to Little Cayman, as they do to hotels in much of the Caribbean. Most of the small resorts shut down September through most of October, during the height of hurricane season.

GETTING HERE AND AROUND

BY AIR

Inter-island service between Grand Cayman, Cayman Brac, and Little Cayman is provided several times daily by Cayman Airways. Edward Bodden Airfield still has an almost provisional feel, a long grassy stretch that accommodates only STOL craft.

BY CAR

Bikes, usually offered in a complimentary basis by the resorts, are the preferred way of getting around the island; dive operations will pick you up, and the hotels also provide airport transfers. A car is suggested only if you rent one of the more isolated villas or if you plan to explore the farther-flung part of the island on a regular basis. Parking is rarely a problem. Another flexible touring option is a moped. McLaughlin Rentals offers mopeds ($54) and SUVs ($80–$100). Scooten Scooters provides rentals for $32 per half-day, $45 for a full day. They also offer free resort delivery/pick-up and free gas, are environmentally friendly, and even give instruction.

Information **McLaughlin Rentals** (✉ By the airport, Village Square ☎ 345/948–1000). **Scooten Scooters** (☎ 345/916–4971 ⊕ www. scootenscooters.com).

BY TAXI

Resorts offer airport transfers. Two companies offer land tours (in addition to fishing, kayaking, and other options). Island tours are usually $50 per person (though each additional person is generally discounted, as are children). LCB Tours has a safari bus for larger groups. Maxine McCoy's MAM's Tours can accommodate up to 15 passengers in two minivans, though she's often off-island.

Information **LCB Tours** (✉ *Little Cayman Beach Resort, Blossom Village* ☎ *345/948–1642 or 345/948–1033*).

MAM's Tours (✉ *65 Mahogany Bay, Candle Rd., West End* ☎ *345/926–0104 or 866/978–5904* ⊕ *www.mamstour.ky*).

RESTAURANTS

The main resorts' dining rooms accept reservations from nonguests pending availability. Otherwise, there are two full-fledged restaurants, both affiliated with villa/condo properties. The choices are limited, with seafood obviously reigning supreme, but the caliber of the few kitchens is generally high.

WHAT IT COSTS IN U.S. DOLLARS					
	¢	$	$$	$$$	$$$$
Restaurants	under $8	$8–$12	$12–$20	$20–$30	over $30
Hotels*	under $80	$80–$150	$150–$250	$250–$350	over $350
Hotels**	under $125	$125–$250	$250–$350	$350–$450	over $450

*EP, BP, CP **AI, FAP, MAP; restaurant prices are for a main course, excluding the customary 10% service charge. Hotel prices are for two people in a double room in high season, excluding the 7½% VAT, customary 10% service charge, and meal plans (except at all-inclusive hotels).

HOTELS

Accommodations are mostly in small lodges, almost all of which offer meal and dive packages. The chefs in most places create wonderful meals despite often limited resources. You won't find any independent restaurants, but if you are staying in a villa or condo you can usually have dinner at one of the resorts (be sure to call ahead). Dive packages represent exceptional savings. Most resorts prefer a five- to seven-night stay in high season, but the minimum isn't always strictly enforced. Still, rooms for shorter stays may not become available until two to three weeks prior to your trip dates.

VISITOR INFORMATION

There is no visitor center on Little Cayman, but each hotel, hotelier, and staffer overflows with information and suggestions. You can also consult the Web sites of the **Sister Islands Tourism Association** (⊕ *www.itsyourstoexplore.com*) for information on Little Cayman.

EXPLORING LITTLE CAYMAN

Little Cayman isn't much for manmade sights and attractions; those that are here essentially serve to explain and promote nature preserved in all her finery, especially underwater, throughout the island. If you're exploring on your own, pick up the *Little Cayman Heritage Sites and Trails* brochure, available at the hotels and National Trust; it lists all the major points of interest.

WHAT TO SEE

Little Cayman Museum. The museum displays relics and artifacts, including a new wing devoted to maritime memorabilia, that provide a good overview of this tiny island's history and heritage. ⊠ *Across from Booby Pond Nature Reserve, Blossom Village* ☎ *No phone at museum; 345/948–1033 for Little Cayman Beach Resort* ⊠ *Free* ⊙ *Thurs.–Fri. 3–5, by appointment only.*

★ **Fodor's**Choice **Little Cayman National Trust.** This traditional Caymanian cottage overlooks the Booby Pond Nature Reserve; telescopes on the breezy second-floor deck permit close-up views of their markings and nests, as well as the other feathered friends. Inside you'll find shell collections, panels and dioramas discussing endemic reptiles, and diagrams on the growth and life span of red-footed boobies, frigate birds, egrets, and other island "residents." The shop sells exquisite jewelry made from Caymanite and spider crab shells, extraordinary duck decoys and carvings of purple gallinules and black-necked stilts by local artist John Mulak, and great books on history, ornithology, and geology. The cheeky movie Calendar Girls inspired a local equivalent: Little Cayman women, mostly in full-ripe maturity, going topless for an important cause—raising awareness of the red-footed booby and funds to purchase the sanctuary's land. Nicknamed, appropriately, "Support the Boobies," the calendar is tasteful, not titillating: The lasses strategically hold conch shells, brochures, flippers, tree branches, etc. Thanks to chair Debbi Truchan's baking skills, this is *the* spot for cappuccino, herb tea, cinnamon buns, and scrumptious homemade ice cream (guava, rum raisin, lemongrass, ginger)—a fantastic place to mingle with residents and visitors. ⊠ *Blossom Village* ☎ *No phone* ⊕ *www.nationaltrust.org.ky* ⊙ *Mon.–Sat. 9–noon and 2–6.*

★ **Little Cayman Research Center.** Located near the Jackson Point Bloody Bay Marine Park reserve, this vital research center

Little Cayman

KEY

Beaches
Dive Sites
Restaurants
Hotels

Restaurants

Blue Lagoon, **1**
Hungry Iguana, **2**
Pirates Point, **3**

Hotels

Blossom Village
Cottage, **6**
Conch Club, **3**
The Club, **4**
Little Cayman
Beach Resort, **5**
Paradise Villas, **7**
Pirates Point Resort, **8**
Sir Turtle Beach Villas, **2**
Southern Cross Club, **1**

Caribbean Sea

East Pt.

Snipe Pt.

Point of Sand

EASTERN BLUFF

Mary's Bay

Crawl Bay

Rosetta Flats

Charles Bight Pond

Charles Bight

LITTLE CAYMAN

Lower Spot Bay

Tarpon Lake

Wearis Bay

Grape Tree Bay

Owen Island

Little Cayman Research Centre

Jacksons Pt.

Little Cayman National Trust

Booby Pond Nature Reserve

Booby Pond

Little Cayman Museum

Blossom Village Park

Jackson Wall

Bloody Bay

Bloody Bay Wall

Spot Bay

South Town

Edward Bodden Airfield

Preston Bay

Anchorage Bay

West End Lighthouse

West End Pt.

Westerly Ponds

0   1 km
0   1 mi

supports visiting students and researchers, with a long list of projects studying the biodiversity, human impact, reef health, and ocean ecosystem of Little Cayman. Its situation is unique in that reefs this unspoiled are usually far less accessible; the National Oceanic and Atmospheric Administration (NOAA) awarded it one of 16 monitoring stations worldwide. The center also solicits funding through the parent U.S. nonprofit organization Central Caribbean Marine Institute; if you value the health of our reefs, show your support on the Web site. Chairman Peter Hillenbrand proudly calls it the "Ritz-Carlton of marine research facilities, which often are little more than pitched tents on a beach." A short video followed by tours explains the center's mission and ecosensitive design (including Peter's Potty, an off-the-grid bathroom facility utilizing compostable toilets that recycle fertilizer into gray water for the gardens); sometimes you'll get a peek at the upstairs functional wet labs and dormitories. To make it layperson-friendlier, scientists occasionally give talks and presentations. The Dive with a Researcher program (where you actually help survey and assess environmental impact and ecosystem health, depending on that week's focus) is hugely popular. ⊠ *North Side* ☎ *345/926–2789 or 345/948–1094* ⊕ *www.reefresearch.org* ⊗ *By appointment only.*

WHERE TO EAT

★ **Fodor's**Choice ✕ **Pirates Point.** Irrepressible Gladys Howard
$$$$ offers Texas-style and Texas-size hospitality at her ravishing little resort. Guests have first privilege, but the kitchen can usually accommodate an extra couple or two. Advance reservations are both a must and a courtesy on this island, where nearly everything is imported at great cost and effort. The resort gardens provide mangoes, Key limes, basil, lemongrass, and other herbs. Gladys wears many hats on island (indeed, if you stumble upon her at a special occasion, she may be wearing a bear mask, bobby cap, or crab pincers). Her lighthearted antics belie the serious food. Gladys trained with Julia Child, James Beard, and Jacques Pepin, and at the legendary Cordon Bleu in Paris; she still supervises everything with an eagle eye. Memorable three-course prix-fixe dinners (wine but not tip included), served on Wedgwood, could feature anything from filet mignon béarnaise with potatoes dauphinoise to kingfish Creole with couscous and ratatouille. It all comes with heaping helpings of bon mots and bonhomie. ⊠ *Pirates Point, Preston*

Pirates Point resort

8

Bay ☎ *345/948–1010* ⚓ *Reservations essential* ═ *MC, V* ⊘ *Closed Sept.–mid-Oct.*

$$–$$$ ✕ **Blue Lagoon.** This little waterfront hangout is daubed in edible colors from its lime and blueberry facade to salmon and mint walls hung with little driftwood signs espousing its philosophy (YEAH MAN, CHILLIN, RELAX). Picture windows afford wondrous views of Kingston Bight, especially when the setting sun triggers a laser show across the bay as smooth and finely hued as Murano glass. The Bight is the island's only truly safe harbor, and everyone has moorings here, so the BL is filled with character and characters. Food is incidental but more than serviceable (though half the extensive menu usually isn't available). Fish-and-chips (fresh catch), lasagna, red-bean soup, chicken tikka masala, turtle steak, and pepper-crusted tuna are usually reliable. ✉ *Kingston Bight* ☎ *345/948–1015 or 345/948–0117* ═ *AE, MC, V* ⊘ *No dinner Sun.*

$$–$$$ ✕ **Hungry Iguana.** The closest thing to a genuine sports bar and nightclub on Little Cayman, the "Iggy" caters to the aquatically minded set with a marine mural, wood plank floors, mounted trophy sailfish, lots of fishing caps, and yummy fresh seafood. Conch fritters are near definitive, while corn-crusted calamari with Scotch bonnet salsa are mouth- and eye-watering. It's a great hangout for (relatively) cheap eats; prix-fixe theme nights between CI$18 and CI$40 offer fine value: pizza, fajitas, curry, and more. Drink in the smashing sunset views on the delightful patio

Iggin Out

An estimated 2,000 prehistoric-looking Little Cayman rock iguanas roam the island, by far the largest population in Cayman. Gladys Howard, former chair of the Little Cayman committee of the nonprofit National Trust for the Cayman Islands, has taken the good fight for the boobies and applied it to the "iggies." Visitors can feed these large (up to 5 feet), fierce-looking but docile vegetarians by hand at the residential Mahogany Bay neighborhood, where the creatures' preferred delicacies—fruit trees and flowers from bananas and papayas to hibiscus—flourish. But Gladys hopes to purchase coastal land to serve as a nesting sanctuary. She knows it's a crucial component of ecotourism and, noting how the same species has all but disappeared on the Brac (while the blue iguana still faces extinction on Grand Cayman), says, "We want to avoid that fate. We must preserve them because so few of that species remain on our planet."

overlooking the water, and also drink of the house specialty Iguana Punch (rum, rum, more rum, and coconut rum with orange and pineapple juices). ⊠ *Paradise Villas, Blossom Village* ☎ *345/948–0001* ⊟ *AE, MC, V* ⊘ *No dinner Sun.*

WHERE TO STAY

Accommodations are mostly in small lodges, many of which offer meal and dive packages. The meal packages are a good idea; the chefs in most places create wonderful meals.

PRIVATE VILLAS

A few private villas on Little Cayman can be rented, most of them basic but well maintained, ranging from one to four bedrooms. Rental fees are reasonable, and normally the price for extra couples in the larger units is only $200 per week, representing substantial savings for families or couples traveling together, while the kitchen helps reduce the price of dining out. In addition, government tax and often a service fee are sometimes included in the quoted rate (be sure to verify this). As a general rule of thumb, properties are thoroughly cleaned before your arrival; you must pay extra if you want daily maid service. Rates are sometimes discounted in the off-season. Most villa owners mandate a three- to seven-night minimum stay in high season, though this is often negotiable. Unless otherwise noted, properties have landline phones; local calls are usually free, but phones are generally locked for international calls.

$$$$ ⊤ **Blossom Village Cottage.** *Private Villa.* This century-old beachfront cottage charms with hardwood floors, corrugated tin mansard roof, and coffered ceilings. The original building contains one bedroom; an adjacent annex holds two more, both en suite. Frilly decor conjures a sweet maiden aunt, with white wicker galore; hand-painted powder blue, pink, or seafoam green tracery; floral curtains; rocking chairs; seashells; and landscape paintings. Both buildings feature delightfully breezy screened-in porches. The rental rate includes tax. **Pros:** pretty beach; central location; historic ambience. **Cons:** no dishwasher; shower only; no laundry facilities; some might find the decor too frilly. ⊠ *Blossom Village* 🕾 *No phone* ⊕ *www.caymanvillas.com* ⌁ *3 bedrooms, 3 baths* ⌂ *Dishwasher, DVD, Wi-Fi, beachfront* ▭ *AE, MC, V* ⟲ *3-night minimum high season.*

$$$– ⊤ **The Club.** *Vacation Condos.* These ultramodern, luxuri-
$$$$ ous three-bedroom condos are Little Cayman's newest (from 2002) and nicest units, though only five are usually included in the rental pool. Each comes fully equipped, from kitchen to bedroom, with Italian marble, Turkish tiles, etched-glass doors, elegant accents like arches and crown moldings, state-of-the-art gadgetry from rainfall showerheads to flat-screen TVs, upscale furnishings like four-poster beds, and patios or balconies with scintillating water views. The complex has an outdoor pool with waterfall and hot tub along the beachfront, as well as a dock with inviting hammocks. Guests can use the amenities and sign up for a meal plan at Little Cayman Beach Resort, under the same ownership; it's about a five-minute walk from the Club. Some residences can be locked off into one- and two-bedroom units. **Pros:** luxurious digs; lovely beach. **Cons:** housekeeping not included; rear guest bedrooms dark and somewhat cramped; handsome but heavy old-fashioned decor. ⌂ *Box 51, South Hole Sound, Blossom Village, Little Cayman KY3-2501* 🕾 *345/948–1033, 727/323–8727, or 800/327–3835* ⊕ *www.theclubatlittle-cayman.com* ⌁ *8 3-bedroom condos* ⌂ *In-room: kitchen, DVD, Wi-Fi. In-hotel: pool, beachfront, bicycles, laundry facilities* ▭ *AE, MC, V* ⦿ *EP.*

$$$– ⊤ **Conch Club.** *Vacation Condos.* The handsome ocean-
$$$$ front development grafts Caribbean-style gingerbread
⟳ onto New England maritime architecture with gables and dormers. Condos are well equipped and ideal for fami-

8

lies or small groups (units 15–20 tend to be quieter). The town-house-style units have vaulted ceilings, full kitchens, private patios, and balconies that look out onto the pool and ocean. Despite individual decorative flourishes, a fussy grandmotherly-style look out of a Sunbelt retirement community predominates. Diving is offered through Conch Club Divers. Guests can also enjoy the amenities at the Little Cayman Beach Resort (a sister property). Meal plans are available for an additional charge. **Pros:** splendid views; gorgeous beach; added shuttle to Little Cayman Beach Resort; beachfront hot tub. **Cons:** long walk to Little Cayman Resort's facilities; dated decor; housekeeping surcharge. ⌂ *Box 51, Blossom Village, Little Cayman KY3-2501* ☎ *345/948–1033 or 888/756–7400* ⊕ *www.conchclub.com* ⏎ *18 2-bedroom condos, 2 3-bedroom condos* ⌘ *In-room: kitchen, DVD, Wi-Fi. In-hotel: pools, spa, diving, bicycles, laundry facilities, Internet terminal, Wi-Fi hotspot* ⊟ *MC, V* ⊚ *EP.*

$$$ ⊤ **Little Cayman Beach Resort.** *Resort.* This two-story hotel,
☾ the island's largest, offers the most options for fun-seekers
★ and modern facilities yet a boutique vibe. The stylishly contemporary rooms received a complete refurbishment in 2008 (flat-screen TVs, iPod docking stations, curved shower rods, malachite and marble accents, carved Honduran hardwood furnishings). They overlook either the pool area or the ocean (the latter are quieter, especially the 300 block, farthest from the occasionally raucous Beach Nuts Bar, where divers congregate at 5 PM to watch the day's top high-definition videos). A full-service spa offers massages utilizing mostly marine-based ingredients, as well as hair and nail treatments. The Mermaid Boutique is the island's most upscale shop. Meals, which have greatly improved under executive chef Anthony Pizzarello, are generally served buffet style. Diving packages represent excellent value. The resort is gradually upgrading various areas and experimenting with ecofriendly practices such as using green-approved organic chemicals. But island warmth remains: It's family-run by Brackers, the children of beloved Linton "Mr. T" Tibbetts, an inspiring self-made millionaire who was awarded an OBE (Order of the British Empire) for his passionate efforts to promote tourism while preserving Caymanian heritage. **Pros:** extensive facilities; fun crowd; state-of-the-art technology; glorious LED-lit pool. **Cons:** less-intimate feel than that of other island resorts; tiny patios; fee to rent bikes. ⌂ *Box 51, Blossom Village, Little Cayman KY3-2501* ☎ *345/948–1033 or*

800/327–3835 ⊕ www.littlecayman.com ⤴ 40 rooms ⚹ In-room: safe, kitchen (some), refrigerator, Wi-Fi. In-hotel: restaurant, bar, tennis court, pool, gym, spa, beachfront, diving, water sports, bicycles, Internet terminal, Wi-Fi hotspot ⊟ AE, MC, V ⨯◯⨯ FAP.

★ Fodor'sChoice ⊠ **Pirates Point Resort.** *Resort.* The large repeat
$$$– clientele attests that everything from the comfortable rooms
$$$$ to the fine cuisine lives up to the billing at this hideaway nestled between sea grape and casuarina pines on a sparkling sweep of palapa-dotted sand. There are 11 bungalow-style rooms, some air-conditioned, others swept by crosswinds through louvers. Walls duplicate the soft colors of a Caribbean dawn; floors and furnishings are immaculate. In true Caribbean getaway tradition, TV is banished to the main cottage (where Wi-Fi is available). You'll likely become fast friends with effervescent owner Gladys Howard, whose down-home welcome belies her upscale meals (ask to hear anecdotes of her studies with Julia Child, James Beard, and Jacques Pepin). She still watches the kitchen staff like a hawk while finding time to host weekly champagne parties on the verandah of her adjacent home and play dominoes after dinner. Somehow Gladys always wins, slamming tiles down with classic Caribbean vigor. Weekly stays (preferred) represent huge savings, especially the dive packages, which include an open bar; guests who are not on dive packages just get wine with dinner. **Pros:** fabulous food; fantastic beach; dynamic dive program; fun-loving staff and owner. **Cons:** everyone respects honeymooners' privacy, but this isn't a resort for antisocial types; tasteful rooms are fairly spare; occasional Internet problems. ⬚ *Box 43, Preston Bay, Little Cayman KY3-2501* ☎ *345/948–1010* ⊕ *www. piratespointresort.com* ⤴ *11 rooms* ⚹ *In-room: no TV. In-hotel: restaurant, bar, gym, beachfront, diving, water sports, bicycles, Internet terminal, Wi-Fi hotspot, no kids under 5* ⊟ *MC, V* ⊘ *Closed Sept.–mid-Oct.* ⨯◯⨯ *FAP.*

★ Fodor'sChoice ⊠ **Southern Cross Club.** *Resort.* Little Cayman's
$$$$ first resort was co-founded in the 1950s as a private fishing club by the CEO of Sears-Roebuck and CFO of General Motors, and its focus is still on fishing and diving. The adventure and barefoot elegance motifs are struck in the semi-open lobby with African masks, trophy game fish, hand-painted cabinets, and magnificent indoor-outdoor bar. Psychedelically hued duplex cottages sit on Little Cayman's most spectacular white-sand beach, with views of the uninhabited Owen Island and romantic private outdoor showers. Rooms feature vivid colors and hardwood

8

Southern Cross Club

furniture, including several four-poster beds. Some have separate living rooms; the newest incorporate ecologically sound aspects like gray-watered gardens and solar-heated water. Dive services are superb—set your gear up once, and the rest is done for you during your stay. The food is exceptional, served in various venues, including an air-conditioned split-level dining room with panoramic views. **Pros:** barefoot luxury; complimentary use of kayaks and snorkel gear; splendiferous beach; international staff regales you with globetrotting exploits. **Cons:** not child-friendly (though families can rent a separate cottage). ✉ *Box 44, South Hole Sound, Little Cayman KY3-2501* ☎ *345/948–1099 or 800/899–2582* ⊕ *www.southerncrossclub.com* ⤳ *11 rooms, 3 suites, 1 2-bedroom cottage* ♿ *In-room: refrigerator (some), no TV. In-hotel: restaurant, bar, gym, spa, beachfront, diving, water sports, bicycles, Internet terminal, Wi-Fi hotspot, no kids under 10* ☐ *AE, MC, V* ⊙ *Closed mid-Sept.–mid-Oct.* ⦿ *FAP.*

$$ ▦ **Paradise Villas.** *Vacation Villas.* The cozy, sunny one-bedroom units have beachfront terraces and hammocks and are simply but immaculately appointed with rattan furnishings, marine artwork, painted driftwood, and bright abstract fabrics. A recent overhaul added stylish touches like flat-screen TVs. If you tire of cooking for yourself in the well-equipped kitchen, fine island-style food (not to mention the island's only real bar) is steps away at the nutty, nautically themed Hungry Iguana (affectionately dubbed

"The Iggy") restaurant. Affiliated Conch Club Divers provides transfers and offers good service despite being off-site; room/dive packages are a sensational value. **Pros:** good value; friendly staff. **Cons:** noisy some weekend nights in season; poky beach; now a (minimal) charge for bike use; dive shop no longer on-site (though the contracted operation runs smoothly). ⌂ *Box 48, South Hole Sound, Little Cayman KY3-2501* ☎*345/948–0001 or 877/322–9626* ⊕*www.paradisevillas.com* ⌑*12 1-bedroom villas* ⌂ *In-room: kitchen. In-hotel: pool, beachfront, bicycles* ☐*AE, MC, V* ⊗ *Closed mid-Sept.–late Oct.* ⊙*EP.*

$$$$ ⚓ **Sir Turtle Beach Villas.** *Vacation Villas.* Two gorgeous nautical-style villas—Boobie's Nest and Man O' War Roost—both with four bedrooms and two bathrooms and identical inverse layouts, sit on a splendid stretch of sugary sand. The extensive old-style wooden verandahs are made for sunset-watching, but the strategic location guarantees nonpareil views of the Caribbean and the Booby Pond on either side, with 360-degree panoramas from the top floor. Simple but smart decor favors splashes of vivid color (scarlet or turquoise sofa contrasted with hardwood furnishings, including rockers galore, and paneling) and glorious half-moon handmade stained-glass windows depicting cavorting mermaids astride dolphins. Loft rooms function as terrific family rooms, with daybeds to sleep additional kids. **Pros:** marvelous views; beautiful beach; outdoor Jacuzzi; stylish and high-tech. **Cons:** no pool; shared bathrooms; smallish guest bedrooms. ⌧ *South Hole Sound* ☎ *No phone* ⊕ *www.sirturtlebeachvillas.com* ⌑*4 bedrooms, 2 baths* ⌂ *Dishwasher, DVD, Wi-Fi, hot tub, beachfront, laundry facilities* ☐*AE, MC, V* ☞ *3-night minimum.*

BEACHES

The southwest part of the island seems like one giant beach; this is where virtually all the resorts sit, serenely facing Preston Bay and South Hole Sound. But there are several other unspoiled, usually deserted strands that beckon beachcombers, all the sand having the same delicate hue of Cristal Champagne and just as apt to make you feel giddy.

Blossom Village Park. Developed by the local chapter of the National Trust, this site of the first albeit temporary Cayman Islands settlement in the 1660s is lined with traditional cottages; bricks are dedicated to old-time residents and longtime repeat guests. There are picnic tables, a play-

ground, and a dock. The beach is small but has plenty of shade trees, good snorkeling, and calm water.

★ Fodor'sChoice **Owen Island**. This private, forested island can be reached by rowboat, kayak, or an ambitious 200-yard swim. Anyone is welcome to come across and enjoy the deserted beaches and excellent snorkeling. Nudity is forbidden as "idle and disorderly" in the Cayman Islands, though that doesn't always stop skinny dippers (who may not realize they can be seen quiet easily from shore on the strands facing Little Cayman).

★ Fodor'sChoice **Point of Sand**. Stretching over a mile on the easternmost point of the island, this secluded beach is great for wading, shell collecting, and snorkeling. On a clear day you can see 7 mi (11 km) across to Cayman Brac. It serves as a green- and loggerhead turtle nesting site in spring, and a marvelous mosaic of coral gardens blooms just offshore. It's magical, especially at moonrise, when it earns its nickname, Lovers' Beach. There's a palapa for shade but no facilities. The current can be strong, so watch the kids carefully.

SPORTS AND THE OUTDOORS

Little Cayman is a recreational paradise on land and especially underwater, with world-class diving, light-tackle angling, and bird-watching the star attractions. Befitting an ecocentric destination, nature owns the island, and you're strictly cautioned about dos and don'ts. But lectures are given with a smile, and then you're free to explore this zoo without cages, and aquarium without tanks.

BIRD-WATCHING

Little Cayman offers bountiful bird-watching, with more than 200 indigenous and migrant species on vibrant display, including red-footed boobies, frigate birds, and West Indian whistling ducks. Unspoiled wetland blankets more than 40% of the island, and elevated viewing platforms (carefully crafted from local wood to blend harmoniously with the environment) permit undisturbed observation—but then, it's hard to find an area that doesn't host flocks of warblers and waterfowl. Brochures with maps are available at the hotels for self-guided bird-watching tours. The Web site of the **National Trust** and the **Sister Islands Tourism Authority** (⊕ *www.itsyourstoexplore.com*) has information on bird-watching.

★ **Booby Pond Nature Reserve** is home to 20,000 red-footed boobies (the largest colony in the Western Hemisphere) and Cayman's only breeding colony of magnificent frigate (or man-of-war) birds; other sightings include the near-threatened West Indian whistling duck and vitelline warbler. The RAMSAR Convention, an international treaty for wetland conservation, designated the reserve a wetland of global significance. Near the airport, the sanctuary is open to the public and has a gift shop and reading library.

BIRD-WATCHING SITES

Grape Tree Ponds on the North Side is a splendid wetland spot for West Indian whistling ducks, with some lovely shore walks.

Jackson's Pond is a vast mangrove-fringed body of water offering excellent viewing of herons, ducks, rails, stilt, plovers, and sandpipers.

Tarpon Lake lures more than anglers. A long deck extends into the writhing tangle of red mangrove roots where white herons, ospreys, and whistling ducks dive-bomb for fiddler crabs and mosquito fish skittering through the brackish water alongside sun-silvered pirouetting tarpon.

West End Lighthouse offers magnificent sunset views and serves as arrivals check-in for migrant shorebirds.

Westerly Ponds is composed of shallow wading pools in the ironshore by Preston Bay lined by low buttonwood trees and herbaceous vegetation where killdeer, willet, black-necked stilt, and American coot perform an aerial ballet.

DIVING AND SNORKELING

A gaudy, voluptuous tumble of marine life—lumbering grouper to fleet guppies, massive manta rays to miniature wrasse, sharks to stingrays, blue chromis to Bermuda chubs, puffers to parrotfish—parades its finery through the pyrotechnic coral reefs like a watery Main Street on Saturday night. Gaping gorges, vaulting pinnacles, plunging walls, chutes, arches, and vertical chimneys create a virtual underwater city, festooned with fiery sponges and sensuously waving gorgonians draped like come-hither courtesans over limestone settees.

Expect to pay around $95 for a two-tank boat dive and $25–$30 for a snorkeling trip. The island is small and

Bloody Bay Wall

susceptible to wind, so itineraries can change like a sudden gust.

DIVE AND SNORKEL SITES

Snorkelers will delight in taking Nancy's Cup of Tea or "scaling" Mike's Mountain, as well as enjoying Eagle Ray Roundup, Three Fathom Wall, and Owen Island. The areas around the East End are difficult to access from shore due to the jagged ironshore (boats are often preferable) but are worthwhile: Mary's Bay, Snipe Point, and Lighthouse Reef (which has stunning Brac vistas).

Among the many superlative dive sites are the Great Wall, the Meadows, the Zoo, Coconut Walk Wall, School Bus Stop, Sarah's Set, Black Hole, Mixing Bowl, Charlie's Chimneys, and Blacktip Boulevard.

★ **Fodor's** Choice **Bloody Bay Wall** (the beach was site of a spectacular 17th-century sea battle) was in fact declared one of the world's top three dive sites by no less than the *maîtres* Jacques and Philippe Cousteau and forms part of a protected marine reserve. It plunges dramatically from 18 to 6,000 feet, with a series of staggeringly beautiful drop-offs and remarkable visibility. Even snorkelers who are strong swimmers can access the edge from shore, swimming among shimmering silver curtains of minnows, jacks, bonefish, and more. The critters are amazingly friendly, including Jerry the Grouper, whom dive masters joke is a representative for the Cayman Islands Department of Tourism.

★ Adjacent to Bloody Bay, **Jackson Wall** and reef are nearly as stunning. Conditions are variable, the water now glassy, now turbulent, so snorkelers must be strong swimmers. There's a mini-wall 50 yards from shore and a dramatic drop-off another 100 yards out. It's renowned for Swiss-cheese-like swim-throughs; though it's not as precipitous as Bloody Bay, the more rugged bottom results in astonishing rock formations whose tunnels and crevices hold pyrotechnic marine life.

RECOMMENDED OPERATORS

Conch Club Divers (☎ *345/948–1026* ⊕ *www.conchclub.com*) is a personable, experienced outfit that often customizes trips on its 42-foot Sea-esta.

Pirates Point Dive Resort (☎ *345/948–1010* ⊕ *www.pirate-spointresort.com*) has fully outfitted 42-foot Newtons with dive masters who excel at finding odd and rare creatures and encourages computer diving so you can stay down longer.

Reef Divers (☎ *345/948–1033*) at Little Cayman Beach Resort also offers a full-service photo and video center; its custom boats' state-of-the-art outfitting includes AEDs (defibrillators).

The **Southern Cross Club** (☎ *345/948–1099 or 800/899–2582* ⊕ *www.southerncrossclub.com*) limits each of its boats to 12 divers and has its own dock. It's particularly good with specialty courses and mandates computer diving.

FISHING

Bloody Bay is equally celebrated for fishing and diving, and the flats and shallows including South Hole Sound Lagoon across from Owen Island, Tarpon Lake, and the Charles Bight Rosetta Flats offer phenomenal light-tackle and fly-fishing action: surprisingly large tarpon, small bonefish, and permit (a large fish related to pompano) weighing up to 35 pounds. Superior deep-sea fishing is available right offshore for game fish including blue marlin, dolphin, wahoo, tuna, and barracuda.

Walter Rhyan, longtime resident, can often be seen relaxing at the gazebo on his gorgeous dock, headquarters for **Little Cayman Fishing Club** (✉ *Head O' Bay* ☎ *345/948–0038 or*

345/925–2921), opposite Owen Island. Captain Steve Pace commandeers the 37-foot Hatteras *Donna Lorraine* (after Walter's sister's and mother's names), which was specially rigged to navigate Little Cayman's shallower waters while offering big-time comfort for up to six anglers. The cabin is air-conditioned, with an L-shaped couch, refrigerator, TV/DVD, CD player, microwave, electric toilet, and four separate bunks for overnight trips. Non-alcoholic drinks, snacks, and tackle are provided; the cost is $700 for up to five hours; smaller boats are $350 per half-day. You can also go bonefishing ($220) in the Sound on a 17-foot Boston Whaler that can accommodate two to three anglers with Captain Jeremy Loercher, who's also a crackerjack fly-fishing instructor.

MAM's Tours (✉ *65 Mahogany Bay, Candle Rd., West End* ☎ *345/926–0104 or 866/978–5904* ⊕ *www.mamstour.ky*) is run by energetic local Maxine McCoy, who comes from fishing royalty of sorts (she, her mum, dad, and five brothers ran McCoy's Diving and Fishing Resort). Deep-sea fishing costs $125 per hour for up to four people; those angling for tarpon and bonefish pay $50 per hour. Maxine also runs snorkeling trips to Owen Island and will take you conching in season. She's spending more time on the Brac, so call in advance to ensure she'll be on island.

The **Southern Cross Club** (☎ *345/948–1099 or 800/899–2582* ⊕ *www.southerncrossclub.com*) offers light-tackle and deep-sea fishing trips.

HIKING

Flat Little Cayman is better suited to biking, but there are a few jaunts, notably the **Salt Rocks Nature Trail,** where you pass ancient mule pens, abandoned phosphate mines, and the rusting tracks of the original narrow-gauge railway now alive with a profusion of flowering cacti and scrub brush.

Travel Smart
Cayman Islands

WORD OF MOUTH

"The island is small. I would suggest renting a car . . . we did for the entire week we were there . . . it was not expensive at all . . . and worth it."

—CaribbeanChick

GETTING HERE AND AROUND

Grand Cayman is a relatively small island, and the longest distance you can travel should take no more than a couple of hours. You can get by on Grand Cayman using a combination of tours and local buses (especially if you are staying in the Seven Mile Beach area), but if you want to explore on your own, it's easier with a rental car. Although driving is on the left, British style, Grand Cayman's well-paved road system makes independent travel fairly easy, though signage is not always clear. Cayman Brac and Little Cayman are even tinier and can be navigated by bike or moped.

▍ AIR TRAVEL

Several carriers offer frequent nonstop or direct flights between North America and Grand Cayman's Owen Roberts Airport. Flying time from New York is about four hours, just over an hour from Miami. Only small STOL propeller aircraft serve Cayman Brac and Little Cayman.

AIRPORTS

Grand Cayman's Owen Roberts Airport (GCM) is a modern facility located in the western, busier section of the island, roughly 2 mi (3 km) east of George Town. The current multimillion-dollar expansion and general upgrade (to meet the projected increase in arrivals over the next two decades) should be completed by late 2012. The airport is about 15 minutes from hotels situated along Seven Mile Beach, about 30 to 45 minutes from the East End and West Bay lodgings, and 10 minutes from George Town. Cayman Brac's Gerrard Smith Airport (CYB) can accommodate smaller jets, while Little Cayman's Edward Bodden Airstrip can only accommodate prop aircraft due to runway limitations.

Airport Information Owen Roberts Airport (*GCM* ✉ *Grand Cayman* ☎ *345/943–7070*). **Gerrard Smith International Airport** (*CYB* ✉ *Cayman Brac* ☎ *345/948–1222*). **Edward Bodden Airstrip** (*LYB* ✉ *Little Cayman* ☎ *345/948–0021*).

GROUND TRANSPORTATION

In Grand Cayman, ground transportation is available immediately outside the customs area of the airport. Taxis aren't metered, but fares are government-regulated (about $15–$30 to resorts along Seven Mile Beach, $60 to the East End). Be sure, however, to confirm the fare before getting into the taxi and whether the price quoted is in U.S. or Cayman dollars.

Round-trip airport transfers are generally included (or at least offered) by hotels on the sister islands, where most accommodations sit within 10 minutes' drive of the airports.

Taxis are always available at Grand Cayman's airport. They don't dependably meet flights on the sister islands, so make sure your resort or villa company has made arrangements.

FLIGHTS

All nonstop and direct air service is to Grand Cayman, with connecting flights to Cayman Brac and Little Cayman on a small propeller plane. Cayman Airways offers nonstops from several destinations, including Miami, New York–JFK, and Tampa. All operate several times weekly except Miami, which is daily. American offers nonstop daily service from Miami. Continental flies weekly from Newark and Houston. Delta flies weekly from Detroit, Minneapolis, and New York–JFK, and several times weekly from its Atlanta hub. U.S. Airways offers daily nonstop service from Charlotte and weekly flights from Boston and Philadelphia. Cayman Airways also flies to both Cayman Brac and Little Cayman. There's also inter-island charter service on Island Air.

Airline Contacts **American Airlines/American Eagle** (☎ 345/949–0666 or 800/744–0006 ⊕ www.aa.com). **Cayman Airways** (☎ 345/949–2311 or 800/422–9626 ⊕ www.caymanairways.com). **Continental** (☎ 345/916–5545 or 800/534–0089 ⊕ www.continental. com). **Delta** (☎ 345/945–8430 or 800/221–1212 ⊕ www.delta. com). **Island Air** (☎ 345/945–0241 ⊕ www.islandair.ky). **US Airways** (☎ 345/949–7488 or 800/622–1015 ⊕ www.usairways.com).

▌ BIKE AND MOPED TRAVEL

When renting a motor scooter or bicycle, remember to drive on the left and wear sunblock and a helmet. Bicycles ($15 a day) and scooters ($50 a day) can be rented in George Town when cruise ships are in port. On Cayman Brac or Little Cayman your hotel can make arrangements for you (most offer complimentary bicycles for local sightseeing).

Rental Companies **Island Scooter Rentals** (⊠ George Town, Grand Cayman ☎ 345/949–2046).

▌ BUS TRAVEL

On Grand Cayman, bus service is efficient, inexpensive, and plentiful, running roughly every 15 minutes. Minivans marked OMNI BUS are mostly independently operated (there are 38 buses and 24 owners) and run from 6 AM to midnight from West Bay to Rum Point and the East End. All routes branch from the George Town terminal adjacent to the library on Edward Street and are described in the phone book; color codes denote the routes. The one-way fare from George Town to West Bay via Seven Mile Beach is CI$1.50, to East End destinations CI$2, and from West Bay and northern Seven Mile Beach to East End CI$3. Some bus stops are well marked; others are flexible. Respond with a wave; then the driver toots his horn.

▌CAR TRAVEL

Driving is easy on Grand Cayman, albeit on the left (British-style). Most visitors, especially if they're staying along Seven Mile Beach, are content taking taxis or a one-day tour to see the sights rather than renting a car. Traffic on the road from Seven Mile Beach to George Town then onto Bodden Town in Grand Cayman is terrible, especially during the 7 to 9 AM and 4:30 to 6:30 PM commuting periods, despite construction of a bypass road. Fortunately, roads are generally well marked and well maintained. One major coastal highway circumnavigates most of the island (remember that no shortcuts divide the extensive East End), though you can get lost in the tangle of side roads in primarily residential West Bay. Exploring Cayman Brac on a scooter is fun and straightforward. You won't really need a car on Little Cayman, though there are a limited number of Jeeps for rent; bikes are the preferred mode of transport.

GASOLINE

In Grand Cayman, you can find gasoline stations in and around George Town, the airport, and Seven Mile Beach. Although times vary, most open daily with hours that extend into the evening; a few remain open 24 hours a day. There are two gasoline stations on Cayman Brac and one on Little Cayman. Prices are exorbitant, even compared to those in the U.S. and most of the Caribbean, especially on the Sister Islands.

PARKING

Park only in approved parking areas. Most hotels offer free parking. Many airport, Camana Bay, George Town, and Seven Mile Beach parking lots are free, but increasing development has prompted some major shopping centers to charge a fee if you park for more than 15 minutes (about $2.50 per hour); however, if you purchase something, parking should be validated and free. There is limited street parking, but watch for signs indicating private parking (in lots as well). Private enforcement companies are employed to discourage interlopers, placing a boot on the wheel and charging CI$75 for removal.

ROAD CONDITIONS

Grand Cayman has well-paved roads that follow the coastline. A network of main highways and bypasses facilitates traffic flow into and out of George Town. Small signs tacked to trees and poles at intersections point the way to most attractions, and local people are helpful if you get lost. Remote roads are in good repair, yet lighting can be poor at night—and night falls quickly at about 6 PM year-round.

Cayman Brac has one major road that skirts the coast, with a shortcut (Ashton Reid Drive) climbing the Bluff roughly bisecting the island. Little Cayman also provides a coastal route; unpaved sections in less-trammeled areas can become almost impassable after heavy rain. Other than that, goats, chickens, cattle, and the occasional iguana have the right of way.

ROADSIDE EMERGENCIES

Each car-rental agency has a different emergency-assistance provider. In the event of theft, accidents, or breakdowns, call your car rental agency and follow instructions.

RULES OF THE ROAD

In the Cayman Islands, drive on the left, British style. Be mindful of pedestrians and, in the countryside, occasional livestock walking on the road. When someone flashes headlights at you at an intersection, it means "after you." Be especially careful negotiating roundabouts (traffic circles). Observe the speed limit, which is conservative: 30 mph (50 kph) in the country, 20 mph (30 kph) in town. George Town actually has rush hours: 7 to 9 AM and 4:30 to 6:30 PM. Park only in approved parking areas. Always wear your seat belts—it's the law!

CAR RENTAL

To rent a car in The Cayman Islands, you must have a valid driver's license and major credit card. Most agencies require renters to be between 21 and 70 years of age, though the minimum age may be 25. Those over 75 may need a certified doctor's note indicating a continuing ability to drive safely. A local driver's permit, which costs $7.50, is obtained through the rental agency. Several dozen agencies rent cars, 4WD vehicles, and SUVs; rates are expensive—ranging from $40 to $95 per day (or $250 to $600 or more per week) in high season, depending on the vehicle and whether it has air-conditioning. Many firms offer significant discounts in low season, as well as reduced three-day rates. The rental generally includes insurance, pick-up and delivery service (or shuttle service to your hotel or the airport), maps, 24-hour emergency service, and unlimited mileage. Car seats are usually available upon request.

The major agencies have offices to the left as you depart from the airport terminal in Grand Cayman; the closest, Andy's, is to the right. All require that you walk outdoors for a hundred yards. Make sure your luggage is portable, because there's no shuttle; if there are two of you, one can watch the bags while the other gets the car. Many car-rental firms have free pick-up and drop-off along Seven Mile Beach (or second branches) so you can rent just on the days you want to tour. Consider security when renting a Jeep that cannot be locked. Midsize cars here often mean subcompact, so you may end up with a car that you wear unless you check the model.

Grand Cayman Agencies **Ace Hertz** (✉ *Owen Roberts Airport, Grand Cayman* ☏ *345/949–2280 or 800/654–3131* ⊕ *www.acerentacarltd.com*). **Andy's Rent a Car** (✉ *Owen Roberts Airport, Grand Cayman* ☏ *345/949–8111* ⊕ *www.andys. ky*). **Avis** (✉ *Owen Roberts Airport, Grand Cayman* ☏ *345/949–2468* ⊕ *www.aviscayman.com*). **Budget** (✉ *Owen Roberts Airport, Grand Cayman* ☏ *345/949–5605 or 800/527–0700* ⊕ *www.budgetcayman.com*). **Coconut Car Rentals** (✉ *Owen Roberts Airport, Grand Cayman* ☏ *345/949–4037, 345/949–7703, or 800/941–4562* ⊕ *www.coconut-*

carrentals.com). **Dollar** (✉ Owen Roberts Airport, Grand Cayman ☎ 345/949–4790 ⊕ www.dollarlac. com). **Economy** (✉ Owen Roberts Airport, Grand Cayman ☎ 345/949–9550 ⊕ www.economycarrental.com. ky). **Thrifty** (✉ Owen Roberts Airport, Grand Cayman ☎ 345/949–6640 or 800/367–2277 ⊕ www.thrifty.com).

Cayman Brac Agencies **B&S Motor Ventures** (✉ West End, Cayman Brac ☎ 345/948–1646 ⊕ www. bandsmv.com). **CB Rent-a-Car** (✉ Gerrard-Smith Airport, Cayman Brac ☎ 345/948–2424 or 345/948–2847 ⊕ www.cbrentacar.com). **Four D's Car Rental** (✉ Spot Bay, Cayman Brac ☎ 345/948–1599).

Little Cayman Agencies **McLaughlin Rentals** (✉ Airport Village Square, Little Cayman ☎ 345/948–1000).

CAR INSURANCE

If you own a car, your personal auto insurance may cover a rental to some degree, though not all policies protect you abroad; always read your policy's fine print. If you don't have auto insurance, then seriously consider buying the collision- or loss-damage waiver (CDW or LDW) from the car-rental company, which eliminates your liability for damage to the car.

Some credit cards offer CDW coverage, but it's usually supplemental to your own insurance and rarely covers SUVs, minivans, luxury models, and the like. If your coverage is secondary, you may still be liable for loss-of-use costs from the car-rental company. But no credit-card insurance is valid unless you use that card for *all* transactions, from reserving to paying the final bill. All companies exclude car rental in some countries, so be sure to find out about the destination to which you are traveling.

▮ TAXI TRAVEL

On Grand Cayman, taxis operate 24 hours a day; if you anticipate a late night, however, make pick-up arrangements in advance. Call for a cab to be dispatched, as you generally cannot hail one on the street except occasionally in George Town. They carry up to three passengers for the same price. Fares aren't metered; the government sets rates, and they're not cheap, so ask ahead. The tariff increases with the number of riders and bags. To travel in style by limo, you can call A. A. Transportation or Elite Limousine Services. Drivers are courteous and knowledgeable; most will narrate a tour at an hourly rate of about $25 for up to three people. Be sure to settle the price before you start off and agree on whether it's quoted in U.S. or Cayman dollars.

Taxis are scarcer on the sister islands; rates are also fixed and fairly prohibitive. Your hotel will provide recommended drivers.

Taxi Companies **A. A. Transportation Services** (☎ 345/926–8294 or 345/949–6598 ⊕ www.burtons.ky). **Charlie's Super Cab** (☎ 345/949–4748). **Elite Limousine Services** (☎ 345/949–5963). **Webster's Taxi Service** (☎ 345/947–1718).

ACCOMMODATIONS

Grand Cayman offers a wide range of lodgings in all price categories (though it ranks as one of the more expensive Caribbean destinations). You'll find luxury resorts, hotels both large and intimate, fully equipped condos, stylish individual villas, B&Bs, and more affordable locally run guesthouses. Quality, professionalism, high-tech conveniences, and service all rank among the region's best. With a few notable exceptions, condo resorts rule Seven Mile Beach (most hotels lie across the coastal "highway"). These are particularly attractive family options, as they include kitchen facilities. Cayman Brac and Little Cayman accommodations emphasize function above glitz and glamour (though most lack neither character nor characters), befitting the sister islands' status as top-notch scuba-diving destinations. Both have villas, condo resorts, and small hotels that often run on an all-inclusive or meal-plan basis and simple, family-run inns.

CATEGORY	COST
Choice	Under $80
$	$80–$150
$$	$150–$250
$$$	$250–$350
$$$$	Over $350

All prices are for a standard double room in high season, based on the European Plan (EP) and excluding tax and (usually) 10% service charge.

■TIP→ Assume that hotels operate on the European Plan (**EP**, no meals) unless we specify that they use the Breakfast Plan (**BP**, with full breakfast), Continental Plan (**CP**, Continental breakfast), Full American Plan (**FAP**, all meals), Modified American Plan (**MAP**, breakfast and dinner) or are all-inclusive (**AI**, all meals and most activities).

COMMUNICATIONS

INTERNET

In Grand Cayman most hotels and resorts provide Internet access—either free or for a small fee—for their guests; wireless is increasingly prevalent, including at the airport in Grand Cayman. You'll also find Internet cafés in George Town and at the easternmost point of the East End. Rates range from $2.50 for 15 minutes to $10 per hour. Several restaurants also advertise free Wi-Fi hot spots. Although there are no cybercafés on the sister islands, most of the small hotels have high-speed access in rooms and/or public spaces. Those lacking Wi-Fi or high-speed Internet connections in rooms usually have a public computer or permit use of the office facilities. A few individual villas offer Wi-Fi.

Grand Cayman Internet Cafés

Café del Sol Internet Cafe (✉ *Marquee Plaza, Seven Mile Beach* ☎ *345/946–2233*). **The Thirsty Surfer Liquor Store and Internet Cafe** (✉ *Reef Resort, Colliers, East End* ☎ *345/947–2337*).

PHONES

The area code for the Cayman Islands is 345.

CALLING WITHIN

In the Cayman Islands local calls are free from private phones; some hotels charge a small fee. For directory assistance, dial 411; international directory assistance is 010. Calls from pay phones cost CI$0.25 for five minutes. Prepaid phone cards, which can be used throughout Cayman and other Caribbean islands, are sold at shops, attractions, transportation centers, and other convenient outlets.

CALLING OUTSIDE

From the Cayman Islands, direct dialing to the United States and other countries is efficient and reasonable, but always check with your hotel to see if a surcharge is added. Some toll-free numbers cannot be accessed, especially on the sister islands. To charge your overseas call on a major credit card or U.S. calling card without incurring a surcharge, dial 800/225–5872 (1-800/CALL-USA) from any phone.

The country code for the United States is 1.

Information AT&T (☎ 800/872–2881). **LIME** (☎ 345/949–7800 in Grand Cayman).

CALLING CARDS

Lime phone cards, which can be used for both local and international calls, are available for purchase in various denominations at many retail outlets, including supermarkets and gas stations. They can be used from any touch-tone telephone (including pay and cell phones) in the Cayman Islands. The rates on island are competitive with those of online servers and more reliable.

MOBILE PHONES

If you're bringing your own mobile phone and it's compatible with 850/1900 Mhz GSM network or TDMA digital network, you should be able to make and receive calls during your stay, especially from Grand Cayman. Be sure, however, to check with your home provider that you have roaming service enabled, and note that charges can be astronomical depending on your calling plan. Renting a cell phone if you're planning an extended vacation or expect to make a lot of local calls may be a less expensive alternative than using your own. Mobile-phone rental is available from LIME (formerly Cable & Wireless) and Digicel; you can stay connected for as little as CI$5 per day plus the cost of a calling card (denominations range from CI$10 to CI$100). International per-minute rates usually range from CI$0.35 to CI$0.60. You can rent phones for use on-island from either LIME or Digicel

Mobile Phone Companies LIME (✉ Anderson Square Bldg., Shedden Rd., George Town, Grand Cayman ✉ Galleria Plaza, West Bay Rd., Seven Mile Beach, Grand Cayman ☎ 345/949–7800 ⊕ www.time4lime. com). **Digicel** (✉ Cayman Financial Center, 3rd Floor, 36A Dr. Roys Dr., George Town, Grand Cayman ☎ 345/623–3444 ⊕ www.digicelcayman.com).

▌ CUSTOMS AND DUTIES

Contacts **Cayman Islands Customs**
(⊕ *caymanislandscustoms.com*).

▌ EATING OUT

Obviously seafood reigns supreme in the Cayman Islands, where it's served everywhere from tiny family-run shanties to decadently decorated bistros. But befitting Grand Cayman's reputation as a sophisticated, multinational destination (with residents from 113 countries at last count), you can find a smorgasbord of savory options from terrific Tex-Mex to Thai to Italian. Menus could highlight by-the-book bouillabaisse or barbecue, kebabs or cannelloni, seviche or sushi. This is one destination where larger resorts generally have excellent restaurants. Two must-try local delicacies are conch, particularly fritters and chowder, and turtle (protected but farmed); the latter is stewed or served like a steak. Many restaurants offer kids' menus, and vegetarians should find acceptable options. *For information on food-related health issues, see Health, below.*

MEALS AND MEALTIMES

Most restaurants serve breakfast from 7 to 10 AM, lunch from 12 to 3 PM, and dinner from 6 to 11 PM. But these hours can vary widely, especially at remote resorts on Grand Cayman's East End and West Bay, as well as on the sister islands, which have few independent eateries. Every strip mall along Grand Cayman's Seven Mile Beach has at least one restaurant open late (often doubling as a lounge or nightclub); many beachfront bars also offer late dining, especially on weekends. Restaurants are likeliest to shutter on Sundays, especially in the less-trafficked areas. Since most markets also close, prepare for contingencies, especially if you're staying at an individual villa or condo. If you arrive on Saturday, when most villa and condo rentals begin, make sure you do your grocery shopping that afternoon. Most grocery stores will be closed on Sunday.

Unless otherwise noted, the restaurants listed in this guide are open daily for lunch and dinner.

PAYING

Major credit cards are widely accepted, even on the sister islands, though some smaller local establishments only accept cash.

For guidelines on tipping see ⇨ Tipping, below.

CATEGORY	COST
¢	Under $8
$	$8–$12
$$	$12–$20
$$$	$20–$30
$$$$	Over $30

All prices are per person for a main course at dinner

RESERVATIONS AND DRESS

Grand Cayman is both cosmopolitan and conservative, so scantily clad diners are frowned upon or downright refused seating. Many tonier establishments require long pants and collared shirts for gentlemen in the evening (lunch is generally more casual). Footwear and something to cover bathing suits (a sarong or sundress for women, T-shirt and shorts for men) are required save at some beach-front bars. The sister islands are far more casual. Reservations are strongly recommended for dinner at most restaurants throughout the islands.

We mention dress only when men are required to wear a jacket or a jacket and tie.

WINE, BEER, AND SPIRITS

Beer, wine, and spirits are readily available at most restaurants. Some pricier restaurants take great pride in their wine lists. Aficionados of local products may want to try the refreshing Caybrew beers (the nutty, smoky dark amber pairs well with many foods) and Tortuga rum (the 12-year-old is a marvelous after-dinner sipper in place of Cognac or single-malt Scotch).

▌ ELECTRICITY

Electric current on the Cayman Islands is 110 volts–60 cycles, U.S. standard. Hotels generally have plug adapters and transformers available for guests who bring appliances from countries that operate on 220-volt current.

▌ EMERGENCIES

Emergency Services Ambulance (☎ 911). **Fire** (☎ 911). **Police** (☎ 911).

Foreign Consulates U.S. Consular Agency (✉ Cayman Centre, Unit B1, Dorcy Dr., George Town, Grand Cayman ☎ 345/945–8173 ⊕ travel.state.

> ### WORD OF MOUTH
>
> Was the service stellar or not up to snuff? Did the food give you shivers of delight or leave you cold? Did the prices and portions make you happy or sad? Rate restaurants and write your own reviews in Travel Ratings or start a discussion about your favorite places in Travel Talk on www.fodors.com. Your comments might even appear in our books. Yes, you, too, can be a correspondent!

gov/travel/cis_pa_tw/cis/cis_1084. html.

Hospitals George Town Hospital (✉ Hospital Rd., George Town, Grand Cayman ☎ 345/949–8600). **The Brac Clinic** (✉ Tibbetts Sq., West End, Cayman Brac ☎ 345/949–1777). **Cayman Clinic** (✉ Grand Cayman ☎ 345/949–4234). **Faith Hospital** (✉ Stake Bay, West End, Cayman Brac ☎ 345/948–2243).

Pharmacies Cayman Drug (✉ Kirk Freeport Centre, George Town, Grand Cayman ☎ 345/949–2597). **Foster's Pharmacy** (✉ Foster's Food Fair, Airport Rd., George Town, Grand Cayman ☎ 345/949–0505). **Health Care Pharmacy** (✉ Photo-Pharm Centre, Walkers Rd., George Town, Grand Cayman ☎ 345/949–0442). **Kirk Pharmacy** (✉ Kirk Supermarket, Eastern Ave., George Town, Grand Cayman ☎ 345/949–7180).

Diving Emergencies Cayman Hyperbaric (✉ Hospital Rd., George Town, Grand Cayman ☎ 345/949–2989).

▮ **HEALTH**

Health concerns are minimal in the Cayman Islands, and Grand Cayman offers some of the Caribbean's finest medical facilities. Though there have been isolated cases of dengue fever (one or two annually, contracted elsewhere), the last on-island outbreak was in 2005. Airlift to Miami for serious emergencies is available. Physicians are highly qualified and speak English. Be sure to pack prescription medications; consider wearing a MedicAlert ID tag if you suffer from such chronic conditions as diabetes, epilepsy, or heart disease. Though many hospitals offer reciprocity with U.S. insurers, you can also purchase medical-only insurance (*see ⇨ Trip Insurance under Things to Consider in Before You Go, above*). Tap water is perfectly safe to drink throughout all three islands. Be sure to wash fruit thoroughly or, better yet, peel it before eating. The subtropic sun can be fierce, especially at midday. Be sure to wear sunglasses and a hat, and use high-SPF sunscreen (most U.S. brands are available). Beware of dehydration and heat stroke; take it easy the first couple of days. Insects can be a real nuisance during the wet season (July–November); bring along repellent to ward off mosquitoes and sand flies. Shops also stock numerous name brands.

MEDICAL INSURANCE AND ASSISTANCE

Consider buying trip insurance with medical-only coverage. Neither Medicare nor some private insurers cover medical expenses anywhere outside of the United States. Medical-only policies typically reimburse you for medical care (excluding that related to pre-existing conditions) and hospitalization abroad and provide for evacuation. You still have to pay the bills and await reimbursement from the insurer, though.

Another option is to sign up with a medical-evacuation assistance company. A membership in one of these companies gets you doctor referrals, emergency evacuation or repatriation, 24-hour hotlines for medical consultation, and other assistance. International SOS Assistance Emergency and AirMed International provide evacuation services and medical referrals. MedjetAssist offers medical evacuation.

Medical Assistance Companies AirMed International (⊕ *www. airmed.com*). **International SOS Assistance Emergency** (⊕ *www. intsos.com*). **MedjetAssist** (⊕ *www. medjetassist.com*).

Medical-Only Insurers International Medical Group (☎ *800/628-4664* ⊕ *www.imglobal. com*). **International SOS** (⊕ *www. internationalsos.com*). **Wallach and Company** (☎ *800/237-6615 or 540/687-3166* ⊕ *www.wallach.com*).

Health Information National Centers for Disease Control & Prevention (*CDC* ☎ *877/394-8747 international travelers' health line* ⊕ *www.cdc.gov/travel*). **World Health Organization** (*WHO* ⊕ *www. who.int*).

▮ HOURS OF OPERATION

Banks in the Cayman Islands are generally open Monday through Friday from 9 to 3. Post offices are open weekdays from 8:30 to 4 and Saturday from 9 to 1. Shops are usually open weekdays from 9 to 5; in outer shopping plazas they are open from 10 to 5. Shops are usually closed Sunday except in hotels or when cruise ships are visiting. Pharmacy hours vary, most opening between 7 and 9 AM, closing between 6 and 10 PM.

HOLIDAYS

In the Cayman Islands public holidays include New Year's Day, Ash Wednesday (46 days before Easter), Good Friday (Fri. before Easter), Easter Sunday (usually Mar. or Apr.), Discovery Day (May 19), Queen's Birthday (June 16), Constitution Day (July 7), Remembrance Day (November 17), Christmas, and Boxing Day (Dec. 26). The last refers to boxing extra presents for charity, not prizefighting!

▮ MAIL

Sending a postcard to the United States, Canada, other parts of the Caribbean, or Central America costs CI25¢. An airmail letter is CI75¢ per half-ounce. To Europe and South America, rates are CI25¢ for a postcard and CI80¢ per half-ounce for airmail letters. When addressing letters to the Cayman Islands, be sure to include the new postal codes that have been introduced. You can find them at ⊕ *www.caymanpost.gov.ky* or on leaflets at any of the islands' post offices. The main post office lies at

the intersection of Edward Street and Cardinal Avenue in downtown George Town. There is no home delivery; instead, all mail is delivered to numbered post-office boxes. For faster and reliable service to the United States, Federal Express, UPS, and DHL all have locations in the downtown area. Airmail can take two weeks to be delivered to farther-flung areas, including Australia and New Zealand.

▮ MONEY

You should not need to change money in Grand Cayman, since U.S. dollars are readily accepted, though you may get some change in Cayman dollars. ATMs accepting MasterCard and Visa with Cirrus affiliation are readily available in George Town; you usually have the option of U.S. or Cayman dollars. The Cayman dollar is pegged to the U.S. dollar at the rate of approximately CI$1.25 to $1, and divided into a hundred cents, with coins of 1¢, 5¢, 10¢, and 25¢ and notes of $1, $5, $10, $25, $50, and $100. There's no $20 bill. Traveler's checks and major credit cards are widely accepted. Be sure you know which currency is being quoted when making a purchase.

Prices throughout this guide are given for adults and unless otherwise indicated are in U.S. currency. Substantially reduced fees are almost always available for children, students, and senior citizens.

ATMS AND BANKS

There are more than 600 banks on the Cayman Islands; practically every major international financial operation is represented. ATMs are available 24 hours a day at bank branches, transportation centers, shopping centers, gas stations, and other convenient spots throughout the island. Those at banks usually dispense both Cayman and U.S. dollars.

CREDIT CARDS

Throughout this guide, the following abbreviations are used: **AE,** American Express; **D,** Discover; **DC,** Diners Club; **MC,** MasterCard; and **V,** Visa.

It's a good idea to inform your credit-card company before you travel, especially if you're going abroad and don't travel internationally very often. Otherwise, the credit-card company might put a hold on your card owing to unusual activity—not a good thing halfway through your trip. Record all your credit-card numbers—as well as the phone numbers to call if your cards are lost or stolen—in a safe place, so you're prepared should something go wrong. Both MasterCard and Visa have general numbers you can call (collect if you're abroad) if your card is lost, but you're better off calling the number of your issuing bank, since MasterCard and Visa usually just transfer you to your bank; your bank's number is usually printed on your card.

If you plan to use your credit card for cash advances, you'll need to apply for a PIN at least two weeks before your trip. Although it's usually cheaper (and safer) to use a credit card abroad for large purchases (so you can cancel payments or be reimbursed if there's a problem), note that some credit-card companies *and* the banks that issue them add substantial percentages to all foreign transactions, whether they're in a foreign currency or not. Check on these fees before leaving home, so there won't be any surprises when you get the bill.

▌ PASSPORTS AND VISAS

All visitors to the Cayman Islands must have a valid passport and a return or ongoing ticket to enter the Cayman Islands. A birth certificate and photo ID are *not* sufficient proof of citizenship.

▌ SAFETY

Though crime isn't a major problem in the Cayman Islands, take normal precautions. Lock your room, and don't leave valuables—particularly passports, tickets, and wallets—in plain sight or unattended on the beach. Use your hotel safe. Don't carry too much money or flaunt expensive jewelry on the street. For personal safety, avoid walking on the beach or on unlit streets at night. Lock your rental car, and don't pick up hitchhikers. Using or trafficking in illegal drugs is strictly prohibited in the Cayman Islands. Any offense is punishable by a hefty fine, imprisonment, or both.

▌ TAXES AND SERVICE CHARGES

At the airport, each adult passenger leaving Grand Cayman must pay a departure tax of $25 (CI$20), payable in either Caymanian or U.S. currency. It may be included in cruise packages as a component of port charges; it isn't usually added to airfare—check with your carrier—and must be paid in cash by each traveler prior to entering the secure area of the airport.

A 10% government tax is added to all hotel bills. A 10% service charge is often added to hotel bills and restaurant checks in lieu of a tip. There is no VAT or comparable tariff on goods and services.

▌ TIME

U.S. Eastern Standard Time (EST), five hours behind Greenwich Mean Time (GMT-0500), is in effect year-round on all three islands; daylight saving is not observed.

▌ TIPPING

At large hotels a service charge is generally included and can be anywhere from 6% to 10%; smaller establishments and some villas and condos leave tipping up to you. Although tipping is customary at restaurants, note that some automatically include 10%–15% on the bill—so check the tab carefully. At your discretion, tip another 5% or more to recognize extraordinary service. Taxi drivers expect a 10%–15% tip. Bellmen and porters expect $1 per bag, more in luxury hotels (especially if you bring lots of luggage). Tip the concierge

(if your resort has one) anywhere from $10 to $100, depending on services rendered and length of stay. Tips are not expected simply for handing out maps and making the occasional dinner reservation. Spa personnel should receive 15%–20% of the treatment price (but verify that a service fee wasn't already added).

▌ TOURS

GUIDED TOURS

A sightseeing tour is a good way to get your bearings and to experience Caymanian culture. Taxi drivers will give you a personalized tour of Grand Cayman for about $25 per hour for up to three people. Or you can choose a fascinating helicopter ride, a horseback or mountain-bike journey, a 4x4 safari expedition, or a full-day bus excursion. The prices vary according to the mode of travel and the number and kind of attractions included. Ask your hotel to help you make arrangements.

Costs and itineraries for island tours are about the same regardless of the tour operator. Half-day tours average $40–$50 a person and generally include a visit to Hell and the Turtle Farm at Boatswain Beach aquatic park in West Bay, as well as shopping downtown. Full-day tours ($60–$75 per person) add lunch, a visit to Bodden Town (the first settlement), and the East End, where you stop at the Queen Elizabeth II Botanic Park, blowholes (if the waves are high) on the ironshore, and the site of the wreck of the *Ten Sails* (not the wreck itself—just the site). The pirate graves in Bodden Town were destroyed during Hurricane Ivan, and the blowholes were partially filled. As you can tell, land tours here are low-key. Children under 12 often receive discounts.

A. A. Transportation Services offers taxis and tour buses. Ask for Burton Ebanks.

B. A. McCurley, owner of McCurley Tours, is a free-spirited, free-wheeling midwesterner who's lived in Cayman for 24 years and knows everything and everyone on the East End. Not only is she encyclopedic and flexible, she also offers car rentals and transfers for travelers staying on the East End; don't be surprised if she tells you what to order at lunch, especially if it's off the menu.

Majestic Tours caters mostly to cruise-ship and incentive groups but also offers similar options to individuals and can customize tours; it's particularly good for West Bay, including Boatswain's Beach and Hell.

Tropicana Tours offers several excellent Cayman highlights itineraries on its larger buses, including Stingray City stops, as well as reef-runner adventures across the North Sound through the mangrove swamps.

Your hotel or villa agent can recommend and organize drivers for tours of the sister islands.

Contacts A. A. Transportation Services (☎ 345/949–6598 or 345/926–8294 ⊕ www.burtons.ky). **Majestic Tours** (☎ 345/949–7773 ⊕ www.majestic-tours.com). **Mc-**

Curley Tours (☎ 345/947–9626 or 345/916–0925 ✍ mccurley@cwhiptop.com). **Tropicana Tours** (☎ 345/949–0944 ⊕ www.tropicana-tours.com).

SPECIAL-INTEREST TOURS

Cayman Island Helicopters offers exhilarating eagle-eye views on three itineraries: $75 for a flyover of Seven Mile Beach; $115 for a trip adding Stingray City; and $295 for a thrillingly panoramic island-wide aerial tour (discounts are available if you book via the company's Web site, and shuttle service is free). Though the island is flat and mostly arid, the sight of waters rippling from turquoise to tourmaline is exciting enough.

Cayman Safari hits the usual sights but emphasizes interaction with locals, so you learn about craft traditions, folklore, and herbal medicines.

Contacts Cayman Island Helicopters (☎ 345/949–4354 or 345/525–6967 ⊕ www.caymanislandhelicopters.com). **Cayman Safari** (☎ 345/925–3001 or 866/389–8559 ⊕ www.caymansafari.com).

▌ TRIP INSURANCE

Comprehensive trip insurance is valuable if you're booking a very expensive or complicated trip (particularly to an isolated region) or if you're booking far in advance. Comprehensive policies typically cover trip-cancellation and interruption, letting you cancel or cut your trip short because of illness or, in some cases, acts of terrorism in your destination. Such policies might also cover evacuation and medical care. (For trips abroad you should have at least medical-only coverage (*see Medical Insurance and Assistance under Health, above*). Some also cover you for trip delays because of bad weather or mechanical problems as well as for lost or delayed luggage.

Another type of coverage to consider is financial default—that is, when your trip is disrupted because a tour operator, airline, or cruise line goes out of business. Generally you must buy this when you book your trip or shortly thereafter, and it's available to you only if your operator isn't on a list of excluded companies.

Always read the fine print of your policy to make sure that you're covered for the risks that most concern you. Compare several policies to be sure you're getting the best price and range of coverage available.

Insurance Comparison Sites
Insure My Trip (☎ *800/487-4722* ⊕ *www.insuremytrip.com*). **Square Mouth** (☎ *800/240-0369* ⊕ *www.squaremouth.com*).

Travel Insurers Access America (☎ *800/284-8300* ⊕ *www.accessamerica.com*). **AIG Travel Guard** (☎ *800/826-4919* ⊕ *www.travelguard.com*). **CSA Travel Protection** (☎ *800/873-9855* ⊕ *www.csatravelprotection.com*). **Travelex Insurance** (☎ *888/228-9792* ⊕ *www.travelexinsurance.com*). **Travel Insured International** (☎ *800/243-3174* ⊕ *www.travelinsured.com*).

▮ VISITOR INFORMATION

The Cayman Islands has tourist offices in the United States, where you can get brochures and maps in advance of your trip. There are also tourism offices on the islands for on-site help.

In the United States, **Cayman Islands Department of Tourism** (✉ *Miami, FL* ☎ *877/422-9626 or 305/599-9033 in Miami, 713/461-1317 in Houston, 212/889-9009 in New York, 312/263-1750 in Chicago* ⊕ *www.caymanislands.ky*).

In the Cayman Islands, **Department of Tourism** (✉ *Regatta Office Park Leeward 2, West Bay Rd., Box 67GT, George Town* ☎ *345/949-0623* ✉ *Owen Roberts Airport, Grand Cayman* ☎ *345/949-3603* ✉ *West End Rd., North Side, Cayman Brac* ☎ *345/948-1649*).

ON-LINE RESOURCES
Brac And Little (⊕ *www.bracandlittle.com*) is a useful, privately run adjunct to the official Sister Islands Web sites, offering lots of local news and gossip, photos, and often faster updates.

Caymanian Compass (⊕ *www.caycompass.com*), the online version of the national newspaper, offers news, occasionally provocative commentary, event listings, weather reports, currency converter, photo galleries, interactive map, and the CaymanEye live Webcam.

Cayman Islands Destination Magazine (⊕ *www.destination.ky*) provides information on everything from airlines to accommodations, restaurants to real estate, with useful links.

Cayman Islands Vacations and Business Directory (⊕ *www.gocayman.ky*), funded by private-sector businesses, functions as a de facto Chamber of Commerce adjunct, with extensive transportation, lodging, dining, recreational, bar-hopping, and shopping write-ups, as well as information on everything from marine conservation to culture, weather to weddings.

Cayman Net News Online (⊕ *www.caymannetnews.com*) provides all the daily local news that's fit to cyberprint, with a helpful weekly Sister Islands supplement titled *The Bracker and Little Caymanian*.

Cayman Observer (⊕ *www.caymanobserver.com*) is a weekly business-oriented newspaper with intriguing news items and editorial taking the current pulse of the islands.

Cayman Restaurant Guide (⊕ *www.caymanrestaurants.com*) is a fairly comprehensive listing of eateries with sample menus, maps, reviews, even recipes.

Good Taste (⊕ *www.caymangoodtaste.com*) bills itself as "Cayman's definitive dining and entertainment guide," dishing out menus for dozens of restaurants, alongside articles on local cuisine and charts detailing which eateries offer children's portions, al fresco dining, water views, and more.

Key to Cayman (⊕ *www.keytocayman.com*) is the online version of a thick, stylish quarterly with particular focus on shopping, real estate, heritage, attractions, and crafts.

National Trust for the Cayman Islands (⊕ *www.nationaltrust.org.ky*) is an admirable nonprofit institution dedicated to preserving the cultural, historic, and environmental heritage of the Cayman Islands. Its informative Web site includes information on programs, maps, events, and more.

Nature Cayman (⊕ *www.naturecayman.com*) details the sister islands' rich flora and fauna on land and underwater, along with detailed coverage of Cayman Brac and Little Cayman history and culture.

Sister Islands Tourism Association (⊕ *www.sisterislands.com*) is the Web site of a business group that publicizes its member establishments on Cayman Brac and Little Cayman.

Tourism Attraction Board (⊕ *www.tab.ky*) runs several of Grand Cayman's leading attractions and events, including Pedro St. James historical site, Queen Elizabeth II Botanic Park, and November's annual Pirates Week Festival.

▍ WEDDINGS

Getting married in the Cayman Islands is a breeze, and each year many couples tie the knot here. Most choose to say their vows on lovely Seven Mile Beach, with the sun setting into the azure sea as their picture-perfect backdrop. Underwater weddings in full scuba gear with schools of fish as impromptu witnesses are also possible (kissing with mask on optional). Cathy Church can photograph your underwater wedding *(see ⇨ Shopping in Chapter 2)*.

You can literally leave things up in the air, getting hitched while hovering in a helicopter ("I do; Roger and out," responded one blushing bride over the propeller noise). A traditional church wedding can even be arranged, after which you trot away to your life together in a horse-drawn carriage.

Documentation can be prepared ahead of time or in one day while on the island. There's no on-island waiting period. In addition to the application, you need proof of identity and age (those under 18 must provide parental consent), such as an original or certified birth certificate or passport; a Cayman Islands international embarkation/disembarkation card; and certified or original copies of divorce decrees/death certificates if you have been married before. You must list a marriage officer on the application, and you need at least two witnesses; if you haven't come with friends or family, the marriage officer can help you with that, too. A marriage license costs CI$160 (US$200).

The best way to plan your wedding in the Cayman Islands is to contact a wedding coordinator (resorts such as the Reef, Westin Casuarina, and Ritz-Carlton have one on staff), who will offer a wide variety of packages to suit every taste and budget. All the logistics and legalities will be properly handled, giving you time to relax and enjoy the wedding of your dreams. The Cayman Islands Department of Tourism keeps a list of wedding coordinators. Or you can order the brochure "Getting Married in the Cayman Islands" from Government Information Services. Vernon Jackson, of Cayman Weddings, is a wonderful marriage officer with a soft accent and a kind heart. You can choose from many different styles of services or rewrite one as you wish.

Information Cayman Weddings (☎ 345/949–8677 ⊕ www.cayman-weddings.com.ky). **Deputy Chief Secretary** (✉ Government Administration Bldg., 3rd Floor, George Town, Grand Cayman ☎ 345/949–7900 or 345/914–2222). **District Commissioner's Office** (✉ District Administration Bldg., Stake Bay, Cayman Brac ☎ 345/948–2222). **Government Information Services** (✉ Cricket Sq., George Town, Grand Cayman ☎ 345/949–8092). **Heart of Cayman** (☎ 345/949–1343 ⊕ www.heartofcayman.com).

INDEX

Photo Credits

1, SuperStock/age fotostock. 2, Corbis. 6, FLPA/age fotostock. Chapter 1: Experience Cayman Islands: 8-9, Anne Flinn Powell/age fotostock. 10, JodiJacobson / istock. 11 (top), Allister Clark/iStockphoto. 11 (bottom), Cayman Islands Department of Tourism. 14 (left), Stephen Frink Collection / Alamy. 14 (top right), DurdenImages/iStockphoto. 14 (bottom right), Ocean Image Photography/Shutterstock. 15 (top left), RENAULT Philippe/age fotostock. 15 (bottom left), Rohit Seth/Shutterstock. 15 (top right), Shimon & Tammer. 15 (bottom right), Starwood Hotels & Resorts. 16 (left), mikadx/iStockphoto. 16 (top right and bottom right), Dan McDougall/Cayman Islands Department of Tourism. 17 (left), Zach Stovall. 17 (right), worleyx/Flickr. 18, Dan McDougall/Cayman Islands Department of Tourism. 19, Cayman Islands Department of Tourism. 21 (left), Christian Wheatley/Shutterstock. 21 (right), Michael Macsuga/Shutterstock. 23 (left), Ronald manera/iStockphoto. 23 (right), Dan McDougall/Cayman Islands Department of Tourism. 24, Ivan Cholakov Gostock.net/Shutterstock. 25, Richard Brooks/iStockphoto. 26, Dave Newman/iStockphoto. 27, Byron W. Moore/Shutterstock. 28, Beverly Speed/Shutterstock. 29, Diana Cochran Johnson/Shutterstock. 30, Robert Smith/age fotostock. Chapter 2: Exploring Grand Cayman: 31, Cayman Islands Department of Tourism. 34, allyclark /istock. 39, Cayman Islands Department of Tourism. 42, SSImagesCollection/iStockphoto. 45, 46, and 54-55, Cayman Islands Department of Tourism. Chapter 3: Where to Eat in Grand Cayman: 63, Shimon & Tammer. 67, javajoba/Flickr. 73, Mark Wieland. 74, Starwood Hotels & Resorts. Chapter 4: Where to Stay in Grand Cayman: 93, Courtney Platt. 102, Dan McDougall/Cayman Islands Department of Tourism. 105, aceshot1/Shutterstock. 112-13, PixAchi/Shutterstock. 114, Caribbean Club. 120, The Ritz-Carlton, Grand Cayman. 122, Dan McDougall/Cayman Islands Department of Tourism. 127, Courtney Platt. Chapter 5: Grand Cayman Nightlife and the Arts: 129, Angelo Cavalli/age fotostock. 134, MCHart/Flickr. 140, Danita Delimont/Alamy. Chapter 6: Grand Cayman Sports and Outdoor Activities: 145, Kevin Panizza/iStockphoto. 148-49, Jan Greune/age fotostock. 155, Peter Heiss/iStockphoto. 159, Corbis. 168 and 170-71, Cayman Islands Department of Tourism. 178-79, Ronald J. Manera/iStockphoto. Chapter 7: Cayman Brac: 183, Greg Johnston/age fotostock. 192, J & C Sohns/age fotostock. 198, Jan Greune/age fotostock. 206-207, RENAULT Philippe/age fotostock. 209, Kevin Panizza/iStockphoto. 214-15, Greg Johnston/age fotostock. Chapter 8: Little Cayman: 221, Karen & Ian Stewart/Alamy. 229, Dan McDougall/Cayman Islands Department of Tourism. 234, Cayman Islands Department of Tourism. 236-37, RENAULT Philippe/age fotostock. 240, Chris A. Crumley/Alamy.

NOTES

NOTES

ABOUT OUR WRITER

Jordan Simon worked in various aspects of the entertainment industry, from actor to director, before defecting to journalism. He's served as food and/or wine editor for *Atlanta Homes & Lifestyles, Hamptons, Second Home,* Snow Country, and *Ski Impact*; contributing editor for *TAXI, I-MI,* and *Shermans Travel.* He oversaw development of *Wine Country International* as founding editor-in-chief. He's currently contributing travel editor for *Nikki Style,* columnist for AOL Travel, and lifestyle editor for *Caribbean Living.* He's beachcombed for many magazines and Web sites, including *Caribbean Travel & Life, Condé Nast Traveler, Town & Country, Modern Bride, Diversion,* ShermansTravel.com, *Cooking Light, Interval, Art & Antiques, USAir Magazine, TravelAge,* and *American Way.*

He's written several guidebooks, including the original editions of *Fodor's Colorado* and *Fodor's Branson: The Official Travel & Souvenir Guide.* He co-wrote *The Celestial Seasonings Cookbook: Cooking with Tea* with Mo and Jennifer Siegel; *Astronumerology: Your Key to Empowerment Using Stars & Numbers* with Pam Bell; and *Edge Atlanta* with Jeff Clark, et al.